THE
STORY OF ISRAEL BETWEEN
SETTLEMENT AND EXILE

A Redactional Study of the
Deuteronomistic History

A.D.H. MAYES

SCM PRESS LTD

© A. D. H. Mayes 1983

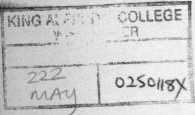
First published 1983
by SCM Press Ltd
26–30 Tottenham Road, London N1

Typeset by Input Typesetting Ltd
and printed in Great Britain by
Richard Clay (The Chaucer Press) Ltd
Bungay, Suffolk

Contents

Preface

If Deuteronomy is central to Old Testament theology, the deuteron-omistic history is no less so for Old Testament historiography. This account, extending from Deuteronomy to the end of II Kings, records the life of Israel in the land until its independent existence was brought to an end by the Babylonians. It has not only brought together many and various traditional materials but has also systematized the different currents of cultural and religious life and thought which Israel fostered. The popular story-teller, the historical novelist, the official chronicler, the prophet and the priest, have all left their imprint here; and even if some aspects of Israel's life, such as its internal structures of government or forms of administration, are not so prominent as they might be, or if large elements of the account are impossibly idealistic or are subordinated to a cultic theme which is historically one-sided, yet the integration of the variety of Israel's experience within the interpretative framework which the deuteron-omist constructed represents a magnificent achievement of historical writing.

Martin Noth's study of the deuteronomistic history was fundamen-tally important in describing the structure of the work and the sources used by its author, and also in the emphasis which it laid on the deuteronomist both as author and as Israel's first historian: it was first by him that a complete account of Israel's history was created from the isolated and fragmentary sources. Though written over forty years ago that study retains its significance, and, like so much of Noth's work, presents a case which, despite the many and serious questions which may be directed to it, continues to resist attempts to construct a satisfactory alternative. However, the wide following it has enjoyed, and the confirmatory studies it has inspired, have in more

vii

recent years come to be outweighed by the numerous critical studies which have weakened its very foundations.

Contemporary study of the deuteronomistic history has not escaped the apparently disintegrating approaches which seem to characterize the study of the rest of the Old Testament; and if it is a healthy sign in the scholarly world that the older 'assured results' are no longer convincing, then the study of the deuteronomistic history is in a vigorous condition. Studies of particular passages, books and topics abound, in all of which the problems of the purpose and the unity of the deuteronomistic history are prominent. The need both for an assessment of the mutual relationship of the results produced by such studies, and for a framework within which they may, even though in modified form, be comprehended, is now a pressing one. The present work is an essay in this category.

The major part of what follows is formed by the five chapters discussing the deuteronomistic editing in each of the books of the deuteronomistic history. The extended introduction sets the scene with a review of the main trends in the study of the work. A complete coverage would be impossible here, but within the limits set I hope it has been possible to present an outline which avoids both obscurity resulting from compression and also insubstantial vagueness resulting from futile efforts at total comprehension. The conclusion, besides performing the usual functions to which such a section is devoted, also addresses itself to the complex problem of the relationship between the deuteronomistic history and the Pentateuch. There are many reasons which suggest the need for a radical re-appraisal of that relationship, but the one which Noth's own work seems to bring to the fore is this: if a deuteronomistic historian, writing either towards the end of the pre-exilic period or during the exile, is Israel's first historian, what does this mean for our understanding of the work and the time of writing of the authors of the Pentateuch?

My indebtedness to colleagues is clear on every page; almost every worthwhile observation has its roots elsewhere. I should like, however, specifically to note that it was the kind invitation of Dr R. E. Clements to write the New Century Bible Commentary on *Deuteronomy* which set in train the course of this study, and that it was in the context of several fruitful conversations with Professor E. W. Nicholson that the work received fresh stimulus. Mrs Margaret Spencer was generous with her help, despite many other pressures, in the task of typing the manuscript. Less immediately obvious is my indebtedness to my wife,

Elizabeth; but without her encouraging cheerfulness and practical support this book would not have been written.

Trinity College, Dublin   *A. D. H. Mayes*

INTRODUCTION

The task of presenting a discussion of some recent developments in the study of the deuteronomistic history, and of suggesting possible ways forward in that discussion, cannot very easily be introduced by an account of the history of the study of this part of the Hebrew Bible. The deuteronomistic history does not form a traditional entity, comparable to the Pentateuch, and so a review of the scholarly treatment of it must in large part be devoted either to a discussion of the study of the individual books which comprise the deuteronomistic history, or to an attempt to elicit the main trends and movements which culminated in the recognition of these books as a particular unit. It is the latter approach which will be followed here, in the hope that it will then be possible to set within its proper context in the history of scholarship the classic presentation by M. Noth that the books from Deuteronomy to the end of II Kings constitute a single literary unit, the deuteronomistic history.[1]

Noth's theory forms the watershed in the study of this part of the Old Testament. It expressed in persuasive form and in convincing detail a theory which had until then been overshadowed by the dominating source criticism associated with Wellhausen; and it replaced source criticism to the extent that from that time on it was source criticism which had to justify itself over against the dominance of the approach expounded by Noth. In this introductory chapter our intention is a threefold one: firstly, to trace those tendencies in scholarship which culminated in Noth's study; secondly, to give a brief presentation to Noth's view; and thirdly, to follow through reactions to Noth up to the present. Into this context the following treatment of the individual books of the deuteronomistic history may then be set.

1

For the pre-Noth period three tendencies may be highlighted. These, rather than being mutually exclusive, represent different emphases along the one line which follows through the process of origins of the books in question.[2] It is more a matter of concern with different stages of development of the books under consideration, than a matter of radically different approaches to the question of the formation of those books. First of all, reference should be made to the source critical approach, for this represented the application to the historical books of classical source criticism as traditionally applied to the Pentateuch. Wellhausen, while reluctant to express any real certainty on the matter, nevertheless noted that Samuel and Kings do contain continuous narrative sources which are to be connected with the Pentateuchal sources J and E.[3] Others who followed in Wellhausen's steps were much more confident. So, by Eissfeldt and others it was felt that Joshua in particular but also in many cases the succeeding books of the deuteronomistic history could be immediately related to the Pentateuchal sources.[4] Joshua especially was emphasized in this connection for here, it was argued, was to be found not only the conclusion to the promises to the patriarchs of land and posterity, but also the climax of the whole theme of the Pentateuch in general.[5] However, the work of the Yahwist was also argued to be even more extensive than this: it provided a presentation of the history of Israel from the creation of the world to the division of the kingdom, and reached its conclusion in I Kings 12.19; thus, it is from the Yahwist that the unified presentation of the books Joshua, Judges, Samuel and I Kings derives.[6] Further reference will be made to this approach in the context of the third section of this introduction – reactions to Noth's presentation – for it is an approach which continued to find, in one form or another, considerable support. At this stage it remains to be emphasized that it was a view by no means altogether incompatible with the second tendency of scholarship on this part of the Old Testament, viz. the understanding that deuteronomistic editing was also to be found in these books; and indeed some source critical scholars argued precisely this, that the books Joshua – I Kings have been subject to deuteronomistic editing, but that in their pre-deuteronomistic stage they constituted continuations of the old Pentateuchal sources.[7]

The recognition of deuteronomistic influence in Joshua – II Kings was widespread before Noth,[8] and without the work of many scholars in this connection Noth's theory would hardly have seen the light of day. One in particular is significant in that he not only recognized this influence but also argued for more than one deuteronomistic stage in the production of Joshua – II Kings. This was A. Kuenen who, first in 1861, argued for a pre-exilic and a post-exilic stage in development of what came to be known as the deuteronomistic history.[9] The reason adduced for this distinction was that while some passages, belonging to the framework of Kings, presuppose the exile, others clearly do not. Passages presupposing the exile were found in for example, I Kings 9.1–9; II Kings 17.19f.; 20.17f.; 21.11–15; 22.15–20; 23.26f.; 24.2–4; 24.18–25.30. Pre-exilic passages were found in I Kings 8.8,12–61 (destruction of the temple is not envisaged); 9.21; 10.12; 12.19; II Kings 8.22 (the Davidic dynasty still rules); 17.7–18,23; 17.34,41 (exile of northern kingdom only is presupposed). It was the pre-exilic editor who, in 600 BC, was the real organizer of the material into its present arrangement, while the exilic edition was really an expansion and supplementing of this.

The third tendency is one which may be traced back to the influence of Gunkel; this encouraged an emphasis on the significance of the earliest rather than the latest stage of development of the books. The interest shifted to the smallest units which could be discerned as originally independent elements within the larger secondary connections. Here belongs the work of Gressmann and Alt on the aetiological stories of the book of Joshua, which were recognized as independent traditions in the pre-literary stage;[10] here belongs also Noth's own early work, his commentary on the book of Joshua which first appeared in 1938.[11] In this context the question of the presence of continuous sources is totally subordinate to the investigation of the older independent pre-literary traditions and their separate transmission. It may be that this focus of attention does not necessarily conflict with the possibility of the extension of such continuous sources as JE outside the Pentateuch,[12] but one can nevertheless discern in the developing discussion a trend towards ignoring the possibility of the extension of these sources in favour of an emphasis on the two extreme stages of the process of development: the early pre-literary stage of single units of tradition and the late stage of deuteronom(ist)ic editing.

The appearance of Noth's treatment of the deuteronomistic history in 1943 marked the final exclusion of JE from Joshua – II Kings, and the direct connection of the other two points in the line of development: behind the stage of deuteronomistic editing in these books there are to be discerned no continuous sources but only the isolated units and complexes of tradition. It was the deuteronomistic author who first combined these in order to yield a connected, continuous account of the history of Israel. For Noth, the books Deuteronomy – II Kings had two characteristics: first, the work is a unity, from the hand of a single author; secondly, it is the first presentation of the history of Israel and Judah, and, because of its links with Deuteronomy, it may be known as the deuteronomistic history.

In order to establish the unity of the work Noth made four chief points. First there is the linguistic evidence which 'remains the most reliable basis for attributing parts of the various traditions to Dtr'.[13] The language, which is considered to be easily recognizable and so not requiring detailed description,[14] is said to be 'very straightforward' and without 'any particular artistry or refinement'; it is marked rather by the 'frequent repetition of the same simple phrases and sentence constructions'. However, the style is also characterized by 'the absence of specific stylistic peculiarities', which tends to diminish its fundamental significance in the question of the unity of the deuteronomistic history; and indeed it is admitted that the work has subsequently been added to in the deuteronomistic style.

Secondly, Noth refers to the regular appearance at specific points in the course of the work of speeches or narratives.[15] These passages, which are from the hand of the deuteronomist, function to review the course of history and draw from it practical consequences for the behaviour of the people. The passages in question include Josh. 1, the speech of Joshua concerning the occupation of the land; Josh. 12, the concluding summary of the results of the conquest; Josh. 23, Joshua's farewell speech instructing Israel on its behaviour in the land; Judg. 2.11ff., a preview of the course of history of the period of the judges; I Sam. 12, Samuel's speech to the people on the inauguration of the monarchy, drawing lessons from history for future life; I Kings 8.14ff., Solomon's prayer of dedication of the temple, in which the significance of the new sanctuary for the present and the future is proclaimed; II Kings 17.7ff., a reflection on the disastrous conclusion to the monarchic period in Israel. It is at critical points in the history of Israel that these reflective speeches and narratives have been inserted, in order to bring out the consequences for national history of the obedience and disobedience of the people to the demands of God. They give a particularly strong impression of the unity of the whole work.

The chronology is the third indication of unity in the deuteronom-

4

istic history.[16] For the monarchic period the matter is relatively straightforward: the chronologies of the kings of the two states of Israel and Judah are interlinked in such a way as to provide a total single chronology of the period. For the pre-monarchic and early monarchic periods, however, the matter is more complex. Chronological statements are given in abundance; but a problem resides in linking these with what is clearly intended as an overall chronological statement, deriving from and based on the earlier chronological statements, that given in I Kings 6.1. According to this, 480 years separated the exodus from Egypt and the fourth year of the reign of Solomon when the building of the temple in Jerusalem was begun. Whether or not this figure is taken as artificial, it belongs within the deuteronomistic scheme and must be linked to other deuteronomistic chronological information; it is in making this link, however, that the problem resides, for the total number of years mentioned in Deuteronomy and succeeding books up to I Kings 6.1 amounts to more than 480.

Noth dismisses those attempts to explain the discrepancy which involve either a synchronic approach, taking some of the periods mentioned in Judges as contemporaneous rather than as standing in chronological sequence, or the omission of the so-called minor judges altogether as a late post-deuteronomistic addition.[17] His own proposal involves two points of fundamental importance: first, the chronological statement of Judg. 13.1, that the Philistines ruled over Israel for forty years, is taken as having the purpose of covering the period up to Samuel's defeat of the Philistines referred to in I Sam.7. This means that the statement in I Sam. 4.18 that Eli 'judged Israel forty years' must be understood as an addition, for, since twenty years separated Eli from Samuel's victory (I Sam. 7.2), Eli's rule would otherwise have extended back through the time of Samson to make him contemporary with some of the minor judges. The chronological statement on Eli is a post-deuteronomistic addition intended to include him in the sequence of 'judges' who preceded Samuel. Second, the absence of chronological information on the final years of Joshua and Samuel leaves historical gaps in the total chronology, for this includes chronological information only up to the time of the distribution of the land (in the case of Joshua) and the defeat of the Philistines (in the case of Samuel). These gaps should, however, be understood as conforming to the original intention of the deuteronomist, who probably intended the reader to conclude that these two events marked also the conclusions of the periods of rule of Joshua and Samuel before the onset of the succeeding periods of the judges on the one hand and of the monarchy on the other.

The period of time from the first apostasy preceding the rise of Ehud as deliverer to the death of the last minor judge, Abdon (Judg. 3.8–12.15), was 350 years. This was preceded by the forty years in the wilderness (Deut. 1.3) and the five years it took to conquer west Jordan (Josh. 14.10), and was followed by the two years assigned to Saul's reign (I Sam 13.1), the forty years of David's reign (I Kings 2.11) and the first four years of Solomon's reign (I Kings 6.1). The total of 481 years may be reduced to 480 in conformity with I Kings 6.1, on the assumption that the deuteronomist understood the first year of Solomon's reign to have coincided with the last year of David's reign, Solomon having been anointed king while David was still alive (I Kings 1.11ff.). The resulting conformity of the chronological statements through the work is a strong pointer to its unity of composition.

The fourth indication that the deuteronomistic history is a unity is to be found in the consistency of its theological ideas. Two of these in particular are described by Noth.[18] In the first place, there is a remarkable lack of positive interest in the cult. Insofar as the deuteronomist is not concerned simply with the negative side, the prohibition of certain cultic actions, he prefers to leave the cult more or less unnoticed. The ark is, for the deuteronomist, simply a container for the law tablets; the temple, in which he has such an obvious central interest, is not described in terms of its function as a place of sacrifice (though from the time of Solomon onwards it is because they offered sacrifices away from the temple that the kings are condemned), but rather is portrayed as the place chosen by Yahweh for his name, and as the place in which and towards which Israelites should offer prayer. In the place of a relationship with God founded on sacrificial worship the deuteronomist has substituted a relationship of obedience to law within the framework of election and covenant. Israel was the chosen people of Yahweh, with a relationship with God not enjoyed by any other people. This involved her obedience to the divine demand contained in the law of Moses in Deuteronomy.

Secondly, the deuteronomist 'saw the history of Israel as a self-contained process which began with specific manifestations of power and came to a definite end with the destruction of Jerusalem'.[19] Even when the opportunity presented itself, as it did over and over again, the deuteronomist did not make use of it to sketch out, however perfunctorily, a future for the people beyond the disaster that had overtaken them. Judgment and disaster were appropriately threatened in speeches by Moses (Deut. 4.25–28), Joshua (Josh. 23.15f.) and Samuel (I Sam. 12.25), should the people prove disobedient; but there are also contexts which offered the occasion for reference to the future beyond destruction if this had been in the deuteronomist's mind. The reflections on the destruction of Israel and Judah in II Kings 17.7ff.; 21.12ff. presented such an opportunity; in the latter part of Solomon's prayer of dedication of the temple, where the king mentions the possibility of Israel's being sent into exile for sin and there repenting (I Kings 8.44ff.) the only thing that Solomon can request is that the prayers for forgiveness be heard. The return of Israel to its land lies outside his view. Thus, when the deuteronomist finally reports the release of King Jehoiachin from prison in exile and the improvement in his situation (II Kings 25.27–30), he intends not to hint at the possibility of a new future, but rather to round off his account of the history by reporting what was known to him as a historical fact. The history of Israel and Judah had come to an end, and in conformity with the curse attached to the covenant law the people had suffered destruction.

If for Noth the deuteronomistic history was the work of a single author it was also the first presentation of the history of Israel and Judah. This was the work of an author creating something new; it was not the simple editing of an already existing work. The repetitive style, the frequent recurrence of the same theological statements, warnings, exhortations, are not to be seen as the tedious interpolations of an editor, but rather as the creative work of an author intent on forging a single literary unit out of a wide variety of traditional materials and sources which had come down to him. He divided his presentation into four periods: that of Moses, for which the law of Deuteronomy in its framework constituted his major source; the period of the conquest, which was built on traditional aetiological and other stories in the first half of Joshua; the period of the judges and rise of the monarchy, to portray which the deuteronomist combined stories of major judges and the list of minor judges and brought in stories about Samuel's birth, the ark and the rise of Saul; and the period of the monarchy, for which the deuteronomist had at his disposal traditions of Saul, David and Solomon, the chronicles of the kings of Israel and Judah, together with various prophetic traditions. His attitude to these sources was generally conservative; he intended his work 'to be a compilation and explanation of the extant traditions concerning the history of his people'.[20] The deuteronomist was, therefore, an author who, through the selection and editing of older individual traditions, compiled the first unified presentation of the history of Israel.

In the variety of scholarly reactions to Noth's theory since 1943 it is possible to discern a small number of different trends within which most writings on the subject may fairly easily be classified. The two broad groups of those who accepted the theory and those who rejected it may be broken down into subgroups of those who simply adopted it and those who confirmed it through detailed study, on the one hand, and on the other hand those who rejected it because they saw the continuation of Pentateuchal sources outside the Pentateuch and those who rejected it because they discerned sufficient lack of unity within the deuteronomistic history to make its derivation from a single author unlikely.

Within the first category we may distinguish, then, between those who simply adopt the theory and those who have confirmed it. To the former group belong many straightforward introductions to the Old Testament such as that by Soggin,[21] together with other works, such as that of Engnell. The extent to which the latter is dependent on Noth is, however, unclear. His formulation of the corollary of this theory, viz. that one must think in terms of a Tetrateuch rather than Pentateuch, was apparently carried through independently of Noth. In any case, Engnell, while applying his traditio-historical approach to the deuteronomistic history and so sharply rejecting the validity of literary criticism as a means of distinguishing literary sources, continuous or not, sees Deuteronomy – II Kings as the 'deuteronomic history' deriving from a 'traditionist circle' to be known as the 'D circle'.[22]

It is, however, the second group within this first category which is of more interest at the moment. There are three scholars who deserve special mention for their detailed work on particular parts of the deuteronomistic history, work which has led them to substantial agreement with Noth. First, Jepsen in a study of the sources of kings attempted to discern the history of the books of Kings and argued that a 'royal history' which was composed by priestly circles from earlier records after 587, was later extended by a redactor, showing the influence of Hosea and Jeremiah and guided by Deuteronomy. This redactor is Noth's deuteronomistic historian, and to him Jepsen assigns responsibility for the incorporation of the story of the conquest, of the judges, of Samuel, David and his succession, as well as the prophetic stories from northern Israel now in the books of Kings. Again with Noth, Jepsen emphasized that Deut. 1 is the beginning of a literary unit, extending to II Kings 25, which is independent of the Tetrateuchal sources. The work was composed in the region of Mizpah (II Kings 25.23) about 500 BC.[23]

Secondly, reference should be made to Boecker's study of I Sam. 8–12.[24] This short section has posed great difficulties for the theory of the unity of the deuteronomistic history, and it is, moreover, a favourite hunting ground for source critics seeking to establish connections with the Tetrateuchal sources. Within the section it has for long been customary to distinguish between two sources, one pro-monarchic and the other anti-monarchic.[25] The former, in I Sam. 9.1–10.16; 11, has been identified as J, and the latter in 7.1–8.22; 10.17ff.; 12, as E. Noth[26] modified this by denying any connection with the Tetrateuchal sources and by seeing the anti-monarchic source as deuteronomistic, and as dependent on the older pro-monarchic traditions. The tension between the different accounts Noth tried to explain by saying that the deuteronomist was very faithful to his sources, incorporating them in their original form even when they disagreed completely with his own critical and negative attitude to the monarchy.

This explanation has, not surprisingly, been seen as a great weakness in the theory of the unified structure and authorship of the deuteronomistic history, for it is perfectly clear, especially from the books of Kings, that the deuteronomist selected his material as well as edited it, and censorship by omission would have been a far more obvious method of dealing with the problem posed by the conflict between his own view and that of the ancient sources on the foundation of the monarchy, rather than the method which has apparently been used, that of adding a critical frame to the old pro-monarchic accounts. Boecker's attempt to cope with this problem is directed fundamentally at a new evaluation of what the so-called anti-monarchic passages, identified as deuteronomistic, are in fact saying. For Noth, they are simply anti-monarchic; for Boecker,[27] however, the deuteronomist is not simply concerned with Saul and with expressing opposition to his election. Rather, he is concerned with giving a theological evaluation of the monarchy as an institution. In this the deuteronomist wishes to counter the double danger which the monarchy posed: first, that it sets in question the lordship of Yahweh; secondly, that it oppresses the people in order to allow the royal court to live in luxury. The deuteronomist does not just reject the monarchy; instead, he is at pains to put it in its proper place within the context of the people Israel and its covenant relationship with Yahweh. The deuteronomistic view of the monarchy comes out particularly in I Sam. 12.14f. It is accepted by Yahweh but it is not itself any guarantee of salvation. The people is still subject to the law, and the king also is subject to the law. The deuteronomist has provided a theological framework which does not contradict the older sources, but sets them within the context of a presentation of the theology of the monarchy in Israel. So the unity of the deuteronomistic history may be upheld.

The third scholar to be noted here is Hoffmann, whose recent study of the deuteronomistic history marks a major attempt to re-establish its unity in the face of much criticism.[28] The redaction critical work since Noth, which has attempted to distinguish systematically different deuteronomistic layers in the various books, is regarded by Hoffmann as a result of and a development from an inconsistency of which Noth himself was guilty. While Noth argued in his original study that the deuteronomist was an author, rather than simply an editor, his later work, in his commentaries on Joshua and Kings, adopted a literary-critical approach towards separating deuteronomistic editing from an older written basis. Thus, the deuteronomist could be regarded as a redactor and no longer as a creative original author, and the way was then open towards distinguishing more than one redaction. In order to correct this and to re-establish the original traditio-historical approach of Noth, Hoffmann proposes to study a basic theme of the deuteronomistic history: the accounts of cultic reforms. These are both the negative reforms, relating to the introduction of forms of worship alien to Yahwism in the eyes of the deuteronomist, and positive reforms, relating to the purification of the cult. The accounts are found associated with the framework formulae by which each king is introduced, specifically with that part of the framework which evaluates the king in his relationship to Yahweh.

For the period of the monarchy, the deuteronomist is understood by Hoffmann to provide what is effectively a cult history, which may be divided into five phases. The first, having given the basic cultic tendency of the Davidic kingdom under Solomon (I Kings 11.1–13), goes on to describe fundamental cultic actions in the northern kingdoms (I Kings 12.26–32) and the southern kingdom (I Kings 14.21–24). The second phase begins with the cult measures of Ahab (I Kings 16.30–33) and his successors, Ahaziah (I Kings 22.53–54) and Joram (II Kings 3.1–3), in the northern kingdom, and those of Asa (I Kings 15.9–15) and his successor Jehoshaphat (I Kings 22.43–47) in the southern kingdom. In this second phase Ahab and Asa provide models of cultic behaviour to which their respective successors conform. The third phase is that of revolution and reform, beginning with Jehu (II Kings 9–10) in the north, and Jehoiada (II Kings 11.1–20) in the south. The actions of their respective successors, Jehoahaz in the north (II Kings 13.1–9) and Joash (II Kings 12.5–17) and Jotham (II Kings 15.34–35) in the south, bring to an end the reform periods of their predecessors and prepare the way for the fall of Israel on the one hand and the depravity of the reign of Ahaz on the other. The fourth phase shows a close integration of cult and politics. The end of the northern kingdom did not mean the end of the cult there: II Kings 17.7–23 constitutes a summary account of all the sins of the northern kingdom, leading to its destruction (finding a close parallel in II Kings 21 which likewise catalogues the cultic sins of Judah, here ascribed to Manasseh), while II Kings 17.24–41 portrays a continuing northern cult under Assyrian control, a mixture of the worship of Yahweh with the worship of other gods, so laying the presupposition for the northern aspect of the reform of Josiah. This finds its counterpart in the reforms of Ahaz (II Kings 16.1–20), in which also cultic reform is a political measure. The final epoch is that of the three great reformers in whom the cultic history of Judah and Israel reaches its climax: Hezekiah (II Kings 18.1–6), Manasseh (II Kings 21.1–18), and Josiah (II Kings 22–23). The sins of Judah reach their climax under Manasseh, in whose cultic measures the deuteronomist portrays the reason for the fall of Judah. Manasseh also serves, however, as a negative foil to Josiah, under whom all Manasseh's practices were set aside. Josiah is portrayed as an exemplary king of whom (as also of Hezekiah) it could be said that 'before him there was no king like him . . . nor did any like him arise after him' (II Kings 23.25; cf. 18.5); but he belonged in a general history of corruption and disaster which his personal qualities could not affect. The uniform account of Josiah's reform is the end point to which all previous reform activities point; in this story the deuteronomist's exilic and early post-exilic contemporaries are pointed to the model of Josiah as their example of faithfulness to the law.

Cultic reform is also the organizing principle for pre-monarchic time, and serves as the theme linking the deuteronomistic presentation of pre-monarchic and monarchic Israel. The epoch of the judges falls into three periods, from settlement to Gideon, from Abimelech to Jephthah and from then to Samuel, the conclusion of all of which is marked by cult notices: Judg. 6.25–32 (the reform of Gideon); 10.6–16 (the introduction to Jephthah); I Sam. 7.2–17 (Samuel). Saul too is a cultic reformer (I Sam. 28.3–25).

For the earlier period there are two cult reformers: Moses and Joshua. Josh. 24 recapitulates and concludes the Pentateuch while at the same time it introduces a new theme: that of the alternative between Yahweh and the gods, a theme which is the major thread holding together the deuteronomistic history in the periods of the judges and the monarchy. The reform of Moses (Deut. 9.7–29) presents an ideal programme and model for all future cult reformers in the deuteronomistic history. It prefigures the reform of Josiah, Moses the first reformer and Josiah the last belonging closely together, both following the requirements of the deuteronomic law.

It is not to be denied that there were cultic reforms in the course of Israelite history; such reforms did take place, especially under Jehu, Hezekiah and Josiah. The presentation of these is, however, in all particulars a deuteronomistic presentation. For the deuteronomist cultic reform is a basic datum of Israelite history, determining its course. That is not the case with the sources used by the deuteronomist. Thus, there is much more to be credited to the work of the deuteronomist than is commonly understood. His contribution covers not just the generalizing framework with its evaluation of the kings, using general cult terminology long recognized as deuteronomistic (for example, walk after, bow down to, fear other gods; do evil in the sight of Yahweh; turn aside from following Yahweh; the vocabulary of child sacrifice, magic, cult prostitution and high places), but also includes the detailed accounts of reforms, using specific cult terminology (verbs relating to the institution or removal of cult objects; cult objects themselves – Asherah, Mazzebah, altar; foreign gods, Baal, host of heaven, etc.). The accounts of the reforms are throughout uniform deuteronomistic compositions, the detail being the deuteronomistic way of giving historic verisimilitude to his account. The vocabulary used to detail the measures of the individual reforms proves to be typical rather than specific and singular, to belong to a literary presentation rather than to reflect historically verifiable events. While it is not excluded that there was some later supplementing of the account (II Kings 17.34–41 is taken to be from a later deuteronomistic hand; II Kings 16.10–18 is said to be priestly), it is not possible to connect such secondary additions into a stage of redactional history of the work of the deuteronomist. Rather, the study of the reform stories confirms the basic unity of the deuteronomistic history, while putting greater emphasis on the work of the deuteronomist as an author.

The three works mentioned are very different in their presentations and in the questions which they set out to answer. Jepsen's under-standing of the deuteronomist as a redactor rather than an author establishes a certain level at which the work is to be seen as a unity, but leaves the way open towards treating this unity as more or less superficial. Boecker's study is confined to a particular section and a particular theological theme, and does not really impinge essentially on the possibility that the deuteronomistic history had a redactional history which may be discerned in a consideration of literary phenom-ena and other theological themes. It is the question of the overall authorial unity of the deuteronomistic history which is the direct concern of Hoffmann, and which corresponds most closely to the issues which are involved here.

Hoffmann's is an impressive attempt to arrest a trend which has been strongly established in recent years, and, whether successful or not, it must lead to a better appreciation of the present structure of the deuteronomistic history. There are certain weaknesses which must, however, be considered. In the first place, there is no discussion of the issues which have been raised especially by Smend, Cross and Weippert, as indicators of lack of unity in the deuteronomistic history. The literary critical observations of Smend in Joshua (see below) remain valid; the tension which Cross has discussed between promises to David and condemnation of Jeroboam does exist and does not correspond with the course of reform and counter-reform which Hoffmann finds to be so significant; the formulaic language of the judgments meted out by the deuteronomist on the kings shows significant enough variation to require the kind of answer that Weippert gives (see below), and cannot easily be absorbed into Hoffmann's scheme.

Secondly, it is difficult to find a relevant background and context for the work of the deuteronomist when it is taken to be the unity that Hoffmann describes. It is surely inconceivable that the exilic or early post-exilic periods would present a suitable context for a presentation of Israel which emphasized that no matter how good the individual might be the end of the nation could only be destruction. Josiah's goodness could not compensate for Manasseh, and because of the evil of the latter the nation had to be destroyed. Josiah cannot act as an example for the deuteronomist's audience, if it requires just one Manasseh to bring about perdition.

Thirdly, Hoffmann's treatment of at least II Kings 17 and 22f. is highly questionable. Not only is he forced to admit the presence of a second deuteronomistic hand in II Kings 17, an admission which opens the way to finding other associated passages from the same hand, but also his argument for the unity of II Kings 22f. (as indeed of other passages) can scarcely withstand examination (see below).

Finally, Josh. 24 is said to be programmatic for the remainder of the deuteronomistic history, in setting before Israel the alternative of Yahweh or the gods as the object of Israel's allegiance. Yet, it is doubtful if the way in which that alternative is expressed in Josh. 24 is in fact to be set on the same level as the deuteronomist's later descriptions of reforms and counter-reforms which, for the deuteronomist, marked the course of Israelite history. There is one passage where that alternative is brought to expression in a way similar to that of Josh. 24, in which the worship of Yahweh and that of other gods is explicitly presented as incompatible, and that is in what Hoffmann takes to be the later deuteronomist's addition to II Kings 17. The alternative described in Josh. 24 does not so much set the theme for the remainder of the deuteronomistic history, as rather draw out to its starkest limits what is perhaps implicit in the rest of the deuteronomistic history, passing, just as does II Kings 17.34–41, a theological judgment on an already existing work rather than setting the programme for that work. There may, therefore, be a strong element of unity in the deuteronomistic history; but it is a unity expressed by a number of different factors, among which one must add the theme of cult reform to the other signs of unity argued for by Noth, none of which can at this stage be taken to preclude the possibility that the deuteronomistic history may also have undergone systematic redaction.

Those who have expressed disagreement with Noth may likewise be treated within two general groups: first there are those who find the Pentateuchal sources continued into Joshua and subsequent books of the deuteronomistic history; secondly, there are those who find sufficient lack of unity to indicate that more than one author was responsible for the compilation of these books. These are not two totally independent groups, for those who belong to the first also belong to the second; on the other hand, however, those of the second group do not always see the lack of unity in the deuteronomistic history in terms of the continuation there of the old Pentateuchal sources.

Those who find Pentateuchal sources in the deuteronomistic history do not form a homogeneous group. The extent to which such sources are traced differs widely, many tracing them only into Joshua or the beginning of Judges, others going so far as Samuel and Kings. The most ambitious in this respect are perhaps Eissfeldt and Freedman,[29] who agree in treating the whole deuteronomistic history as based on Pentateuchal sources. The latter provides no detailed argument for this view, while the former does, and so it is to the work of Eissfeldt that the following remarks are addressed. First, Eissfeldt expresses a general objection to Noth: Noth pays more attention to the early history of the material and not enough to its literary stage; a close examination of the pre-deuteronomistic parts of Joshua – II Kings shows that many apparently isolated fragments are in fact parts of well constructed wholes which may be reconstructed in spite of certain gaps that cannot be filled; 'all the analogies suggest that Israelite historical writing began when Israel had reached or just passed its zenith, i.e. under or soon after David or Solomon; and that it did not restrict itself to the immediate present or to a section of the past closely connected with it, but presented the whole development of the people from its beginnings, linked with the beginning of the world and of mankind, right down to the contemporary scene.'[30] Thus, in effect, Noth is here criticized for short cutting the process of growth of the deuteronomistic history by omitting the intermediate literary stage which comes between the old isolated traditions and the later fully developed work.

Three passages may be taken to illustrate Eissfeldt's attempt to demonstrate the existence of pre-deuteronomistic literary sources: Josh. 1–4; Judg. 7; I Sam. 7–12. In the first of these, Josh. 1 is taken to be reminiscent of E; it finds its continuation not in Josh. 2 but in Josh. 3.2. Josh. 2 'is itself equally clearly made up of two parallel narratives, which may be assigned to L and J'. These three strands continue into chapters 3f.: so, the taking up of the twelve stones is ordered three times ('from here', i.e. the eastern bank of the river, 4.3; from the middle of the Jordan, 4.3; from the middle of the Jordan, 4.5); and likewise, the setting up of the twelve stones is noted three times (4.8, at the halting place; 4.9, in the middle of the Jordan; 4.20, at Gilgal).

Eissfeldt's subsequent analysis of Joshua may be held to be based on the three sources thus analysed in these first four chapters.

In Judg. 7, v. 18 shows that we are dealing with a narrative which only knows of the sounding of trumpets and battle cries as the means of intimidating the enemy, and this story may be recovered more or less complete from vv.16ab*a*, 17b–19ab*a*,22. Beside it are traces of another narrative in which the shattering of jars makes the noise intended to intimidate the enemy, and the hands then set free hold torches and swords. This narrative too, though it suffered considerable loss when the two were combined, may be restored with certainty. In addition, the double reference to the flight of the enemy in vv.21f. shows that we are here dealing with two parallel narratives and not with the expansion of one basic narrative.

I Samuel 7–12(15) has already been noted to be a favoured passage for source analysis, in which the pro-monarchic source is seen as J and the anti-monarchic as E; Eissfeldt follows this general approach and so can see all the passages mentioned as proof texts for the distinction of continuous Pentateuchal sources in these books.

It need hardly be remarked that the proof is weak indeed: it does not reckon adequately with alternative reasons for the presence of doublets; it is inconsistent;[31] it does not result in coherent narrative strands;[32] and it fails to appreciate the function, not only of Josh. 1 but also of the so-called E passages in I Sam.7–12, to act as a theological framework to the traditions they take up.

Of course, the criticisms here expressed apply also to those who trace Pentateuchal sources into Joshua only, or to the beginning of Judges, for no more pressing literary critical arguments than those brought forward by Eissfeldt have been brought to bear on the question. Yet there is one reason in particular for making more detailed reference to both von Rad and Bright in this context: their view that JE is to be traced in Joshua is not based on a literary analysis of Joshua into these strands, but rather on the argument that the nature of JE in the Pentateuch demands the presence of JE in Joshua. Von Rad's presentation of this case[33] takes its starting point in the observation that the Pentateuch or Hexateuch is basically a series of credal statements which have been vastly elaborated through the inclusion of all kinds of diverse materials. These credal statements do, in fact, appear together in the literary form of an actual creed in a number of passages within the Hexateuch, the classic one being Deut. 26.5b–9. This creed is, for von Rad, the basis of the Hexateuch. It is a recital of Israel's saving history, leading up to her acquisition of the land, her settlement of Palestine; it is that event and the confession of God's gift which makes it possible, that is the whole point of the creed. Thus, the book of Joshua, wherein Israel's settlement of the land is recounted, is an essential conclusion to the books which precede, so that the only appropriate literary unit is a Hexateuch.

This is primarily a form-critical argument, and one which has come in for much criticism. However, the validity of its conclusion, viz. that Joshua belongs with the Pentateuch as a single literary unit, is not wholly dependent on the correctness of the observation that the short historical creed is basic to the Hexateuch. That possibility has come under strong attack on account of the largely deuteronomic formulation of the creed,[34] so that the creed is probably better understood to derive from the later rather than the earlier stages of the history of the growth of the Pentateuch/Hexateuch. Nevertheless, other observations may be made which lead to much the same result without the weak form-critical basis of von Rad's view. So Bright has listed three reasons for finding JE in Joshua:[35] first, the major emphasis of J from Gen. 12 onwards and of E from Gen. 15 onwards is that the people will inherit the promised land (cf. Gen. 12.1–3,7; 13.14–17; 15.7, 13–16 *et passim*), and so J and E must then go on to tell of the actual settlement; secondly, JE in Num. 32.1–17, 20–27, 34–42 tell how the Transjordanian tribes received their territory, and it is therefore likely that JE went on to tell of how the other tribes fared; thirdly, Num. 25.1–5 describes Israel as encamped at Shittim, and it is precisely at Shittim that Josh. 2.1 takes up the story.

The force of this argument is not as great as might at first appear, and indeed, insofar as it is intended as an argument against Noth's view that the deuteronomistic history begins something new and does not incorporate the old Pentateuchal sources, it must be considered as largely irrelevant. The third of Bright's points is a minor one: Shittim is a natural halting place before the actual crossing of the Jordan and its appearance in Josh. 2.1 could also be the result of a conscious link being established with Num. 25 rather than the result of an identity of authorship of the material in both passages. The major points are the first two which say in effect that the nature of JE in the Tetrateuch is such that they must have told of the settlement of Canaan by the Israelite tribes. With this argument one can only agree; but the conclusion does not necessarily follow that JE is present in Joshua. In this respect Bright has overlooked some fundamental aspects of the literary criticism of the Pentateuch adopted by Noth, which Bright in part follows. For Noth[36] it is the priestly writing which, as the latest of the Pentateuchal documents, forms the framework within which the others have been fitted; it is therefore the interests of P and the extent of P which are determinative for what JE can tell. A fundamental point is that P is absent from the book of Joshua:[37] the interests of P are centred on the event at Sinai and the figure of Moses, and with the death of Moses the priestly writing also comes to an end. Since this framework is that into which JE was then fitted, so also the JE account of the conquest of Canaan, which did originally exist, has been lost. The argument against Noth can, therefore, be effective only on the basis of a different understanding of the nature of P, quite apart from the additional necessity that the presence of parallel strands in the books which follow Deuteronomy should also be demonstrated.

If the argument for the presence of JE in Joshua has not been effectively presented, the question of the unity of the deuteronomistic history is not thereby resolved, for quite independently of the question of the presence there of documents as such, it is clear that a strong case can be made for lack of unity in a rather different way. The work of von Rad[38] is again fundamental at this point, for it has drawn attention to the startling lack of consistency of editorial presentation within the books of the deuteronomistic history. This inconsistency lies both in the quantity of editorial material discernible and also in the very nature of that editorial activity. Whereas the book of Judges has been heavily edited, there is little sign of any deuteronomistic contribution in the books of Samuel after I Sam. 12, and not until I Kings 3 is an extensive deuteronomistic presence once again discernible. Furthermore, while in the book of Judges the history of Israel is presented by the deuteronomist as 'cycles of apostasy, enemy oppression, repentance and deliverance', in the books of Kings 'the Deuteronomist lets the sin mount up throughout whole generations so as to allow Jahweh to react in judgement only at a later day'.[39]

This argument may in part at least be countered by the observation that the extent and nature of deuteronomistic editorial work depends on the extent and nature of the sources being incorporated and edited; such differences as those to which von Rad has pointed should not then be taken immediately to mean that different deuteronomistic hands have at various times and in various ways edited the individual books.[40] It will become clear, in any case, in the course of our study that as far as extent of deuteronomistic editing is concerned there is little to justify the argument for lack of editorial unity. With regard to the ideas expressed in the editing, the particular discrepancy to which von Rad has pointed will be seen to arise largely from the different natures and ideas present in the sources being used, and to be balanced by an evident editorial attempt to ameliorate disagreement by the subtle introduction of a more consistent presentation.[41]

This is not to say that we must then conclude that the deuteronomistic history has the unity for which Noth originally argued, for there remains one further form of disunity rather different from those hitherto discussed. While it may not be the case that different hands are responsible for the deuteronomistic versions of each book, the possibility is still open that different hands have in turn edited the whole deuteronomistic corpus to which these books belong. It is in this direction that several recent studies have pointed. The most significant contributions to this proposal have come from Cross and Nelson, the latter consciously intending to supplement and strengthen the former by supplying a firmer literary critical foundation. Cross[42] has adopted a thematic approach, in which he has distinguished two major themes in the deuteronomistic history: first, there is the sin of Jeroboam and his successors, bringing judgment on the northern kingdom (I Kings 13.34; 15.29; 16.1–4 etc.); and, secondly, there is the promise of grace to David and his house (II Sam. 7; I Kings 11.12f., 32,34,36; 15.4; II Kings 8.19; 19.34; 20.6 etc.). The climax is Josiah's extirpation of the cult of Jeroboam and his attempt to restore the Davidic kingdom in the context of his reform. This episode is treated at length by the deuteronomist; his whole account may indeed then be seen as propaganda for Josiah's reform, aimed at the north and the Israelites remaining there, and telling them to return to Judah and Jerusalem. This must, therefore, have been a pre-exilic deuteronomistic history; it was then edited during the exile by a deuteronomistic editor who extended it to its present limits, and who also turned the work into an address to the Judean exiles and a call to repentance. Nelson confirms this by studying the regnal formulae by which kings are introduced and dismissed: the formulae relating to the last four kings of Judah, following Josiah, differ from the others and derive from a different, later author.[43]

A major characteristic of Cross's study, which is that there is an interpretative process at work in the updating of the material to meet new situations, is explored at length by Polzin's compositional analysis of the deuteronomistic history.[44] This work represents a notable

attempt to apply modern literary critical approaches to the deuteronomistic history, at least as far as Judges. Although the validity of
traditional literary critical considerations is not denied, the emphasis
is shifted towards an attempt to understand the text as it now stands,
its tensions and inconsistencies being used in order to bring out the
overall thrust of the present text.

Polzin distinguishes reported from reporting speech in the deuteronomistic history, finding the latter minimal in Deuteronomy (only in
56 verses) but predominant in Joshua—Kings, while in Deuteronomy
it is the reported speech which dominates. The effect is to lay the
foundation of the history in a reported prophetic word, on the basis of
which the narrator then presents the history. The narrator, however,
validates his presentation of the history through what he does in
Deuteronomy, for here he achieves the end of presenting himself
ultimately as the authoritative voice: while the overt voice in Deuteronomy is that of Moses presenting the law in the past, the hidden
voice which gradually comes to exalt itself at the expense of Moses'
uniqueness is that of the narrator applying the law to this day. Thus
we are led to dissent from the declaration that there has arisen no
prophet like Moses (Deut. 34.10), and to agree to the proclamation
(Deut. 18.15–18) concerning the new prophet like Moses to whom
Israel should listen and to identify the narrator with this new prophet.

In Deut. 1–3 Moses reports the past, and then in chapter 4 interprets
it and analyses it in relation to the present and the future. This
distinction between past and present, between the report of the
authoritative word and the reinterpretation of it, is gradually broken
down, so that in the end the authority of the author of Joshua – II
Kings in interpreting and applying the law to the history may be
validated. Deuteronomy 5.28–31 authenticates the central teaching
role of Moses, and Deut. 18.17–20 authenticates the narrator's
teaching role in the history he presents to us. The overriding voice of
Deuteronomy, contradicting such passages as Deut. 13.1, is against
an immutable orthodoxy that would petrify the living word of God.
There is a shifting emphasis from past to present to future coincident
with the diminishing sound of the voice of Moses and the increasing
sound of the voice of the narrator, whose words become more
prominent in the collection of Moses' final sayings. So the ground is
prepared for the words of the narrator to take the central place in the
history.

There is much of value in this approach, though it is not clear if

Polzin believes that the distinction between reported and reporting speech, or between one view of the word of God and another, may have an effect on any form of traditio-historical or redaction critical approach to the text. The importance of recognizing the work as it stands as a creation to be studied and appreciated in its own right is often thought of as a useful corrective to atomizing tendencies: but the value of the more traditional approach cannot be undermined by modern literary criticism. These are in fact essentially different approaches, neither exclusive of the other; if confusion is to be avoided, it is difficult to see how they can interact.[45]

In what follows the major characteristics of the work of Cross and Nelson are represented: in general it is understood that the process at work is one of interpretation, by which older accounts are made to serve new purposes in new situations; it is also argued that interpretation is an ongoing process which has left a mark to be discerned in the literary criticism (in the more traditional sense) of the text, so that one may distinguish different levels in that ongoing process; and it is also recognized that this process belongs to concrete situations and is designed to respond to the definite needs of particular historical communities.

1

Deuteronomistic Editing of
DEUTERONOMY

The deuteronomic law in Deut. 12–26 is now framed by material which is related in varying degrees to the law which it incorporates. Some of it is very closely related, referring directly to the law and having the object of encouraging obedience to it; other parts of the framework have only a remote and indirect connection, and this aim of inculcating obedience is not the first concern. This is the case in particular with Deut. 1–3, chapters which relate the history of Israel from the point of its leaving Horeb to its arrival on the border of the promised land, an account which is then continued in Deut. 31ff. Deuteronomy 3 concludes with the two commands made to Moses by Yahweh: that he should ascend Mount Pisgah and from there view the land into which he himself was not to be permitted to enter, and that he should institute Joshua as his successor since it was to be Joshua who would bring Israel into the land. Moses' institution of Joshua is then recounted in Deut. 31.7f., an act which then receives divine confirmation in Deut. 31.23 and Josh. 1.6;[1] while in Deut. 34 the fulfilment of the first divine command to Moses, that he should ascend Mount Pisgah, is related.

The relationship between this historical account and the law of Moses is not an obvious one, and it is this clear difference of concern which prompted Noth[2] to see in Deut. 1–3 not primarily an introduction to the deuteronomic law, but an introduction to an account of Israel's history which continued at the end of Deuteronomy and then was to be traced through the following books of Joshua, Judges, Samuel and Kings: the so-called deuteronomistic historical work. Others have gone even further than this and have denied any original connection between the deuteronomic law and the history introduced by Deut. 1–3. While Noth considered that the deuteronomistic

22

historian had incorporated the deuteronomic law as the basis of his account, and as the criterion according to which the events and the personalities were to be judged, and ultimately as the criterion by which the whole history of the people was to be judged, it has been considered by others that this deuteronomic law did not form part of the original deuteronomistic history, but was brought into that context only at a secondary editorial stage.[3]

This latter view has a simplicity and clarity which recommends it: it allows us to see Deut. 4 as a transitional passage through which the connection between the history of chapters 1–3 and the law book with its introduction in chapters 5–26 was effected, and it effectively explains the remarkable lack of reference to the deuteronomic law in chapters 1–3. Moreover, this view supplies a credible motive for what we shall see to be a very clear second deuteronomistic stage of development having taken place at all: the purpose of the deuteronomistic editor who succeeded the deuteronomistic historian was to introduce the deuteronomic law. However, there are at least two fundamental difficulties here. In the first place, the work of the deuteronomistic historian in Deut. 1–3 is not immediately continued in Deut. 31ff.; rather, there is material particularly in chapters 5,9f. which must be assigned to his hand. It is to the deuteronomistic historian's stage of writing that the story of Israel at Horeb and its receiving there the decalogue, together with the subsequent account of Israel's breach of the covenant at Horeb, is to be assigned.[4] It is in this renewed reference to Horeb that the whole point of the historical introduction in Deut. 1–3 is revealed: it was at Horeb that something definitive happened which has a significance also for the Israel which Moses is addressing now at this later time. That Moses should begin his historical account in Deut. 1 by referring to Horeb, rather than, for example, to the patriarchs or to the exodus from Egypt finds its point and explanation in Deut. 5; it was in the event which took place there that the basis of the history of the people was laid. This basis consisted of the proclamation to the people of the decalogue and of the establishment there of a covenant relationship through which the people undertook to obey the demands of this covenant. However, that same event included also the fear of the people before the divine presence and the request to Moses that he should act as mediator between Yahweh and the people. Moses, in performing this function, received from Yahweh further commandments which he is now to deliver to the people. It is clear, therefore, that Deut. 1–3 leads up to

23

Moses' reference back to Horeb when he received from Yahweh commandments in addition to the decalogue which had been imparted directly. The deuteronomistic historian's account, therefore, leads directly into the deuteronomic law.

Secondly, just as the decision of the deuteronomistic historian to begin Israel's history at Horeb finds its explanation in the Horeb story in the context of which Moses received the law, so also the presentation of that history as a first person account of Moses can be understood only in the context of the inclusion within that story of the deuteronomic law understood as law of Moses. If the deuteronomistic history did not include the law of Deuteronomy but continued in chapters 31ff. and then subsequently in the following books, it is impossible to explain why it should have begun by using this first person style. This style breaks down in chapters 31ff. and in the following books, to become a third person impersonal account. If, however, the deuteronomistic historian intended to incorporate into his work the deuteronomic law, an already existing body of law understood as the law of Moses declared directly by Moses to Israel on the border of the promised land, then the first person style of Deut. 1–3 may be appreciated as an inevitable consequence. For this reason too, therefore, the deuteronomic law must be seen as part of the deuteronomistic history, brought in by that historian as an already existing corpus.

It may be presupposed, therefore, that in Deut. 1–3 we have an account of Israel's history from the hand of the deuteronomistic historian who here intends to set the scene for the deuteronomic law which is to follow. The story of Israel's history is continued in Deut. 31ff. and then subsequently in Joshua and the following books up to II Kings, but it now stands under the shadow of the deuteronomic law on the basis of which that history is intended to be judged. Yet this does not solve the problem of Deuteronomy; it supplies only the framework for our understanding the history of growth of that book. There is much in it which can be assigned to neither the original deuteronomic law nor to the hand of the deuteronomistic historian, and it is this which reveals that there is more than one (deuteronomistic) stage of redaction to which the book has been subjected.

Fundamental to the view of different redactional stages put forward here is the relationship which may be established between Deut. 1–3 and Deut. 4.1–40, a parenetic passage now functioning to link the historical survey of chapters 1–3 with the decalogue demand and other laws delivered to Moses in chapters 5ff.[5] The opening words of

Deut. 4.1–40, 'And now, O Israel . . .', indicate that there is some relationship: something is presupposed as preceding what is now to be said; and this relationship has on occasions been described as one of original unity.[6] If this were so, then the deuteronomistic historian in 4.1–40 would be drawing out the consequences for Israel of its history just narrated. In other words, the form of Deut. 1.1–4.40 would closely resemble that of the covenant formulary. However, there are basic problems here. In the first instance, the presence of such a formulary as an original form presupposes that the history narrated in Deut. 1–3 is focused on the relationship between Yahweh and Israel, so that now the implications of that relationship may be spelled out in terms of laws governing present behaviour. However, this is not the nature of Deut. 1–3. The history here is an account of Israel's progress from Horeb to the border of the land; it is a history which has its starting point indeed in the command of Yahweh, but it is not a history which has its focus on what Yahweh has done for Israel and how Israel has reacted towards Yahweh. It is not history used in the parenetic way of Deut. 8.2–6, for example, where it quite inevitably culminates in a reference to the law and Israel's obedience to it. The connection between the history of Deut. 1–3 and the parenesis of Deut. 4.1–40 where the law is central does not, therefore, appear to be an original one.

Secondly, there is a strong element of discontinuity between chapters 1–3 and 4.1–40 which confirms the conclusion that the connection between them is a secondary one. The transition from history in chapters 1–3 to parenesis in chapter 4 is much too abrupt to be original, and chapters 1–3 make no preparation whatever for the change through providing some indication that the history is being related as a foundation to a demand for obedience to law. Moreover, when 4.1–40 makes reference to events in Israel's history as a basis for the demand for obedience it is striking that those very events do not figure in the preceding chapters. So 4.3 alludes to an incident at Baal-peor unknown to chapters 1–3 where Baal-peor appears only as a stopping point of Israel on its journey (3.29). The theophany at Horeb is central to 4.1–40 (vv.9–14,33,36), but again appears in chapters 1–3 only as a stage in Israel's journey, this time its starting point (1.2ff.). Israel's exodus from Egypt is likewise important for this parenesis (4.20,34,37), but it has only very incidental reference in the first three chapters, in the story of the spies (1.27,30), and its significance there is by no means unequivocal; 4.1–40, on the other hand, presents this event as an unquestioned, basic datum of Israelite origins.

One possible approach to this situation is to see all of chapters 1–4 as being together the result of a process of bringing together of strands or the supplementation of layers by further layers.[7] However, this approach will not work in the present case, because it is clear that Deut. 1–3 (excepting probably just one or two passages) and Deut. 4.1–40 are in each case single units which have not undergone this form of editorial activity. In Deut. 1.1–3.29 a general historical and geographical introduction in 1.1–5 is followed by a historical review with a regular construction and presentation.[8] A framework in 1.6–8,19; 2.1,8,13b–15; 3.1,8,12 uses the first person plural style, and makes constant reference to the land as promised by Yahweh to the ancestors and which the descendants of the present generation will possess. This framework links together traditional material which can often be paralleled in the traditions of Genesis—Numbers. Deuteronomy 1 takes up the old traditions of the appointment of divisional heads of the people and the charging of the judges (paralleled in Ex. 18.25f.; Num. 11.16),[9] together with the story of the spies (Num. 13f.). In Deut. 2.1–3.11 there is an account of Israel's encounters with five peoples on its way to the land. There is a fairly consistent pattern of presentation of these encounters,[10] a pattern which is clearly of deuteronomistic origin since it is not evidenced in the sources which the deuteronomist used. The final part of the historical review, in 3.12–29, refers to the settlement of east Jordan by the two and a half tribes, the command that these tribes should help the others in their conquest of west Jordan, and the command to Moses to relinquish his leadership of the people to Joshua.

Characteristic of the author of Deut. 1.1–3.29 is his use of sources and indeed perhaps even a certain expectation that his readers know these sources.[11] The actual relationship between the deuteronomistic historian and his sources is difficult to establish since the precise nature and extent of the sources available to him are now unknown. However, the allusiveness of the spy story in Deut. 1.19–46, insofar as it reveals neither the reason for the fear of the people at the report of the spies (vv.27–28) nor the reason for the exception of Caleb from the general sentence of exclusion from the land pronounced on the people (v.36), apparently presupposes that the readers can fill in the detail from their knowledge of (a form of) the tradition now also contained in Num. 13f.; this may indicate a situation and an attitude in which the deuteronomistic historian felt able to allude to and make free use of the sources available to him in order to promote his particular theological point of view. Such a freedom is suggested by his general arrangement of the accounts of Israel's encounters with the peoples, where he modified the traditional account of Israel's meeting with Edom (Num. 20.14–21) in order to fit in with the general context of his view that Israel did not have the military assistance of Yahweh before the death of the rebellious generation (so there was no war with Edom), but did have this subsequently (so Israel defeated Sihon and Og).[12]

The situation in Deut. 4.1–40 is wholly different. As with Deut. 1.1–3.29, so here we have essentially a single unit, but its character and purposes are utterly different from those of Deut. 1.1–3.29 to the extent that common authorship must remain out of the question. The discontinuity between the two passages is important to establish clearly for this is the foundation on which it is possible to build the view that in these first four chapters of Deuteronomy there lie the beginnings of two clearly differentiated deuteronomistic redactions of the book.

It is to Braulik and Lohfink in particular that credit is due for establishing the unity of Deut. 4.1–40.[13] This has been done on the basis of the study of the language, form and content of the passage. Particularly striking are the stereotyped language and motifs which are distributed regularly throughout the passage. Israel's taking possession of the land is referred to in vv.1,5,14,21,22,26,38,40 using the three verbs *ntn*, 'give', '*br*, 'cross over', and *bw*', 'enter'. There is frequent reference to the promulgation of the law, with the verb *ṣwh*, 'command', and with either Moses or God as subject (vv.2,5,13,14,23,40). Certain words appear so frequently that they become catchwords characteristic of the passage: *bānîm*, 'children', in vv.9,10,25,40; *hyh*, in either verbal or nominal forms, 'live', 'life', in vv.1,4,9,10,33; *yāmîm*, 'days' in vv.9,10,26,30,32,40; *naḥ⁼lāh*, 'possession', 'inheritance', in vv.20,21,38; '*ênayim*, 'eyes' in vv.3,6,9,19,25,34; *nepeš* and *lēbāb*, 'soul', 'heart', in vv.9,15,29,39.

As far as its form is concerned, the passage may be broken down into six sections, vv.1–4, 5–8, 9–14, 15–22, 23–31, 32–40; each of these is self-contained, and all of them, except for the last, begin with a warning to obey the law and this warning is then reinforced through a reference to what history has taught. But these sections have been brought together within a credible overall framework, and a framework which, moreover, to some extent cuts across the divisions according to sections. A general principle of order, consisting of history, command, sanction, governs the sequence of thought, which thus reflects a pattern typical of the extra-biblical treaties. It is difficult to be precise here, for there are parts of the chapter, particularly its prologue in vv.1–8 and its epilogue in vv.32–40, where it is difficult to establish the existence of influence from the form of the treaty. It is in the central section, vv.9–31, that we find a mixture of exhortation and historical allusion followed by the prohibition of making images and finally by the curse and blessing.

Deuteronomy 4.1–40 cannot be claimed to be a treaty document; rather, it is a speech or sermon in the background of which there stands the form of the treaty. The rhetorical style, the repetition and expansiveness, represent a development far beyond any rudiments of parenesis which may be discerned in the treaties.[14] The treaty form has been used as a basic tool for the parenetic inculcation of a single prohibition, that of making images, a concern which appears throughout the whole central section in vv.9–31. The complete passage is then bound together by a prologue and epilogue in vv.1–8, 32–40, two passages which are themselves connected by many points of contact: v.40 takes up 'statutes' and 'commandments' from vv.1–2, the same phrase used of the law, 'which I command you', is found in this form only in vv.2,40; '(in order) that', as the introduction to a promise, is found only in vv.1,40; there is emphasis on what the eyes have seen in vv.3,34; the adjective 'great' is used frequently, in vv.6,7,8 and vv. 32,34,36,37,38; finally, the two sections are characterized by an explicit universalism of outlook which sets Israel in the context of the other peoples of the world.

The unity of Deut. 4.1–40 suggested by the language and form is confirmed by the content. The prologue refers in general to the law promulgated by Moses; the central section elaborates on what is taken to be the chief commandment of this law: the prohibition of images; and the epilogue affirms that Yahweh alone is God. This last section, in vv.32–40, is only from a superficial point of view loosely related to its context. In fact, its affirmation is an inevitable consequence of the prohibition of images, given the way in which Deut. 4.1–40 understands that prohibition. Just as in the decalogue in Deut. 5,[15] so here this prohibition relates not simply to the making of images of Yahweh, but more generally to the worship of other gods. For the author of 4.1– 40 the very attempt to make a representation, whether of Yahweh or otherwise, carries with it the worship of another god who is not Yahweh. Yahweh is imageless; to worship an image of him is to worship that which is not Yahweh, and so is the worship of another god. The fundamental reason, therefore, for the prohibition of images is that Yahweh alone is God, and it is this which the epilogue affirms.

In addition to this, Lohfink[16] has noted another connecting link in the content of the whole passage. When the author refers to past or future he apparently reaches progressively further backwards and forwards in each succeeding section: v.3 refers to Baal-peor and an incident there which belongs to Israel's most recent past; the references to wisdom and possibly also to the building of the Jerusalem temple (through which Yahweh is near to his people) in vv.6–8 point forward to the near future, the reign of Solomon; vv.10–14 refer to Israel at Horeb; vv.16–19 may refer to the images set up in the monarchic period; v. 20 looks back to the exodus; vv.25–28 look forward to the Babylonian exile; finally, in vv.29–31 the writer brings together the furthest past and furthest future by proposing the renewal of Israel in exile on the basis of the covenant with the patriarchs.

If the unity of Deut. 4.1–40 is thus established,[17] then another explanation will have to be found for that characteristic which Deut. 4.1–40 shares with many other parts of Deuteronomy and which has often been used to argue the case for lack of unity here: change of address from second person singular to second person plural and vice versa.[18] However, the argument that such inconsistency is evidence of lack of unity by which an original singular (or plural) text was later supplemented by an editor using the plural (or singular) form of address, really begs the fundamental question of why an editor did not conform to the style of address of the passage which he was in the process of supplementing. If it is answered that for this editor the difference in form of address has no significance then the ground for making any distinction between original work and editorial supplementation on this basis is immediately removed. It is, in fact, much more likely that a stylistic explanation is the most probable for this phenomenon, or perhaps a stylistic explanation in combination with that approach which has seen in the phenomenon a sign of different authorship.

It is probably the case that the deuteronomic law with its original parenetic introduction was formulated in the second person singular form of address; when this law with its introduction was incorporated into the deuteronomistic history it was brought into a context which made extensive use of the second person plural form of address.[19] The author of the deuteronomistic history, using the plural form of address, intended that the deuteronomic law, composed in the singular, should be understood as a quotation independent of, yet incorporated within, his work. If our own conclusion that Deut. 4.1–40 is later than the work of the deuteronomistic historian may be anticipated, the mixture of styles in 4.1–40 may then be explained as a deliberate device which has as its primary purpose the fuller integration of the deuteronomic law within the deuteronomistic history through the disguising of its character as quotation.[20] The use of the different forms of address in the composition of the passage was thus deliberate; moreover, the places where changes were introduced were not chosen simply arbitrarily; rather, there is some indication of a conscious attempt to use the changes deliberately for purposes of effect and emphasis, to highlight certain significant statements, and perhaps to allude to other theological statements outside 4.1–40.[21] There is certainly no basis here for literary critical division of the text.

The character of Deut. 4.1–40 has become clear on the basis of this discussion of its language, form and content. It is a sermon concerned with inculcating obedience to the law in general and to the prohibition of images in particular. A historical concern is far from central to it; there is no evidence of the use of sources in the manner of chapters 1–3; there are only a few historical allusions – to the covenant making at Horeb, the exodus from Egypt, the events at Baal-peor – which are, however, immediately subsumed beneath a weighty mass of preaching. This reinforces the conclusion already suggested by the elements of discontinuity already referred to: Deut. 4.1–40 is not from the author of Deut. 1–3. However, the matter cannot be left there. The introductory 'And now . . .' in Deut. 4.1 makes what follows dependent on what precedes whether or not it is an original continuation of what precedes. Deuteronomy 4.1–40 was, therefore, composed later than chapters 1–3 and was inserted after chapter 3 as its continuation. The connection is a secondary one, but it is, nevertheless, a deliberate connection.

If this establishes the presence in Deut. 1.1–4.40 of two authors, the deuteronomistic historian in chapters 1–3 and a later author in 4.1–40, our task must be now to confirm that in these chapters we also have the beginnings of two stages in the redaction of the book, rather than, perhaps, one stage with an isolated supplement.[22] The tracing of the continuation of chapters 1–3 later in the book presents little problem, for the story of these chapters is quite clearly taken up again towards the end of Deuteronomy. Our major concern is with discovering the hand responsible for Deut. 4.1–40 later in the book, so that one may think in terms of a clear stage of redaction of Deuteronomy in this connection. However, we must first refer to at least one point in connection with the contribution of the deuteronomistic historian.

We have already noted at the beginning of this chapter that the divine commands to Moses in 3.27f. find their fulfilment in Deut. 31 and 34. The deuteronomistic historian may, therefore, be credited with the authorship at least of Deut. 31.1–8,14f.,23; and most of 34.1–6. However, there is also one other major contribution which he apparently made. This is the introduction of the decalogue in Deut. 5 and the story of covenant breaking in Deut. 9f. The decalogue is introduced in the context of a story of covenant making at Horeb, and although it is quoted in its totality the tone and emphasis of the account lies on the history rather than the law. This common historical concern, together with connections in language, establish the common authorship of the stories of covenant making and covenant breaking in chapters 5,9f. Moreover, their ascription to the deuteronomistic historian is also probable. It is only here in an otherwise parenetic context that the historical interest, which has been noted for the deuteronomistic historian, emerges once again; as before, so now there is the use of sources.

This positive connection between the deuteronomistic historian and chapters 5,9f. is reinforced by the fact that chapters 5,9f. are suited neither as the work of the later author apparent in 4.1–40 nor as original parts of the deuteronomic law incorporated by the deuteronomistic historian. The later author of 4.1–40 apparently presupposes the presence of the decalogue in Deuteronomy, to which, in his sermon on the prohibition of images, he is referring; yet the intention behind the form of the decalogue in Deut. 5 is not the intention of the decalogue in the understanding of the author of 4.1–40, and so we cannot think in terms of this later editor as responsible for the introduction of the decalogue into Deuteronomy.[23] At the other extreme, it is also unlikely that the decalogue in the context of the story of covenant making in Deut. 5 is an original constituent of Deuteronomy from the time before the work of the deuteronomistic historian. The original heading to the deuteronomic law may be discerned in Deut. 4.45, and the original parenetic introduction is scattered through chapters 6 – 11. This introduction, composed in singular form of address, has no historical reference, and is clearly concerned only with the law proclaimed by Moses to Israel on the border of the promised land and not with events at Sinai as related in Deut. 5,9f. It is therefore most probably to the deuteronomistic historian that we owe these insertions. Through them he has not only provided a general historical setting and context for the deuteronomic law which he was incorporating, but he has also provided a precise origin for this law. It was that which was delivered to Moses by Yahweh on the occasion of the covenant making at Horeb, when the people feared to hear any more directly from the mouth of God.[24]

The contribution of the deuteronomistic historian has, therefore, been a twofold one. On the one hand he has provided a historical framework and a continuing historical presentation of the history of Israel from the time of Moses, a history which in its totality stands under the shadow of the law of Moses, the original deuteronomic law which he incorporated into the beginning of his work. On the other hand, however, he has also provided a particular historical context for the original deuteronomic law which it did not formerly have. Moses was traditionally known as the lawgiver of Israel, and around that figure the deuteronomic law gradually accumulated; it derived its authority from its connection with this venerable figure of Israel's past – it was the law of Moses. The time at which that law was given to Israel was not of pressing concern originally; it was accepted simply as having been imparted to Israel by Moses before his death just prior to Israel's having entered the land. So it was known as 'the testimonies, the statutes, and the ordinances, which Moses spoke to the children of Israel when they came out of Egypt' (Deut. 4.45). It was only its authorship which was of importance. The work of the deuteronomistic historian, however, had the effect of connecting this law of Moses (*a*) with the covenant made between Yahweh and Israel on Horeb; and (*b*) with the moment of entry into the land. The law was given to Moses by Yahweh on the occasion of that covenant making at Horeb; the fear of the people prevented its being delivered directly to the people and so Moses must act as mediator. The law thus stands in essential relationship to that covenant made at Horeb. However, the law is now given to the people, the new generation which has grown up after the death of the old rebellious generation, on the eve of their conquest of the land. This new generation is thus brought into immediate connection with both the original Horeb covenant and with the land which was promised to the fathers but which the former generation had forfeited. These two aspects of the work of the deuteronomistic historian are of considerable significance for subsequent editorial work on Deuteronomy, and for our understanding of the purpose with which the deuteronomistic historian composed his work.

The work of the author of Deut. 4.1–40 was clearly not at an end in that passage. Apart from some detailed additions which he made to the deuteronomistic historian's account of the covenant making at Horeb,[25] most significant contributions may be discerned both within chapters 6 – 11 and later in chapters 27ff.[26] Within chapters 6 – 11 the distinction between history and parenesis is not one which is particularly or generally useful in marking out the contribution of the author of 4.1–40, for, apart from the addition by the deuteronomistic historian to chapters 9f. there is, in fact, no historical material present. Rather, it is evident that otherwise within chapters 6 – 11 there are combined two parenetic layers. The one which we are mainly concerned here to note is distinguishable by its affinities with 4.1–40 in emphasizing the law in general, the worship of other gods in particular and in generally using the style and vocabulary familiar from 4.1–40. The other, which is evidently the earlier of the two, has its focus on Israel on its way into the land, and is chiefly concerned with encouraging Israel in the face of the opposition to its settlement which it will meet, and with ensuring that Israel when she finally does expel the inhabitants of the land and settles there herself, will remember who is the true author of her prosperity. Since this parenetic layer is the basis on which both the deuteronomistic historian's addition in chapters 9f. and the later editor's contribution have been built, it is clear that in this layer we have the oldest and probably the original introduction to the deuteronomic law. It is this introduction, with the following law, which was incorporated by the deuteronomistic historian and later edited.

The literary unit within which the decalogue was introduced extends up to 6.3. Within the remainder of chapter 6 a distinction is to be made between vv.4–9, 20–25 on the one hand, and vv.10–18(19) on the other. The former uses a literary form of child's question associated with a cultic action, which has been broken by the later insertion of vv.10–18(19), a passage which, like 4.1–40 but unlike the remainder of chapter 6, alludes to the decalogue and is concerned with the worship of other gods, shows the same use of change from second person singular to second person plural form of address in order to introduce particular emphasis, and shares a stock of common vocabulary.[27]

In Deut. 7 a distinction is to be made between vv.1–3, 6, 17–24 on the one hand, and vv.4–5, 7–15, 25–26 on the other. These passages deal with two different subjects: the destruction of the peoples of the land, and the avoidance of the worship of their gods, and these two subjects are abruptly brought together in the linking verse 16. It is the second of these subjects which corresponds with the interests of the later editor: it is here that we find common contact with the decalogue, especially the prohibition of images/other gods, and also common style and vocabulary, including the change between singular and plural forms of address at significant points.

Deuteronomy 8 likewise deals with two subjects. The link between them is formed by the word 'forget'. For the older parenetic layer in vv.7–11a (beginning the translation by 'When the Lord your God brings you . . . .'), 12–14a, 17–18a, the subject is the possibility that Israel, once settled in the land and enjoying all the benefits which it confers, will forget that it is to Yahweh that she owes all this prosperity, and will ascribe her success to her own power. In the later parenetic layer in vv. 1–6, 11b, 14b–16, 18b–20, 'forget' means to forget the commandments. This conforms with the interests of the later editor; and this connection is confirmed by the allusion in vv.14b, 19 to the decalogue, by the stylistic change between singular and plural forms of address and by common vocabulary.

Between 9.1 and 10.11 there is a basic parenetic layer, which belongs to the original introduction to the deuteronomic law, which has been supplemented by the deuteronomistic historian. The later editor does not appear again until 10.12–11.32, the final section of the parenetic introduction to the deuteronomic law. Here, however, there is no older parenetic layer to be discerned; the section as a whole apparently derives from the hand of the later editor.[28]

In form, content and language 10.12–11.32 shows a remarkable resemblance to 4.1–40, and creates the clear impression that here the later editor is rounding off his contribution to the parenetic introduction to the deuteronomic law, just as he began it, with a long sermonic exposition. Both passages begin with 'And now . . .', establishing a secondary link between what follows and already existing deuteronomistic historian's material. In both passages the influence of the covenant or treaty form is obvious, especially in the succession of history-demand-sanction: in the present instance 11.2–7 is a historical prologue, 11.8–9 is the demand; and 11.13–15 is the blessing. Here too there is no actual covenant or treaty document; rather, the form of such a document provides the basic pattern or framework for a sermon. This sermon breaks down into sections which parallel the structure of 4.1–40. Both passages begin (4.1–8; 10.12–22) with a prologue which refers in general to the commandments, to Israel's history and to her exclusive worship of Yahweh, concluding with a descriptive phrase of the greatness of Israel in the present ('a great nation,' 4.7f.; 'as the stars of heaven for multitude', 10.22). Next comes a historical prologue (4.9–14; 11.1–7) which emphasizes that which 'your eyes have seen'. This leads into a general warning against disobedience concluding with a reference to the land (4.15–22; 11.8–12). Next there comes a section (4.23–31; 11.13–25) which looks to the future, holding out the prospect of curse and blessing dependent on Israel's attitude to the law. Finally (4.32–40; 11.26–32), the sermons come to an end with an epilogue which in each case contains a general exhortation to obey the law in 'the land which the Lord your God gives you'.

Both passages share a substantial stock of common vocabulary, and in both there is the same stylistic change between second person singular and second person plural forms of address. One aspect of this change is perhaps especially noteworthy. Whereas in 4.1–40 the first part of the sermon (vv.1–31) was basically in plural form of address with only occasional change to singular, and the remainder (vv.32–40) in singular with only one change to the plural, in the sermon of 10.12–11.32 the first part (10.12–22) is mainly singular with only one change to plural address,[29] and the remainder (11.1–32) is mainly in the plural with occasional change to the singular. This may be a deliberate inversion of this stylistic phenomenon, intended to emphasize the function of 4.1–40; 10.12–11.32 to embrace the whole parenetic introduction as complementary parts of a framework.

It is clear, therefore, that the later editor has made a very considerable contribution to the present parenetic introduction to the deuteronomic law, building both on the deuteronomistic historian's work and also on the older, original parenetic introduction. It is very probably true that both the deuteronomistic historian and the later editor have also contributed to the deuteronomic law itself; however, it is not until the end of that law that substantial and quite clearly discernible contributions from both of these editors of Deuteronomy again come to the fore.

After the conclusion of the deuteronomic law in 26.15[30] it is difficult to see anything which may be reckoned as part of the original book as it lay before the deuteronomistic historian.[31] The concluding chapters are rather composed of contributions from the deuteronomistic historian, the later editor and even later additions. The immediately following section, 26.16–27.26, which is, broadly speaking, concerned with establishing the deuteronomic law as the law of the covenant between Yahweh and Israel to which both parties assent, has as its basis 26.16–19 and 27.9–10. These two passages belong closely together, both in vocabulary and content. Israel's status as the people of Yahweh is formally established and then formally affirmed. The express concern of both passages with the exclusive relationship between Yahweh and Israel links them with the dominant interest of the later editor, a connection which is confirmed by the close language contacts with the author of 4.1–40 and other passages already seen to derive from his hand.[32] The blessings and curses which then follow in 28.1–68 represent a collection of traditional materials which, however, have been introduced here only late. The chapter is not uniform, but has clearly gradually developed to its present proportions. It goes back to a basic parallel series of blessings and curses in vv.3–6, 16–19. These, however, show no connection with law or covenant; they have been provided with such a connection through the introductions now given to them in vv.1–2,15. Through these verses, moreover, a connection may be established with the late editor of 4.1–40 through vocabulary and concerns. It is he who first introduced blessings and curses into the context of the deuteronomic law, and it is probably also he who was responsible for a large part at least of the elaboration of those blessings and curses through the gathering together of traditional materials derived from the long-established tradition of blessing and cursing in the treaty context.

Deuteronomy 29.1 opens a section which extends to 30.20, 31.1 being probably a corrupted form of an original concluding formula which was modified only after the introduction of further words of Moses.[33] The two chapters consist of a series of speeches or sermons, which together constitute a sermon on the theme of covenant obedience to the law which has been proclaimed. There is a coherent order: first (29.1–9) obedience is advocated on the basis of what history has taught; then (29.10–15) the two parties to the covenant are identified; the third part (29.16–28) declares the curse which will inevitably follow on disobedience; the fourth (29.29–30.14) proclaims the blessing and restoration which will follow on destruction; finally (30.15–20) the whole is summarized with renewed exhortation to obedience. The ground here is familiar. It is not a covenant document which appears, but a sermon, which alludes to basic treaty elements and uses them for its construction and elaboration.[34] Just as in 4.1–40, so here the treaty scheme of history, law, sanction is the background framework for an expansive sermon which almost transcends its limits. In addition to many connections in vocabulary, the two passages also share a remarkable form of presentation of curse and blessing. In the treaty form these are alternatives which will follow on disobedience and obedience respectively; but in 4.25–31 and 30.1–10 the blessing is presented as a state which will follow on the curse rather than as an alternative possibility to the curse.[35]

We have already seen that the work of the deuteronomistic historian is continued in 31.1–8,14f.,23 and 34.1–6, passages where the fulfilment of the divine commands to Moses in 3.27f. is related. The material which remains to be considered consists chiefly of the Song of Moses with its introduction, to be found in 31.16–22,30; 32.1–44, and the Blessing of Moses in chapter 33, both of which are late isolated interpolations into Deuteronomy. Aside from these there is material which may be identified as coming from the hand of the priestly writer, in 32.48–52 and 34.7–9 both of which passages, together with the even later 34.10–12, belong to the time of the bringing together of the deuteronomistic history with the Tetrateuch and the subsequent separating off of the Pentateuch as a distinct entity. This leaves three passages: 31.9–13, 24–29 and 32.45–47.

Deuteronomy 32.45–47 offers a suitable conclusion to the layer which begins in 4.1–40, and there are close contacts in thought and vocabulary which suggest that the verses should be seen as deriving from that same hand. Here the later editor brings to a close his very extensive contribution to the present form of Deuteronomy.

The other two passages, however, stand apart. They are clearly related: both are concerned with the law, the first with its future public proclamation and the second with its preservation as witness against Israel in the future; both are concerned with the Levites, as the ones who have the responsibility of proclaiming and preserving the law; both make reference to the ark of the covenant of the Lord which is carried by the Levites; and both passages stand apart from their contexts. There is some suggestion that the hand of the later editor which we have already extensively traced is present here too, since in both cases there is a concern with the law, and, insofar as the public reading of the law is required and reference is made to witness (31.26), there is apparently a link in these two passages with the treaty tradition which is so strong in the thought of the later editor. However, the interest shown by these two passages in the Levites, in ritual and ceremonial, sets them apart from that editor, and indeed it is difficult to see them as a good continuation of the work of that editor as represented in chapters 29–30. Rather, these passages find their closest association with other passages which we have already noted as coming from a hand even later than that of the later editor: 11.29–30; 27.1–8, 11–26.[36] Through all these passages ritual, the Levites, the ark and the law are recurrent features, and they apparently constitute a distinct layer within the book which is later than the editorial layer in 4.1–40 and so many other passages.

With the work and significance of the author of the latest layer here noted we shall be concerned later, since further material from his hand is probably also to be found in Joshua.[37] It does not represent a major redactional stage of development of the deuteronomistic history, additional to the two stages whose beginnings we have now traced in Deuteronomy. For the moment, we may conclude our discussion of Deuteronomy by bringing together some of the points which have been made in order to present a picture of the general development of the book. The original book of Deuteronomy with its parenetic introduction[38] is to be found within chapters 6–11, 12–25. It is composed of earlier books of law which have been brought together into a collection governed by the principle of centralization of worship; to this a parenetic introduction addressing Israel on its way into the land has been added. The work was known as the law of Moses. The deuteronomistic historian incorporated this at the beginning of his work, providing a setting for it through the addition of chapters 1–3, together with the account of the making and breaking of the covenant in chapters 5, 9f. He completed his framework of the original book by the addition of material now found in chapters 31 and 34 relating to the appointment of Joshua as leader and Moses' death. The intention of the deuteronomistic historian was to provide a standard by which his readers should judge the history of Israel which he was now going on to relate. One effect of his work was to bring the law of Moses into close relationship with the covenant making at Horeb, a connection which did not formerly exist: it was at Horeb, on the occasion of the making of the covenant, that Moses received the law. This connection provided the basis for the work of the later editor. For him the law of Moses is also covenant law; this was the implication of its origin as related by the deuteronomistic historian, but, through the introduction of the idea of a covenant as the setting for Moses' giving this law to Israel on the eve of the entry into the land (Deut. 29.1), it is now made explicit that this law of Moses is in fact covenant law, the law of the covenant between Yahweh and Israel.

In developing this theme, the later editor has introduced into Deuteronomy covenant or treaty categories which did not originally belong to it.[39] This was a fruitful innovation, for it allowed the editor to make a particularly effective contribution to the problem of the theological understanding of the situation in which his contemporaries found themselves. This was undoubtedly an exilic situation. The parallels between the work of this later editor in Deut. 4.1–40; 6–11*; 26.16–19; 27.9–10; 28; 29–30 and 32.45–47 on the one hand, and Second Isaiah on the other,[40] confirm their common exilic context and background. The people of this time had experienced the destruction of the nation and the exile to Babylon. The only theological explanation for this, which could be consistent with a belief in the omnipotence of Yahweh, was that it represented punishment for sin. This is declared through the use of the covenant form. However, the editor has modified that form in order to ensure that this should not be the last word on the subject. Whereas the treaty form presented curse and blessing as alternative possibilities depending on one's attitude to the law, this editor has put them in historical succession (4.25–31; 30.1–10): the curse of the law is that which Israel in exile is now experiencing; but there is the blessing to follow. Israel in exile is encouraged with the promise of renewal and restoration.

2

Deuteronomistic Editing of
JOSHUA

We have seen that the book of Deuteronomy has experienced more than one stage of development which may be classified as deuteronomistic. The fundamental argument, that the work of the deuteronomistic historian in Deut. 1–3 is supplemented rather than directly continued in the parenetic sermon of Deut. 4.1–40, has been confirmed by the distinction which may be observed between two parenetic layers within Deut. 6–11: the older of these is apparently the original introduction to the law of Moses incorporated by the deuteronomistic historian, and the later is the work of the deuteronomistic editor at work in Deut. 4.1–40. That same editor is, moreover, to be distinguished again from the deuteronomistic historian towards the end of Deuteronomy: while the historian continues his account in Deut. 31.1–8, 14f., 23 and 34.1–6, before taking up his story in the book of Joshua, the later deuteronomistic editor, after substantial contributions to Deut. 26ff., brings his work in Deuteronomy to a close in Deut. 32.45–47.

These two editions have been distinguished consistently on the basis of their language and purpose: the deuteronomistic historian has introduced the law of Moses as a criterion of judgment on the history he presents; this historico-theological interest is determinative for his work. The later editor has built on this, taking as his starting point the connection now established between the law of Moses and the covenant made between Yahweh and Israel at Horeb: the law of Moses is no longer that alone, it is now the law of the covenant between Yahweh and Israel; it was received by Moses at the original covenant making at Horeb, and it is now delivered to the new generation of Israelites who had not participated in the first event. To this generation, with which the contemporaries of the later deuteronomistic editor would quickly identify, the editor speaks a word of warning, of threat, but also of encouragement, concerning their inheritance of the land promised to the fathers. It is now our task to examine the book of Joshua in order to determine if the pattern of development shown for Deuteronomy may be seen also here.

The many levels at which the continuity between Deuteronomy and Joshua may be established clearly indicate that the latter book has experienced a process of redaction which closely parallels that of Deuteronomy. The straightforward narrative continuity, according to which Joshua fulfils the task for which he was commissioned by Moses (Deut. 3.28; 31.7f., 23; Josh. 1.6), is reinforced by a consistence of theological and literary presentation in both these books. At least four theological motifs link the two books,[1] to the extent that they both reflect a single theological outlook.

First, Israel is presented as a single whole. All Israel is the frequent object of address (Deut. 1.1; 5.1; 11.6; 27.14; 29.9; Josh. 3.7,17; 4.14; 7.23f.; 8.21,24; 23.2 etc.) and its constitution as a people of twelve tribes is made explicit in the lists of tribes in Deut. 27.12–13 and Josh. 13–19. It is, however, in the context of stories of the danger of division and disruption, as when the two and a half tribes occupy territory in east Jordan separate from their fellow-tribes in the west, that the insistence on the unity of the people becomes explicit. It is only on condition that these transjordanian tribes help the others in their settlement of the west that Moses permitted them to take land for themselves in east Jordan (Deut. 3.12–20; Josh. 1.12–15; 4.12) and when the possibility arises that these transjordanian tribes might establish themselves as an independent cult community in the east this is vehemently opposed (Josh. 22.1–34).

Secondly, this single people stands in covenant with Yahweh in both Deuteronomy and Joshua. The covenant mediated by Moses between Yahweh and Israel on the plains of Moab (Deut. 29.1) on the eve of crossing over into the land, is renewed by Joshua when the conquest and distribution of the land has been completed (Josh. 24.1–28). In fulfilment of the demand of Moses (Deut. 27.1–8), the law which is the content of that covenant, is inscribed and read before the people at Mount Ebal as soon as opportunity offered after entry into the land has been effected (Josh. 8.30–35). On several occasions explicit reference is made to the law of the covenant (Deut. 17.18; 31.24,26; 28.61; 29.20; 30.10; 28.58; 29.19,26; Josh. 1.8; 8.30–35; 23.6,16) but it is also clear that the stories in Joshua often implicitly presuppose that law and are told from its point of view. The crime of Achan, in taking from the devoted things on the occasion of the battle against Ai (Josh. 7) was a violation of the war law of Deut. 20.10–18, and his punishment, death by stoning, is in conformity with that prescribed in Deut. 13.10. The war law of Deut. 20 was also violated in the covenant made between Israel and the Gibeonites, and it is only against the background of that law that the actions of the Gibeonites may be fully appreciated.[2] The bodies of the five kings killed by Joshua were taken down at sunset from the trees on which they had been hanged, in conformity with the demand of Deut. 21.23.

Thirdly, the single people Israel is led by one leader. The parallels clearly observable in the presentations of Moses and Joshua go beyond a common stereotype, so that it is evident that it is a specific idea of leadership, reflecting a particular point of view, which informs the descriptions. Many of these parallels, such as that of the leader of the people on dry land through water, that of the leader celebrating the Passover, and encountering Yahweh or a messenger of Yahweh, relate to Exodus (15.8; 14.21f., 29; 3.5; 12) and Joshua (3.13, 17; 5.10,15) rather than Deuteronomy and Joshua. But as specific links between Deuteronomy and Joshua in this connection one may point to the function of both leaders as intercessors when the people or an individual sin (Deut. 9.25–29; Josh. 7.7–9), and also to the parallel between Moses as leader of the people into East Jordan and his assignment of that territory to the transjordanian tribes (Deut. 3.12–17) on the one hand, and Joshua's leadership of the people into West Jordan and his assignment of that territory among the tribes, on the other.

Fourthly, the means by which Israel gained possession of the land, according to the book of Joshua, was not simply a war of conquest; rather, it was a holy war, a religious undertaking, a war waged under the leadership of Yahweh, and one which consequently involved the observance of certain ritual prescriptions. There is undoubtedly very ancient tradition behind the stories of Joshua, but the presentation of the events described there now follows the ideals of holy war as these come to expression in the book of Deuteronomy. The latter, in both its old parenetic introduction (see especially Deut. 7.1–3, 6,17–24; 9.1–6) and its laws (Deut. 20), is imbued with a martial spirit, to the extent that the Israel to which it is addressed is an Israel in camp preparing for war against its foes. Although the leadership of Yahweh in war had long been an article of faith, carrying the assurance of power and victory, it is first in Deuteronomy that this receives systematic presentation in the form of a holy war ideology.[3] According to Deuteronomy, Israel is to destroy all the inhabitants of the land which she is to enter, making no peace or covenant with them, for it is only thus that the purity of her relationship with Yahweh will be preserved. She is not to fear the might of these nations, for it is Yahweh who brought Israel out of Egypt, who is her leader and guarantor of victory. With those of Israel's enemies outside her land who seek to make peace with her, Israel may make covenants, but not with her enemies within the land. Total destruction is the only means by which Israel may come to full possession of the land sworn to her fathers and so to the 'rest' which Yahweh has promised her. It is precisely in these terms that Israel's taking of the land in the book of Joshua is described, so that in the end Yahweh gave Israel 'rest on every side just as he had sworn to their fathers; not one of all their enemies had withstood them, for the Lord had given all their enemies into their hands' (Josh. 21.44). The conquest was a total conquest, involving the utter destruction of the former inhabitants of the land; the dismay of Israel on finding that because of the deception of the Gibeonites these Canaanites had to be excepted from that general destruction illustrates the concern of the book of Joshua to present Israel's conquest of the land in deuteronomic terms.[4]

This strong linking of Joshua to Deuteronomy may be the further strengthened on a different level by the literary critical approach adopted by Polzin.[5] The book of Joshua exhibits the same concerns as were manifest in Deuteronomy: what Deuteronomy sets forth as word of Moses to Israel or to Joshua is in Josh. 1 set forth as word of God: this exalts not only the authority of the word of Moses but also the role of the narrator as Moses' successor.[6] The process of authoritative application and interpretation appears also in the direct utterances of God in Josh. 1–12: here God is presented as interpreting and applying his own earlier utterances (either direct words of God or through Moses or Joshua). The word of Yahweh in the book of Joshua, as in Deuteronomy, is not static but open to further understanding, interpretation and application. So it is enlightening to interpret the stories of Joshua in the context of their relation to the holy war laws of Deuteronomy or as interpretative meditations on parts of Deuteronomy. In Josh. 2 Rahab is preserved alive despite holy war provisions relating to enemies in the land who should be wholly exterminated. In this there is expressed, from the point of view of the dispossessed nations, the theme of Deut. 9.4f.: in the latter Israel is told that she is to occupy the land not because of her own righteousness but because of the wickedness of the nations; in Josh. 2 it is not because of Rahab's merit that she and her household continue to occupy the land but because of the wickedness and lack of faith of Israel as exemplified in the sending of spies. Joshua 5.9 is a direct allusion to Deut. 9.28, the reproach of Egypt being Egypt's interpretation of Israel's not being given the land as proof of God's inability to do what he promised and also his hatred of Israel. Israel's covenant with the Gibeonites in Josh. 9 parallels Yahweh's covenant with Israel and has a literary foreshadowing in Deut. 9f., 29: the Gibeonites, whose clothing and sandals should have been new but are displayed as old and worn out remind us of Israel whose clothing and sandals should have been old but were good as new; the Gibeonites eat dry and mouldy bread, Israel had no bread; the Gibeonites remind Israel of her victory over Og and Sihon just as Moses does in Deut. 29; neither the Gibeonites nor Israel deserves the covenant, and of this the Gibeonites shall be a constant reminder to Israel in the context of its covenant with Yahweh. Thus, the deuteronomistic account of the occupation, while using traditional stories, is in fact a 'hermeneutic meditation on the word of God', both interpreting and showing the need for such interpretation.

Certain of the detailed interpretations involved in this approach are far from convincing,[7] though these of themselves are perhaps not of very great significance. What is more important is that it must be recognized that this approach belongs to a quite different level of understanding from that which seeks to discover the seams within the narrative resulting from its redactional development. Polzin's approach is often helpful towards an appreciation of the deuteronomistic history as a literary totality, but it is not to be confused with, nor does it undermine the validity of, the literary critical quest for the redactional history of the books within the deuteronomistic history. So it may be that the only way to take Josh. 21.43–45 within the present book of Joshua is ironically, and to see it, in Polzin's terms, as the voice of authoritarian dogmatism which is subdued through most of Josh. 13–21 (see also Josh. 23.9,14 in relation to Josh. 23.11–13, 15–16) by the voice of critical traditionalism; but this understanding is neither supplementary to, nor a corrective of, but simply different from the recognition that Josh. 21.43–45 belongs to a stage in the history of the book which may be discerned more widely and which in its present wider context is being reinterpreted.

The literary observations which must provide the valid basis to the theological characteristics which hold Deuteronomy and Joshua together were given their classic expression by Martin Noth.[8] Here Josh. 1 was seen to be the continuation of the deuteronomistic history which has its introduction in Deut. 1–3 and reappears in Deut 31* and 34*. The book of Joshua was recognized to exhibit characteristics which bind it in with that history: in particular, the use of reflective speeches or narratives at decisive points in the course of the history. The narrative of Josh. 1 opens the conquest period; that of Josh. 12 completes it; and the departure speech of Joshua in Josh. 23 concludes the deuteronomistic presentation of the conquest by setting before the assembled Israel the law in obedience to which she may enjoy life and prosperity in the land. Clearly Josh. 1 cannot be understood as the beginning of a new work, and it is particularly in Deut. 1–3, according to Noth, that some of its necessary presuppositions are to be found. The spies story of Deut. 1.19–46, relating an unsuccessful attempt to penetrate the land from the south, explains why the invasion had to take place from the east, as the book of Joshua relates. The presuppositions for the Caleb story of Josh. 14.6–14 are also to be found in that story of the spies, for it is to Caleb and Joshua alone among the generation of the spies that entry into and possession of the land are promised.

The literary continuity indicated here in general terms is open to detailed demonstration through a study of those texts in Deuteronomy and Joshua relating to the transfer of leadership of Israel from Moses to Joshua (Deut. 3.28; 31.7f., 23; Josh. 1.6,9b).[9] The task for which Joshua is instituted has two aspects: he is to go over into the land at the head of the people, and he is to put the people in possession of the land. The first of these is a command to conquer the land, the second a command to divide the conquered land among the tribes, thus corresponding to the division of the book of Joshua itself into an account of the conquest (Josh. 1–12) and an account of the division of the land (Josh. 13–21).[10] The initial divine command to Moses in Deut. 3.28 mentions these two tasks together, while the account of Moses' institution of Joshua in Deut. 31.7f. likewise mentions them together. The divine confirmation of this action, however, in Deut. 31.23 refers only to the first, that of bringing Israel into the land, while the divine confirmation of the second task does not appear until Josh. 1.6. That this is an intentional stylistic device, which has the effect of binding the two periods, that of Moses and that of Joshua, closely together, is clear from the fact that quite distinctive formulaic language is common to the institution accounts. In the three passages, Deut. 31.7f.; Deut. 31.23 and Josh. 1.6,9b, there is used a formula for institution to an office, a formula which may have had a fixed form in pre-deuteronomistic time and may have had an actual life situation, but which is found complete in only these three deuteronomistic passages. It consists of three elements: *(a)* the formula of encouragement, 'be strong and of good courage'; *(b)* the description of the task for which the subject of the task is being instituted, introduced by 'for you . . .'; *(c)* the formula of divine support giving the assurance of the presence of Yahweh, 'the Lord will be with you'/'I will be with you'. Through the use of this formula a strong literary link is provided to connect the Moses and the Joshua tradition in the deuteronomistic presentation.

It is clear, however, that further refinement is necessary. The book of Joshua has a strong literary and theological link with Deuteronomy, which may be explained on the basis of common deuteronomistic authorship or editing in both books. Yet, within the book of Joshua, as within Deuteronomy, it is evident that editing was not a uniform process or a single event. Most obviously is this the case in relation to Josh. 23 and 24.1–28. Since Josh. 23 is intended as a final speech from Joshua who is 'old and well advanced in years' and 'about to go the way of all the earth' (vv.2, 14), Josh. 24.1–28, where no such indication of Joshua's imminent departure is given or presupposed, cannot constitute the original continuation. Yet Josh. 24.1–28 has too much in common with Josh. 23, in terms of its setting, expression and subject, for it to be considered totally independent of Josh. 23, a chapter normally and rightly ascribed to deuteronomistic authorship. In both chapters Joshua summons the Israelite tribes to himself, makes a speech to them, and, with reference to the past, gives them directions for their future behaviour.[11]

However, it is not here that we may find the primary indication that the book of Joshua has been subject to a process of editing analogous to that which determined the present shape of Deuteronomy. Smend in particular in connection with other passages in Joshua has shown that two stages in the editing of the book may be distinguished, the first being marked by a concern with history and the second by a concern with the law.[12] The first indication of this dual editing is to be seen in Josh. 1.6ff. There is a clear break between v.6 and v.7: whereas in the former the phrase 'be strong and of good courage' is properly and exactly used in order to encourage Israel in the face of the forthcoming battle, in the latter it is used loosely and generally with reference to doing one's best to obey the law. While v.6 proclaims Israel's success in taking the land on the basis of the divine promise, in v.7 Israel's success is dependent on her obedience to the law. Verse 6, therefore, represents the basic text, from which distinctive vocabulary has been taken and applied in a quite different, and not wholly suitable, way in v.7; the latter verse must be seen, then, as the later of the two. Verse 7 is continued by v.8[13] and v.9aa, forming a passage concluding with the same words with which it opened. The basic text takes up again in v.9abb 'be not frightened, neither be dismayed; for the Lord your God is with you wherever you go'. This part of v.9 constitutes the third, concluding part of the formula of institution to an office, of which the first two parts are found in v.6.[14] The basic text is quite clearly that of the deuteronomistic historian, which, in Josh. 1.1–6,9abb and following, continues the historical account of Deut. 1–3,31*,34*. The supplement in vv.7–9aa has a strong concern for the book of the law; its language[15] and subject link it immediately with the later deuteronomistic editor identifiable in Deuteronomy.

In Josh. 13.1–7 a similar picture emerges. The literary construction of v.1aba closely parallels that of Josh. 1.1,2a: that is, an introductory sentence sets the scene and gives the presupposition for what follows. The divine speech begins by repeating this presupposition. However, while Josh. 1.2b then immediately continues with the divine command introduced by 'and now . . .', this command is not found in chapter 13 until v.7. This suggests that vv.1bb–6 are a later intrusion breaking the original connection of v.1aba and v.7, a suggestion which is supported by at least three other points: first, the geographically very detailed list of vv.1bb–6 is unlikely as original divine speech; secondly, the subject of these verses, the land which yet remains to be conquered, is not that of the context which deals with the division of the conquered land among the tribes; thirdly, the verses conclude with a command to allot the land to Israel, a most improbable immediate prelude to the command to divide the land among the nine and a half tribes which follows in v.7.

The subject of the intruding verses, the incompleteness of Israel's conquest of the land under Joshua does not conform with the general picture of the deuteronomistic historian which concludes in 21.43–45 with an assertion of total conquest, but it is a presentation which is open to close harmonization with the ideas of the later deuteronomistic editor. The latter consistently presents obedience to the law as the necessary presupposition of success in the occupation of the land, and the present reference to the incompleteness of the conquest conforms closely with the conditional note which he introduced in Josh. 1. Once again, therefore, there is a basic text which continues the account of the deuteronomistic historian, by relating how the nine and a half tribes were given land just as earlier the two and a half transjordanian tribes had been given their land (Deut. 3.12–17);[16] this text has been edited in a quite new direction through the presentation of the conquest as quite incomplete.

The deuteronomistic historian's account of the conquest comes to a conclusion in Josh. 21.43–45, a passage which gives expression to the characteristic deuteronomistic themes of the land promised to the patriarchs, total conquest of that land, and the rest which Israel as a result enjoys from her enemies.[17] Joshua 23, which is treated by Noth as a speech composed by the deuteronomistic historian and set in the mouth of Joshua to mark the conclusion of the conquest period, has close connections with Josh. 21.43–45. Many of the phrases in the latter passage, particularly those relating to Israel having rest (v.44a), to Israel's enemies not being able to withstand them (v.44b), and to the fact that none of Yahweh's good promises had failed (v.45), are taken up in Josh. 23 (vv.1a,9b,14b); and so there is clearly a close connection between the two passages. Yet, as Smend has noted, the differences between the two preclude common authorship. Joshua 23 also speaks of the peoples that remain, who have not yet been conquered by Israel (vv.4,7,12), and it resolves the contradiction between this and the reference to the fact that not one of Israel's enemies has been able to withstand her by the use of the phrase 'to this day' (23.9b). So far, Israel's conquest of the land has been successful; those of her enemies whom she has already come against have been defeated. Others still remain, however, and against these Israel will be successful only if she is 'very steadfast to keep and do all that is written in the book of the law of Moses, turning aside from it neither to the right hand nor to the left' (23.6, cf. 23.12f., 16). The references to those that remain in the land connect this chapter not with the deuteronomistic historian but with the later deuteronomistic editor in Josh. 13.1b*b*–6; and, that it is this later editor at work in Josh. 23 is confirmed by the declaration that success is dependent on obedience to the law, as in Josh. 1.7–9a*a*.

If Josh. 23 is the work of the later deuteronomistic editor rather than that of the deuteronomistic historian, then it is clear that the duplication of Josh. 13:1a in Josh. 23.1b is not to be explained along the lines suggested by Noth,[18] viz. that Josh. 13.1a is secondary and modelled on 23.1b, and was brought in as a result of the secondary incorporation into the deuteronomistic history of the account of the division of the land among the tribes in Josh. 13–19. The relationship is, in fact, the reverse, Josh. 23.1b being modelled on Josh. 13.1a. The latter is part of the deuteronomistic history and introduces the account of the division of the land as an original part of that history. This view is supported by the consistent presentation by the deuteronomistic historian of the task of Joshua as a twofold one involving not only the conquest of the land but also its division among the tribes (Deut. 31.7f., 23; Josh. 1.6).

This account of the work of the deuteronomistic historian and that of the later deuteronomistic editor in Joshua throws into sharp relief the problem of the place of Josh. 24.1–28. This is by no means a new problem; even in the context of the view that the deuteronomistic historical work is the work of a single author, the origin and authorship of this passage have been by no means clear. It is obviously not the original continuation of Josh. 23. In the latter Joshua is an old man 'about to go the way of all the earth' (vv.1f.,14), and it is clear that the only acceptable continuation to the chapter is a notice of Joshua's death. In Josh. 24.1–28, however, Joshua is apparently at the height of his powers of leadership, and the subject of his old age and death is quite outside the view of the author.

On the other hand, however, the connections between the two passages are not to be denied. There is a clear link between 23.2 and 24.1; in both Joshua makes a speech to the assembled people; in both speeches he makes reference to the history of the people, and in both he draws consequences from this history for the future behaviour of the people. There are, in fact, strong reminiscences of the covenant or treaty form in both chapters.[19] Such connections suggest that one passage is then dependent on the other, common authorship being excluded by the discontinuity between them. Noth originally argued that Josh. 24 was the prototype for Josh. 23, but later expressed doubt about this, thinking instead that the connections between the two passages were too general for such a precise connection. Rather, Josh. 24.1–28 is to be taken as a traditio-historically independent and isolated passage, unknown to both the old settlement tradition of Josh. 2ff. and to the deuteronomist, which was subsequently edited in the style of the deuteronomist and introduced into his historical work because it made a significant contribution to the history of Joshua. Noth later partially reaffirmed this view of the traditio-historical independence of Josh. 24, seeing the passage as dependent on a regularly enacted ritual at Shechem in the context of which the historical figure of Joshua is perhaps to be located; but at the same time Noth reverted to his older view that the kernel of Josh. 24 had been available to the deuteronomist who used it as the prototype for Josh. 23. The deuteronomist did not himself take Josh. 24.1–28 into his work, but replaced it with Josh. 23, and so it is only in a secondary deuteronomistic stage that Josh. 24 was introduced as a supplement.[20] Smend, however, who assigns Josh. 23 to the later deuteronomistic editor, reverses the relationship, taking chapter 23 as the supplement to 24.1–28, so apparently assigning the latter to the hand of the deuteronomistic historian.[21]

Two major difficulties confront this view. In the first place, the work of the deuteronomistic historian has been so far marked by a concern to relate the history of Israel, while that of the later deuteronomistic editor has been characterized by a concern to inculcate obedience to the law. Yet the latter is most clearly the concern of the author of Josh. 24.1–28 as well as of the author of Josh. 23. In both instances, Israel's obedience to the law within the framework of its covenant relationship with Yahweh is the primary concern. It is true that the deuteronomistic historian composed his work in the light of the deuteronomic law, and he intended that his readers should judge that history from the standpoint of the law. However, it is most unlikely that the deuteronomistic historian would have given expression to this connection with the law in the form of Josh. 24.1–28. The covenant categories which are so prominent here find their correspondence not with any other part of the work of the deuteronomistic historian, but rather with the ideas of the later deuteronomistic editor. It was first he who introduced covenant thought and terminology, transforming the law of Moses contained in Deuteronomy into the law of a covenant relationship between Yahweh and Israel in which Moses is merely the intermediary.

Secondly, the work of the later deuteronomistic editor has hitherto been marked by a considerable subtlety. Both in Deuteronomy and in Joshua he has taken considerable pains to work his material into his basic text without causing any more disruption than necessary to that text. By taking up themes and vocabulary, and by avoiding harsh and abrupt connections he has in general produced a work which reads smoothly as a whole and in which his own contribution is to be discerned only by some considerable effort in discrimination. Such cannot be said to be the case with the relationship between Josh. 23 and Josh. 24. It is inconceivable that the latter could have formed part of a basic text into which the later deuteronomistic editor worked in Josh. 23. The abrupt clash of Josh. 23 and Josh. 24 finds no analogy in the work for which the later deuteronomistic editor can be held to be responsible.

Joshua 24.1–28 must, therefore, be taken as an insertion into the text later than the work of the later deuteronomistic editor. This is not to pass judgment on whether or not it was used by the later deuter-onomistic editor as a prototype in his formulation of Josh. 23; the question of the direction of influence between Josh. 23 and 24.1–28 is still open. But one would perhaps be justified at least in starting off on the assumption that it is Josh. 23 which has influenced the form and presentation of Josh. 24.1–28 until the contrary can be shown to be more probable. At any rate, 24.1–28 is to be assigned neither to the work of the deuteronomistic historian, nor to the edition of the deuteronomistic historical work which resulted from the work of the later deuteronomistic editor.[22]

The passage is not, however, completely isolated within the book of Joshua. There is at least one other passage which must be seen as deriving from the same hand. This is Josh. 8.30–35. There are at least four points of contact between the two passages. First, in both cases we have described for us an event which is located at Shechem. Secondly, both passages describe a ceremonial, ritual action involving all the tribes of Israel under the leadership of Joshua who initiates the action. Thirdly, both passages refer to the book of the law, though in the one case (8.31f.) it is the law of Moses, while in the other (24.26) it is the law of God.[23] Fourthly, both passages are abrupt and unexpected in their contexts and clearly disrupt the continuity of the account into which they have been introduced.[24]

Moreover, there is a still wider context to which both Josh. 8.30–35 and Josh. 24.1–28 belong. This context reaches back into Deuteron-omy, and consists of the following passages which have been already seen to be intrusive and to derive from a time later than the second deuteronomistic editor: Deut. 10.8–9; 11.29–30; 27.1–8,11–26; 31.9–13,24–29. The points of contact which indicate a common origin for all these passages are chiefly the following. First, all of them stand out from their contexts, and have been abruptly introduced into these contexts. Secondly, they all share a common concern with ceremonial. Thirdly, they are all either explicitly or implicitly associated with Shechem: this is explicit in Deut. 11.29f.; 27.1–8,11–26; Josh. 8.30–35; 24.1–28; it is implicit in Deut. 10.8f.; 31.9–13,24–29, because of the involvement of these passages with the ark, which, according to Josh. 8.30–35, was located at Shechem. Fourthly, they are all either explicitly or implicitly concerned with the Levites. This is explicit in Deut. 10.8f.; 27.11–26; 31.9–13,24–29; Josh. 8.30–35; it is implicit in Deut. 11.29f.; 27.1–8 and Josh. 24.1–28 because of the connection of all these passages with the law with its blessing and curse, for it is to the Levites, according to Deut. 31.9f., that the law was entrusted.

One must not, however, underestimate the difficulties here. There are differences between these passages which prohibit any simplistic idea that they are all to be seen as the work of a single individual who has composed them for insertion in these places. In particular, one might refer to the discrepancies between Deut. 27.1–8 and Josh. 8.30–35,[25] which are probably only to be resolved on the assumption that in both passages, and indeed also in the other passages marked out, we have older material which was edited only after it had already attained a fairly fixed form, and that it is within the context of this editing that a certain degree of uniformity is to be discerned. The intention of the editor seems to have been to emphasize the connection between Israel's possession of the land and Israel's obedience to the law; entry into the land and entry into the covenant belong so closely together as to be to all intents and purposes identical. The covenant tradition which is closely associated with Shechem, and the settlement tradition which has its focus on Gilgal, are conflated so that Shechem can be seen as the place to which Israel comes immediately on crossing the Jordan into the land, and her entry into the covenant with Yahweh coincides with her entry into the land.[26] In Josh. 24 time is telescoped so that those whom Joshua addresses and to whom he offers the choice of worshipping the gods of the fathers, the gods of the Amorites or Yahweh are Israelites who have just entered the land and are immediately taking on the obligations inherent in a covenant relationship with Yahweh.

It is clear, therefore, that, corresponding to the situation discovered in Deuteronomy, there are in the book of Joshua at least two and more probably three distinct stages of redaction, to be associated with the deuteronomistic school or later, through which the material has gone before reaching its present shape. As far as the pre-deuteronomistic period is concerned, one may follow Noth, at least with regard to Josh. 1–12, in his view that it is not the deuteronomist who is responsible for the primary collection of material.[27] Rather, one may trace signs of a pre-deuteronomistic collection, the hand responsible for which being apparent in Josh. 5.1; 6.27; 9.3,4a*a*; 10.2,5,40–42; 11.1,2,16–20. The collector at work here, who is responsible for the introduction of Joshua into the series of stories, had available to him the aetiological stories of Josh. 2–9 and the war narratives of 10; 11.1–9, which already had all-Israel significance. His work is to be dated *c*.900 BC and to be located in Judah.

The situation with regard to the rest of the material in Joshua is considerably more complex. It is clear that Josh. 13–19, listing the tribal borders, together with the list of cities of refuge and levitical cities in chapters 20 and 21, formed part of the deuteronomistic book of Joshua and are not a subsequent insertion into that edition.[28] Yet the history of the material contained in these chapters and the processes by which it came to be included in the deuteronomistic account are very obscure. It is very likely that at least the tribal borders given in chapters 13–19 rest on very old tribal border descriptions which were concerned primarily with the central and northern tribes of west Jordan: Ephraim, Manasseh, Benjamin, Zebulun, Asher and Naphtali. It is not impossible that such a system goes back into the pre-monarchic period, originally representing agreed borders of a federation of these tribes.[29] Subsequently, however, and probably at different times, this border description has been filled out, primarily in the interests of providing greater detail for the southern part of the land. This has been achieved in part through the provision of further topographical detail on the actual borders, but mainly through the supplementation of the border descriptions with a list of towns lying within the territories of Judah, Benjamin, Simeon and Dan. These cities, noted in Josh. 15.21–62; 18.21–28; 19.2–7,41–46, may have stood together originally in a single list, and this list, given the fact that it relates to only a particular part of west Jordan, is most likely to be seen as having its background in the kingdom of Judah, perhaps of the time of Josiah.[30]

The history of the lists of cities of refuge and levitical cities is also by no means clear. That the former, in Josh. 20, goes back only to the time of Josiah, and is the indirect result of Josiah's abolition of the local sanctuaries which had until then provided the sanctuary which the cities of refuge now provide for, is unlikely. The deuteronomic law on the subject, in Deut. 19, is built on a very clear pre-deuteronomic law which reflects the existence of a very ancient institution. A certain systematizing of that institution, so that six cities of refuge are stipulated, three in west Jordan and three in the east, does, however, represent a considerably later development. The original deuteronomic law on the subject provides for three west Jordan cities of refuge only, and it is an addition by the deuteronomistic historian in Deut. 19.8f. which provides for a further three in the event that Israel's territory should be enlarged.[31] Since Josh. 20 names six cities of refuge, three in west Jordan and three in Transjordan, the chapter should then be seen as deriving in its present form from the hand of the deuteronomistic historian, even though it presupposes a much older institution.

It is unlikely that the same can be said of the list of levitical cities in Josh. 21. The assignment of certain cities for the support of the Levites is not to be dissociated from the action of Josiah in destroying the provincial sanctuaries, thereby depriving the Levites of their erstwhile sources of livelihood.[32] It is, therefore, to the relatively short time between Josiah and the deuteronomistic historian that the origin of the list is to be put. With both lists, their inclusion in their present place is unlikely to ante-date the deuteronomistic historian. They round off the picture of the division of the land in Josh. 13–19, and tie that section in firmly with the provisions of the deuteronomic law and the tasks for which Joshua was instituted as leader of Israel. This is less likely to be the case, however, with Josh. 13–19. Here a fairly good case can be made for the view that the collector responsible for the pre-deuteronomistic collection of traditions connected with the conquest also appended to this an account of the division of the land among the tribes. Negatively, one might argue that insofar as there is no evidence that it was the deuteronomistic historian who expanded the old border description involving six tribes into the present version involving all the west Jordanian tribes, a context and purpose for this expanded description is lacking unless one assigns it to the collector at work in the account of the conquest. On the positive side, it should be noted that the role of Joshua in Josh. 17.14ff., as arbitrator in tribal territorial disputes, forms a not improbable original context for the figure of Joshua alongside his role as leader of a tribal group in battle.[33] Joshua may have been well known in tradition in both roles, and it is that which would have provided the basis on which the collector could then expand his presentation of Joshua, both by introducing him into conquest stories in which he had no original place and by assigning him the function not just of settling the territorial extent of the tribe of Joseph, but of assigning their land to all the west Jordan tribes.[34]

It was, therefore, a well formed account of the life and leadership of Joshua in his bringing Israel into the land and dividing that land among the tribes which the deuteronomistic historian incorporated into his work. It was his contribution to set that account in the wider context of the history of Israel from Moses to the exile. This he did through presenting the time of settlement and division of the land as a complete and self-contained period, marked off historically as the period from Joshua's assumption of leadership of Israel until his death, and in a literary way through the provision of an introduction (Josh. 1) and conclusion (Josh. 21.43–45). The picture of the period was filled out by the deuteronomistic historian who supplied or introduced into the context for the first time from other sources summary accounts of the places captured by Israel in west Jordan (Josh. 12.7–24) and a list of cities assigned to the otherwise landless Levites (Josh. 21) so that now all twelve tribes of Israel were given their inheritance. This same editor also introduced passages which are intended to connect the account of Joshua with the earlier part of his history. So, in Josh. 12.1–6, the story of Moses' conquest of east Jordan in Deut. 3.8ff. is taken up in summary fashion as the first part of a comprehensive deuteronomistic summary of the conquest of the whole land; Josh. 13 relates Moses' division of east Jordan as a prelude to Joshua's division of west Jordan; so also Josh. 11.21–23; 14.6–15 is a deuteronomistic link with Deut. 1.22f.; and Josh. 20 provides the list of cities of refuge prescribed in the deuteronomic law in Deut. 19. Other detailed additions by the deuteronomistic historian to the individual stories which he incorporated are also to be marked out,[35] and these, together with his more substantial additions, resulted in the incorporation of the hitherto independent presentation of Joshua's conquest and division of the land within a uniform and consistent presentation of the history of Israel since Moses. According to this consistent presentation, Joshua succeeded Moses as leader of all Israel and, under the command of Yahweh and through using the practice of the holy war, completed the conquest and settlement begun by Moses in east Jordan by subjecting the west to the same treatment. In the end, 'the Lord gave them rest on every side' (Josh. 21.44).[36]

The later deuteronomistic editor has introduced a quite new aspect to the account. Not content with the simple idea that Yahweh led Israel in its conquest of the land, this editor has described the relationship between Yahweh and Israel in terms of a covenant which involves the observance of law. This has introduced a conditional element into Yahweh's leadership which was not present before, but which now dominates the whole. The means by which this element has been introduced is through the subtle addition of relatively short passages to the basic text of the deuteronomistic historian (Josh. 1.7–9a; 13.1b*b*–6) and in one case through the addition of a long speech put in the mouth of Joshua as his last testimony before the assembled Israel (Josh. 23). While the basic deuteronomistic account described Israel's conquest of the land as complete and concluded with her rest free from her enemies, the later deuteronomist, through distinguishing between Israel's successes 'so far' and her warfare which is yet to come, has managed to introduce the idea that in the end Israel's final success will be completely dependent on her attitude to the law. There still remains much land to be possessed, and Israel's conquest of it will follow if she is faithful to the law of Moses, Deuteronomy.

The final stage of redaction is that which in Joshua has introduced 8.30–35; 24.1–28. The connecting links between these passages, and between them on the one hand and passages in Deuteronomy on the other, have been noted. The possibility exists that one must think in terms of a consistent third redaction of these books, and, moreover, that this redaction has introduced material of an ancient kind independent of that which is contained in the deuteronomistic historian's work. This, in addition to other points noted, marks this third stage off clearly from that of the later deuteronomistic editor. The latter was very much concerned only with editing the existing work of the deuteronomistic historian, and insofar as any sources as such are to be traced in the work of the later deuteronomist these can be seen to be derived from the deuteronomistic historian; there is direct and immediate continuity from one to the other. This is not the case, however, with the third putative stage. Here independent source material has apparently been introduced, material which is marked by its concern with the covenant law, the ark and the Levites. The historical significance of this material and its history until its appearance in its present context are both extremely difficult to evaluate and to trace. The lack of harmony with the context in which it now stands, the particular subjects with which it deals, the evidence that it is not just

56

a matter of simple later composition but rather of late editing of older material, point in the direction of the preservation here of an ancient levitical tradition, associated with Shechem, and possibly reflective of long established covenant practice at the sanctuary there. Whatever the detail of its history may be, it is clear that it was introduced into this context at a very late stage, after the work of the second deuteronomistic editor; the purpose of this late addition seems to have been to bring to even greater prominence the covenant theme, and, through explicit reference to Shechem in this connection, to establish or re-establish the significance of Shechem in the religious history of Israel.

3

Deuteronomistic Editing of
JUDGES

The strong continuity which binds together the books of Deuteronomy and Joshua makes most unlikely the suggestion that different deuteronomistic hands at different stages have been at work in these books. The general thematic continuity is reinforced by clear stylistic continuity: the deuteronomistic historian's account of Yahweh's confirmation of the institution of Joshua as Moses' successor, which begins in Deut. 31, is completed only in Josh. 1.6,9b; the deuteronomistic description of the task for which Joshua was instituted (the conquest of the land and its division among the tribes) is given in Josh. 1–12, 13–21, reaching its conclusion in Josh. 21.43–45 with an affirmation of the completion of that task and Israel's rest in the land. However, this straightforward if rather idealistic account has been subtly modified by later editorial work: success is dependent on obedience to the law (Josh. 1.7–9a*a*), the conquest is not yet complete (Josh. 13.1b*b*–6), and will be completed only if Israel is faithful (Josh. 23)..

It is, therefore, evident that the work of the deuteronomistic movement has proceeded in at least two stages, each of which extends through the books of Deuteronomy and Joshua. The distinction between them, on the basis of the historical concerns of the one and the covenant law concerns of the other, is consistent throughout. That there was a third stage of redaction is less certain; yet some passages in both Deuteronomy and Joshua have been seen to stand out from both deuteronomistic editorial stages and to show a consistency of interest in covenant ceremonial, the Levites and Shechem, to the extent of suggesting strongly yet a third step in the editorial process.

With the book of Judges we move into a dramatically changed atmosphere from that which dominated the book of Joshua. The single people Israel no longer stands to the forefront, nor the single leader; the period is one of dissension, division and apostasy from Yahweh. From the very first chapter onwards the picture of a divided people dominates, and Israel stands as an ideal, an entity which in practice is scarcely ever realized. The framework within which the individual stories of the book stand indeed speaks of Israel; but it is clear that it is not intended that it should disguise what the stories themselves make only too clear: the people does not appear as a single whole; tribes and small tribal groups act in their own self-interest, independently of the people; Israel's existence is to be discerned only dimly and without real substance. The book asserts that it is only in return to Yahweh that Israel will find its unity and its 'rest'; but the realization of this state is constantly inhibited by its own waywardness. In a sense, Abimelech and Jephthah, the accounts of whom stand at the centre of the book, may be taken to epitomize the two ways between which the people should choose: in the one case a military adventurer who in selfish seeking for kingship brings death and destruction, in the other case a judge who brings deliverance and rest.[1]

This discontinuity between Judges and the preceding books does not, however, mean a literary discontinuity. In Joshua and Judges we have presented two sides of a single coin: unity-disunity; faithfulness-unfaithfulness; success-failure. The mind and attitude of the writer(s) involved is no different in each case: both are dominated by the idea of the unity of Israel in covenant with Yahweh.[2]

On the literary level this view is confirmed by a detailed treatment of the Judges material, for this reveals levels of continuity between Joshua and Judges which arise from editorial work of the same nature and from the same hand(s) having been carried out on both books. The deuteronomistic historian's edition of the book of Joshua will not have ended without a reference to the death of Joshua, and indeed Josh. 24.29–30, which would have followed immediately after the epilogue in Josh. 22.1–6, forms a suitable conclusion to this edition. The substance of this note on the death of Joshua is, however, repeated in Judg. 2.6–10, where it is filled out and supplemented in order to set the death of Joshua in the context of the disappearance of the whole Joshua generation, that generation which had had direct experience of the conquest and whose military success derived from Yahweh's leadership. It is probable that Judg. 2.6–10 is a secondary repetition of Josh. 24.29–30, a repetition caused by the introduction of secondary material into the context of the deuteronomistic historian's work, which disrupted the continuity of his account.[3]

This indicates that Judg. 1.1–2.5 should be seen as an insertion into the deuteronomistic history, an insertion whose point and purpose is probably to be discerned in the theological story in 2.1–5.[4] The verses, especially v.3, take up the dominant theme of Judg. 1, the inability of Israel to defeat and drive out all the inhabitants of the land. The reason for this failure is given in the second verse: Israel disobeyed the commandment of Yahweh to make no covenant with the inhabitants of the land. There is conformity between the view expressed here and that of Josh. 23. In both cases the conquest is incomplete, in both cases complete success is dependent on obedience to the law, and this law in Josh. 23.12 and Judg. 2.2 is seen in concrete terms as a prohibition of making alliances with the inhabitants of the land.[5] Despite this connection, however, it is by no means clear that Judg. 1.1–2.5 should be seen as an insertion deriving from the hand of the deuteronomistic editor at work in Josh. 23, as Smend suggests. One of the significant characteristics of the work of this editor has been the subtlety and smoothness with which he has introduced his contributions. Another has been the fact that his work has represented the editing of an existing text by means of his own comments and compositions. Hitherto there has been no sign of his taking up older materials or, at least, materials of uncertain origins. On both counts Judg. 1.1–2.5 does not suit this later deuteronomistic editor. Judges 1.1–2.5 is anything but a smooth and subtle insertion in the context. It clashes with 2.6ff. in that the latter suggests that what has gone before precedes the death of Joshua, and also in that the implication of 2.6ff., that Israel departed from the commandments of Yahweh only after the conclusion of the conquest, is contradicted by 2.1–5. Furthermore, it is not a uniform composition to be identified as the unified work of a single editor; whatever its age and provenance, whatever its historical value,[6] Judg. 1 incorporates materials taken up by the author of 2.1–5 which the author of that latter section has brought in here by means of 2.1–5. This raises the possibility that the editor at work here should be identified with the editor in Josh. 24.1–28 and elsewhere. In all cases there is an abrupt introduction of materials of uncertain origin, in all cases there is a strong concern with covenant and ritual, and in all cases there is a concern with Israel's obedience to covenant law. One may suggest, therefore, that the third editorial layer which has been tentatively identified in Deuteronomy and Joshua is continued in Judg. 1.1–2.5.

The substance of the book of Judges is contained in 2.11–16.31. In a collection of stories of deliverers and judges the pre-monarchic period is portrayed in cyclical terms as a time of recurrent sin, punishment and deliverance.[7] The external threat and danger to Israel's life takes its origin and cause in her internal covenantal unfaithfulness; it is as an illustration of moral and physical instability within the people that the epilogue in 17.1–21.25 serves.

Within the major central portion of the book, 2.11–16.31, it is clear that there is a uniformity of presentation which is largely lacking elsewhere. It is only here that the deliverers and judges appear; it is only here that the recurrent rhythm of sin, punishment and deliverance marks the presentation of the history; and on the literary level it is only here that there is used a quite clearly discernible literary framework to the individual stories which serves to describe the rhythmic pattern of its history.[8] There is not absolute uniformity within chapters 2–16 in the use of this literary framework: some sections fall completely outside it; in others the framework is only partial. Yet, in some measure it is 2.11–16.31 which is touched by it, and this being the core of the book it is in the closer delineation of the way in which the literary framework is here used that our understanding of the literary origin of the book will be advanced.

The framework consists of six elements:[9]

(i) The statement that Israel sinned. This is constant in form and expression: 'Israel did what was evil', and appears in 2.11; 3.7,12; 4.1; 6.1; 10.6; 13.1.

(ii) The statement that Israel was handed over to an enemy. Here some variations appear in the verbs used: 'the Lord sold them into the hand of . . .' (2.14; 3.8; 4.2; 10.7); 'the Lord strengthened . . . against Israel' (3.12); 'the Lord gave them into the hand of . . .' (6.1; 13.1). In each case, however, it is a description of the military defeat of Israel by a foreigner.

(iii) The statement that 'Israel cried to Yahweh' from their oppression (3.9,15; 4.3; 6.6; 10.10).

(iv) The statement that Yahweh 'raised up a deliverer' (3.9,15). The relative infrequency of this element casts doubt on whether it should be included as an independent part of the framework. It is probably subordinate to and a development of the third and fifth elements, in the sense that though a deliverer is raised up in response

to the cry of the people it is, as far as the framework is concerned, Yahweh and not the deliverer who effects the subjugation of the enemy.[10]

(v) The statement that the enemy was subjugated, '. . . was subdued' (3.30; 8.28; 11.33); 'God subdued . . .' (4.23).

(vi) The statement that 'the land had rest' (3.11,30; 5.31; 8.28).[11]

There are some clear indications that this framework must be seen as independent of the stories which it contains and as supplying a secondary context for those stories. In the first place, the distinctive language and style which appear in the framework do not appear in the stories themselves; secondly, there is in general a quite different interest in the framework from that of the stories which it takes up: on the one hand, the stories relate the heroic exploits and acts of courage on the part of individuals and tribes against an enemy; and, on the other hand, the framework relates the sin of the people which brought about the distress from which God delivered them.

It would appear, therefore, that the central part of Judges is composed of stories taken up into an editorial framework and that with the simple removal of this framework one can get back to the older traditional material. However, the matter is rather more complex. The framework as outlined does not embrace all the material within 2.11–16.31, and even when it does appear it is not always complete. It is the story of Ehud's killing of Eglon the king of Moab in Judg. 3.12–30 which has the complete framework in all of its six elements: Israel . . . did what was evil . . . the Lord strengthened Eglon . . . Israel cried to the Lord, the Lord raised up . . . a deliverer . . . Moab was subdued . . . the land had rest. The stories of the victory of Deborah and Barak over Sisera in Judg. 4–5 and of Gideon's victory over the Ammonites in Judg. 6–8 contain all but the fourth element, the latter, however, being probably not essential to the framework. These three stories, therefore, may be seen together as having been edited in a uniform way by a single editor.

This is not to say that the removal of the framework passages surrounding these stories results in the falling apart of the traditions into isolated entities, so that it was the editor who supplied the framework who was also responsible for bringing the traditions together. Rather, it is evident that the material adopted into the framework already existed as a single work: it has a common interest in and reference to Israel, and it is concerned to present the events in which the deliverers were involved as holy wars in which Yahweh delivered his people. In other words, behind the stage at which the framework was added there is an older stage which marks the collection of the ancient traditions into a single work. The tensions between the interests of the collection in Israel and the holy war and those of the traditions in the individual tribes and heroic exploits reveal that older material has been taken up into a pre-framework collection and adapted there to a particular purpose. The collection will have included the stories on Ehud, Deborah-Barak and Gideon, those stories which are now presented in the full form of the framework.[12]

There are difficulties in relation to the following materials within the central portion of Judges: 2.11–3.6, which contain no story but yet exhibit some relationship in language to the framework (elements *(i)* and *(ii)* appearing in 2.11,14); the story of Othniel in 3.7–11 which, besides other peculiarities, lacks element *(v)*;[13] the story of Jephthah in Judg. 10.6–12.6, which lacks elements *(iv)* and *(vi)*; the story of Samson in Judg. 13–16 which lacks elements *(iii)*, *(iv)*, *(v)* and *(vi)*; and the list of those 'judged Israel' in Judg. 10.1–5;12.7–15, where none of the framework elements appears.

The last mentioned in this collection, the list of judges, stands apart from the stories of the deliverers not only in terms of the literary presentation but also in terms of the subject.[14] From a literary point of view it is clearly a single list, though now divided into two parts; it follows a common pattern throughout, in which each judge is connected with his predecessor by the words 'after him', of each it is said that 'he judged Israel for . . . years', and of each it is recorded that '(he) died and was buried in . . .'. It is true that of some individuals more biographical information is given than of others; but the essential uniformity and unity of the list is still clear.[15] It is also clear, moreover, that the list has basically no original connection with the stories of deliverers. The literary form of the framework to these stories does not appear here; it is not recorded of the deliverers that they 'judged Israel';[16] and of the judges it is not recorded that they performed heroic acts of deliverance.

There is one exception to this: Jephthah. At the point where his name occurs in the list of judges there is to be found a story of how he delivered Israel from the Ammonites. It is frequently supposed that the very fact that Jephthah occurred in both the list of judges as a judge and among the deliverers as a saviour of Israel facilitated the bringing together of these two blocks of material. This is not to say that all the judges were also deliverers, the stories of whose exploits are now lost to us; rather, it is the exceptional nature of the fact that Jephthah was both judge and deliverer[17] that allowed the two essentially different literary forms, relating to different individual types to be brought together. In fact, one could then say that the basic nature of the central section of the book of Judges is created by precisely this: the bringing together of the list of judges and the original collection of deliverer stories. Jephthah provided the connecting link, and the effect of the link is that now it is no longer the case that deliverers succeed one another and judges succeed one another in independent series, but that both deliverers and judges succeed one another in the same series. Effectively, both deliverers and judges are set on the same plane and their place and function is identified.

There is a difficulty in this outline which requires a modification and refinement in the process of growth of the central section of Judges which it projects. It is presupposed that the figure of Jephthah and the story of his deliverance of Israel from the Ammonites belongs originally along with the other deliverers and the stories of their exploits, so that Jephthah, since he figures also among the judges of the list, could form the link between these two types of individual and these two forms of record about them. There is no doubt that the Jephthah story in Judg. 10.6–12.6 bears a relationship to the series of deliverer stories: it apparently lacks only one of their substantial framework elements. Yet, it has been argued by Richter that this story is, in fact, independent of the original series, and had its own history before being brought into the context of the other deliverer stories through deuteronomistic editing.[18] There is some considerable force to this argument, because not only is the last element of the framework missing, but the first three elements are embedded within an extensive introduction to the Jephthah story which finds no parallel with the other deliverer accounts.

In an extensive study of the Jephthah tradition Richter argued that the tradition had its own independent history. The stories of Ehud, Deborah-Barak, Gideon and Abimelech were in due course collected into a *Retterbuch*, a book of deliverers, with which the Jephthah tradition was connected only at a secondary stage. The Jephthah story may be broken down into a number of units, the relation between which is not at all times quite clear. The old Jephthah tradition, which originally was concerned with a family feud and was later told in the setting of a dispute between Gilead and Ammon, is found in

Judg. 11.1–11 with 11.34–36. This has been secondarily connected with the explanation given in 11.37–40 of the origin of a particular custom in Israel. A further stage in development is marked by the working in of the Shibboleth incident in 12.5f. and the argument of 11.15–26. Editorial passages, which have the purpose of bringing together the different units, and which are particularly important in the question of identifying the relationship between the developing Jephthah tradition and other stories of the book of Judges, are to be seen in 10.17f.; 11.4,11b,12–14,27–29,32f. It is in these fragments that connections may be seen with the *Retterbuch*; but the connections are with the *Retterbuch* in a developed form. Particularly important is the connection between 11.29,32 and 3.10, for the latter belongs to the Othniel tradition in 3.7–11, a tradition which did not form part of the original *Retterbuch* (see below). The indications are, therefore, that the Jephthah tradition has been brought into this connection in its present developed form by an editor before whom the *Retterbuch* already lay as an existing entity; the object was simply to provide an additional example of the events and the individuals described in the *Retterbuch*.

If this is to be accepted, it may indicate the necessity for only a slight change in the proposal already mentioned for the process by which deliverers and judges came to be connected: it would be modified only through the recognition that the deliverer stories came together unevenly, with the Jephthah tradition being brought into a collection which had already been extended by the Othniel tradition in 3.7–11, before the list of judges in 10.1–5; 12.7–15 was introduced. However, the probable complexities are in this not yet adequately presented. The deliverer stories dealing with Ehud, Deborah-Barak, Gideon (and Abimelech) exhibit the secondary framework we have already outlined, in a form not found in the Jephthah tradition. Insofar as the Jephthah tradition displays a connection with this framework, the connection is almost entirely[19] determined by the extended introduction to the Jephthah tradition in 10.6–16 which finds no parallel in the other deliverer stories. In other words, the Jephthah tradition came into its present place not just later than the primary collection of stories in the *Retterbuch* but probably also later than the edited version of these stories which gave them their distinctive framework. That distinctive framework is presented in an elaborate way in 10.6–16, a passage which is sufficiently similar to the framework and yet also sufficiently different from it to indicate that it was later composed in dependence on the framework. How is this situation to be described in terms of the place of the Jephthah tradition in the process of growth of the book?

The basic observation which lays the foundation for understanding is the existence of the regular framework embracing the traditions of Ehud, Deborah-Barak, Gideon (and Abimelech), together with the point that this framework has been added to an older collection of traditions of these figures and does not mark the first step in their being brought together. In the determination of subsequent stages of development it will be helpful first to examine 3.7–11 which serves as an introduction to the series of deliverer traditions, and, secondly, 10.6–16 along with 2.11–3.6 since these two passages display many close links.

Judges 3.7–11 shows all the elements of the framework already outlined;[20] yet it is distinct in a number of respects. First, the story element is minimal – outside the formulae of the framework and some additional formulaic contributions there remain only the proper names 'Othniel the son of Kenaz, Caleb's younger brother', and 'Cushan-rishathaim king of Mesopotamia'. There is to be found here no old tradition and combination of literary units either or both of which characterize the stories embraced by the framework. Secondly, in addition to the familiar framework formulae, 3.7–11 contains elements not found in the framework: the development of the nature of Israel's sin in terms of 'forgetting the Lord their God, and serving the Baals and the Asheroth' (v.7;) the reference to Yahweh's anger being kindled against Israel (v.8); that 'the Spirit of the Lord came upon him (Othniel) and he judged Israel' (v.10); and the death notice (v.11). It is possible that of these the reference to Othniel having judged Israel and his death notice are simple additions to the passage: the combination of the former with reference to the spirit of Yahweh is unique and hardly suitable, and it is probably best to take both it and the death notice, as additions secondarily brought in from the context in which they are otherwise familiar and undoubtedly original, that of the list of judges in 10.1–5; 12.7–15.[21]

If this is correct, then the section on Othniel in Judg. 3.7–11 is to be judged as dependent on and a development of the framework passages. It has taken up the typical framework passages but has expanded on them and drawn out implications not made explicit in the framework. It is set here as a typical example of events in the period. Stripped of all distracting detail it is presented only in its essentials. Furthermore, it provides at the beginning of the account of the period of the judges an event involving Judah, or a Judean clan, and thus brings Judah, which otherwise plays no role in the period, into the context of events in the period of the judges. It is unlikely that any old traditional story is to be discerned here; it is, rather, an introductory passage providing a model for what was to come, developing and interpreting events along the lines already initiated by the existing collection of stories of deliverers with their framework.

Judges 2.11–3.6 and 10.6–16 also display many connections with and differences from their literary contexts; each stands as an introduction to the material which follows and the connections with the material are close. Yet they are quite clearly introductions which are set in their present places as prefaces to already existing accounts. There are, moreover, signs that neither introduction is a unified composition. So the literary structure and content of each must be examined before any contacts are made with the stages of growth of the book of Judges which have so far been discerned. Judges 2.11–13 is undoubtedly overfull;[22] and there is, moreover, an unlikely combination of two sources of apostasy: the Baals and the gods of the peoples round about. The partial repetition of the beginning of v.12 in v.13 also indicates editorial work, as does the inconsistency between the end of v.12 ('served the Baals') and the end of v.13 ('served the Baals and the Ashtaroth'). Perhaps the most probable resolution is to take v.12abb ('they went after other gods . . . they provoked the Lord to anger') as a secondary expansion from the hand of an editor responsible also for v.13a ('they forsook the Lord') which has been used as the link phrase. The basic text in vv.11, 12aa, 13b, is concerned with Israel's apostasy to the gods of the land which they have conquered, not to the gods of the peoples who remain round about. The peoples around Israel for this basic text are primarily a threat to Israel's secure rest in the land and the enemies into whose power Yahweh sells Israel for sin, not primarily an attraction to apostasy.

Judges 2.17 is also an addition,[23] which has likewise caused a secondary repetition within the context into which it is introduced ('the Lord raised up judges', v.16, repeated in v.18). Moreover, in its assertion that the judges made no difference to Israel's moral and religious behaviour even in their own lifetimes, the verse clearly is incompatible with v.19. Verse 19, however, is not uniform; it has been expanded through the addition of 'going after other gods, serving them and bowing down to them', which is an interpretative addition interrupting the otherwise connected context and belonging clearly to the hand responsible for the addition of vv.12abb,17.

It has often been noted that a conclusion is reached in v.19, and that v.20 marks the beginning of a new section.[24] If vv.20–23 are taken as a unity it clearly is a quite unsuitable continuation of v.19, since the reason given in v.22 for leaving the nations (viz. to test Israel's faithfulness) is quite different from and incompatible with that presupposed by the earlier verses (viz. to punish Israel's faithlessness). Verse 22 is probably, however, a later addition to vv.20f.,23;[25] but in spite of this there are still difficulties in seeing v.20 as a satisfactory continuation of what precedes. Verse 20 takes up the beginning of v.14; but while there the result of Yahweh's anger is immediately described as an element in that series of historical events which characterized Israel in the period of the judges, events which revolve around Israel's relations with peoples outside the land, in v.20 the repeated reference to the anger of Yahweh is used as a means of introducing divine speech offering a theological explanation for the continued presence of peoples in the land.

This new subject – Israel in conflict with the peoples of the land which has been only partially occupied – characterizes all of 2.20–3.6. But within that section there is lack of uniformity.[26] If v.22, introducing the idea of the nations as having been left in the land to test Israel, is secondary, then one should see 3.3f. as deriving from the same supplementary stage. Judges. 3.1f., on the other hand, reinterprets the idea of testing in the sense of gaining experience of warfare and is clearly secondary to 2.22; 3.3f. So Judg. 2.20–3.6 consists of a first layer in 2.20f., 23; 3.5f., to which 2.22; 3.3f. have been secondarily added, with 3.1f. being a further later addition.

Within the whole section 2.11–3.6 there is, therefore, a basic narrative in 2.11,12aa, 13b,14–16,[27] 18abb, 19aab. This narrative explains Israel's suffering at the hands of plunderers as the result of sin and Yahweh's punishment; out of pity for Israel's suffering, however, Yahweh sent judges who saved Israel from her enemies. Yet in the end Israel did not learn; on the death of each judge she reverted to evil and indeed did worse than the previous generations. Israel's sin, which the basic narrative described in terms of serving the Baals, has been more elaborately presented by an editor at work in 2.12abb,13a,17,18aa,19ab,20f., 23;3,5f,[28] The nations into whose power Israel fell according to the primary narrative (v.14) are the very ones whose gods Israel worshipped (v.12abb); it is by no means unlikely that the editor intends to suggest that Israel's enslavement consists precisely in her attachment to these foreign gods.[29] This attachment is seen not only as a violation of the commandments of Yahweh but specifically as a transgression of the covenant which Yahweh made with their fathers (vv.17,20). Because of this, Yahweh will not drive out before Israel those nations which were left in the land when Joshua died.

Minor additions have been made to this second editorial layer in two stages: in the first (2.22; 3.3f.) the nations left in the land are said to be there in order to test Israel's faithfulness; and in the second (3.1f.) this testing is understood to mean the giving to Israel in the post-Joshua period of the experience of warfare.

Judges 10.6–16, the introduction to the Jephthah story, presents similar signs of editing. A basic text in v.6a*a* ('. . . served the Baals and the Ashtaroth'), 7–9, is intended to serve as a historical introduction to Israel's oppression by the Ammonites and later by the Philistines, on which then the Jephthah story, as that recounting the Ammonite oppression, follows immediately in 10.17ff. As in the basic narrative in Judg. 2.11ff., so here Israel sinned in serving the Baals and the Ashtaroth and is punished through being sold into the power of enemies outside the land. Again here, however, this account has been enriched by elaboration of the description of Israel's sin in v.6a*bb* in terms of her worship of the gods of the nations, including those of the nations into whose power she has been given. The same hand is probably also responsible for the addition of vv.10–16. They are unsuitable as an introduction to the Jephthah story, not only in that they come to their own conclusion so that the transition to v.17 is then unexpectedly harsh, but also in that they presuppose as already having happened (deliverance from Ammonites and Philistines, v.11) what the following stories (of Jephthah and later of Samson and Saul) have yet to describe. That the verses derive from the same editor at work in v.6 is more difficult to show. That Israel 'forsook Yahweh' is a characteristic term (vv.10,13) which appears also in the expansion to v.6, and that connection is perhaps reinforced by the contrasting usages 'did not serve him' (v.6), 'served Yahweh' (v.16). There are, furthermore, some links between v.6a*bb*, 10–16, and the first editor of the basic layer in 2.11ff. To forsake Yahweh is a common element (though found also in the basic layer of 2.11ff.), and the phrase 'other gods' which appears in 2.12a*bb*,17,19a*b*, occurs again in 10.13 (cf. also 10.16).[30]

Two differences between the two passages, however, could be held to encourage caution in this connection. In the first place, there is in Judg. 10 no explicit reference to either commandments or covenant, which appear prominently in Judg. 2. Secondly, while Judg. 2 makes no reference to repentance, or even to Israel as having cried to Yahweh for deliverance, that is a prominent feature of Judg. 10. Yahweh's intervention directly follows and is dependent on Israel's confession and repentance. However, there is a possible explanation for these points. Beyerlin has argued that Judg. 10.10b–15 follow the pattern of the *Rib* or controversy, a legal form which was used, both within and outside Israel, in the context of procedures designed to deal with breach of treaty or covenant. On the basis of Isa. 1.2–3,10–20; Micah. 6.1–8; Jer. 2.2–37 and Ps. 50, the structure of this form may be described as follows: an introduction, frequently calling heaven and earth as witnesses, is followed by the hearing. The accusation refers to breach of covenant, calling to mind Yahweh's saving deeds and Israel's ungratefulness. Connected with this there may also be found a reference to the uselessness of the worship of foreign gods. The *Rib* pattern may conclude in two different ways: on the one hand, it can end with a declaration of guilt and an announcement of judgment, in which case the whole form appears as a judgment speech justifying Yahweh's punishing intervention; on the other hand, it may end with a warning that Israel should amend its behaviour and return to covenant faithfulness.[31]

Judges 10.10–16 shows some close contacts with this *Rib* form. An especially clear example is Yahweh's speech of accusation, which makes direct reference to all that he has done on Israel's behalf in the past. In the present context, however, this form has been put to serve a narrative function; here it concludes with neither judgment nor warning, but with Israel's repentance and the restoration of the relationship between Yahweh and Israel as a result of which Yahweh intervenes to save.[32] What is of particular importance at the present point is that the use of this form presupposes covenant thought, and that its application presupposes an earlier use of covenant categories. It is in the second edition of Judg. 2.11ff. that covenant has been introduced and Israel's behaviour has been described as transgression of the covenant (2.20). It is wholly appropriate that the same editor in a later passage should use the *Rib* form in order to open up the future as one of restoration and renewal. The probability that Judg. 10.10–16 derives from the later editor is, therefore, strong, on account of both the connections in vocabulary and the fact that the literary form used presupposes the covenant reference of the editor at work in chapter 2.

Before we attempt to gather together into a coherent picture the various points which have been made, there is one further particular question to be examined briefly: the relationship of these composite passages in 2.11–3.6 and 10.6–16 on the one hand with 3.7–11 and the framework passages on the other. It has already been seen that 3.7–11 is dependent on and a development of the passages which frame the traditions of Ehud, Deborah-Barak and Gideon-Abimelech. The relationship of 2.11–3.6; 10.6–16 to 3.7–11 is of a similar order: there are both similarities and differences.[33] This is not to say that the similarities relate to the basic layers in 2.11–3.6; 10.6–16 while the differences appear only in the secondary editions of these layers; rather, all stages of development of 2.11–3.6; 10.6–16 show similarities to and differences from 3.7–11 and the framework passages.

In all cases Israel is said to have done evil in the sight of the Lord, and 3.7–11 shares with 2.11–3.6; 10.6–16 the reference to Israel having served the Baals and to the anger of Yahweh having been kindled against Israel; in all cases Yahweh gave or sold them into the power of an enemy, and in all but 2.11ff. there is reference to Israel having cried to Yahweh. However, the differences are no less striking. Only in the edited versions of 2.11–3.6; 10.6–16 (cf.2.12f.; 10.6,10,13) is Israel said to have forsaken Yahweh and (cf.2.12,17,19; 10.13) to have gone after 'other gods'. Neither the framework passages nor 3.7–11 uses the phrase 'bow down to them' (2.12,17,19) or the phrase 'provoked the Lord to anger' (2.12), or the term 'plunderers' and the verb 'plundered' (2.14,16); only in 2.14 are both verbs 'gave' and 'sold' used of Yahweh's handing Israel over to an enemy; only in 2.15 is it said that 'the hand of the Lord was against them for evil'; only in 2.16,18f. is Yahweh said to have raised up 'judges' to deliver Israel,[34] and only in 2.19 do the terms *hišḥîtû* ('behaved worse') and *qāšāh* ('stubborn') appear.

There is here a significant quantity of distinctive vocabulary and forms which mark off 2.11–3.6; 10.6–16 from 3.7–11 and the framework passages, and this distinctiveness combined with the similarities and conformities permits only one conclusion: 2.11–3.6; 10.6–16 are in all their layers later than and a development of 3.7–11 and the framework passages. The latter have been used and supplemented in order to provide overall introductions embracing existing materials.

Judges 3.7–11 and the stories with their framework already existed before the author(s) of 2.11–3.6; 10.6–16, who have used these existing materials in the formulation of their own work.

There is a corresponding modification in the thought of 2.11–3.6; 10.6–16 over against the earlier passages. Most clearly this comes to expression in the secondary editorial layer where covenant and *Rib* forms and terminology are used, where Israel's sin is described as disobedience to the commandments and especially as going after other gods. But the basic layer of 2.11–3.6 also marks a significant advance on the earlier passages in more than the vocabulary used; for here for the first time we find the function of judges and deliverers brought together. Whereas 3.7–11 and the framework passages either explicitly (3.9,15) or implicitly[35] spoke of Yahweh raising up a deliverer to rescue Israel from her enemies, in 2.16,18 it is a judge whom Yahweh raises up for this function. This has created a certain tension within the basic layer of 2.11ff., for the judges were occupants of a lifetime office (2.18) and yet the emergency for which they were raised up was by its nature a temporary one. The author of the introductions clearly has before him two traditional sets of materials, the stories of the deliverers raised up by Yahweh to cope with temporary emergencies, and the list of judges in Judg. 10.1–5; 12.7–15, the occupants of a lifetime office. The combination of these two types could not be completely harmonious, but it allowed the author of the basic introductions in 2.11ff. to conflate his materials in order to present a single picture.

Three tasks remain: first, to bring together the various points made in order to reconstruct a total picture of the stages by which the central section of Judges in 2.11–16.31 reached its present form; secondly, to relate these stages of development to the wider context of the redaction of the other books of the deuteronomistic history which have been examined so far; and thirdly, to complete our treatment of the book by reference to its prologue and epilogue.

The basic and earliest materials within the book consist of the stories of deliverers on the one hand and the list of judges in Judg. 10.1–5; 12.7–15 on the other. The latter is a fixed list of uncertain provenance and significance,[36] which is presently broken through the insertion of the story of Jephthah, a figure who also appears in the list of six judges. Apart from this break the list gives no indication of a process of development and redaction. The stories of deliverers, however, present a different picture. An original collection of them included the stories of Ehud, Deborah-Barak, Gideon-Abimelech, a collection which at a later stage received a distinctive editorial framework. Closely associated with this framework, yet distinct from it, there came into existence the story of Othniel in 3.7–11, a story with no discernible traditional basis, and one which served both to introduce Judah into the history of the period in which the deliverers were active and also to provide a paradigmatic account of the history of Israel in the pre-monarchic time. This collection, headed by 3.7–11, still had no connection with the list of judges in Judg. 10.1–5; 12.7–15 or with the Jephthah tradition. This connection was made at the next stage of development, represented by the author of the basic layer in 2.11–3.6; 10.6–16. This stage marked not only the connection between deliverers and judges – it is now 'judges' whom Yahweh raised up to deliver Israel – but also the introduction of the story of Jephthah. It is only from this point that the Jephthah story gains connection with the older collection of deliverer stories.[37] The basic layer of 10.6–16 is from the hand of the author of the basic layer of 2.11–3.6 and without his work the Jephthah story has no link with the other deliverer accounts. The only element of the framework which remains outside 10.6–16 is 'so the Ammonites were subdued before the people of Israel' in 11.33, but this cannot possibly function on its own to provide an original link between the Jephthah story and those of the other deliverers. This link was first forged by the author of the basic layer in 10.6–16 at which stage also the deliverer framework was imitated through the insertion of the penultimate framework element in 11.33. It must inevitably follow that the editor at work at this stage framed the Jephthah story with the two parts into which he divided the list of judges.

A further contribution from the hand of the same editor has not yet been referred to. Judges 10.6–16 in its basic layer refers not just to oppression by the Ammonites but also to oppression by the Philistines (10.7). In making this reference the editor was providing the link by which he might draw in the stories of Samson in Judg. 13–16.[38] There is no indication that this individual hero tale belonged to the original collection of deliverer stories, while such redactional material as it does exhibit links it with both the framework to the deliverer stories and to the list of judges. So in 13.1 the first two elements of the framework to the deliverer stories appear, while in 15.20; 16.31[39] there appears the distinctive terminology of the list of judges. This reflects the stage of growth of the book of Judges at which judges and deliverers were brought together in the aim of producing a uniform presentation of the period of the judges.[40]

The final major stage in the growth of the central section is marked by the editing of the introductions in 2.11ff.; 10.6ff.;[41] through the use of distinctive vocabulary and ideas the sin of Israel is described as disobedience to the commandments and breach of covenant, although the possibility of renewal of the covenant relationship remains. While the sin of Israel had at an early stage been identified as that of serving the Baals (3.7), it is only in the final stage of redaction that the distinctive term 'other gods' appears, and that apostasy is defined as breach of the covenant law. Subsequent additions came in, in 2.22; 3.3f., and then again in 3.1f., but these are isolated and make no comprehensive impact on the redactional shape and significance which the central section of Judges in 2.11–16.31 now projects.

The attempt to relate this process of growth of Judg. 2.11–16.31 to our earlier discussion of Deuteronomy and Joshua belongs within the overall context of the determination of the development of the deuteronomistic history as a whole. So far, we have traced consistent editing on two levels at least through Deuteronomy and Joshua: we have been able to identify two deuteronomistic editors at work at different times on the material contained in these books. The possibility of a third consistent stage of editing, showing a marked levitical interest, has also emerged, but without the comprehensiveness and clarity of the other two. Our task now is to set Judges within that context. In so doing we should be able to decide if the place of Judges within the deuteronomistic history is to be described in terms of its having formed part of these stages of redaction already identified, or if, as occasionally proposed,[42] the (deuteronomistic) editing of Judges is independent of that of the other books within the so-called deuteronomistic history.

The original collection of deliverer stories and the stage at which this collection received its first editing through the provision of its regular framework are not of primary concern here. At this stage the collection is set within a closed framework and neither the collection nor the framework reveal any outside connection or external reference. In other words, neither the language of the primary collection nor that of the framework shows the contact with any of the stages of editing of Deuteronomy and Joshua which would indicate that these deliverer stories were now part of a wider literary context. Moreover, the collection with its framework does not, so far as its content is concerned, presuppose a wider literary context.

In one respect only there is a connection between the language of the framework and wider literary contexts. This lies in the phrase 'did what was evil in the sight of Yahweh', a phrase which is found on several occasions both in Deuteronomy and Kings;[43] but while it is thus typical of deuteronomistic writing, it is by no means exclusive to this context[44] since it is found in at least one passage (I Sam. 15.19) which is in all likelihood not to be assigned to any deuteronomistic editor. Beyerlin may be correct in his view that the phrase should be treated as part of the parenetic vocabulary which is older than Deuteronomy and the deuteronomistic school, and which is taken up into that context. At any rate, this single point of contact is insufficient to justify an alignment of the framework passages with Deuteronomy and the deuteronomistic school.

In connection with the content only one feature of the framework possibly points beyond the otherwise closed collection of deliverer stories: this is the number of years given for which the land had rest when the enemy was subdued. There is present here a desire to set the activities of the deliverers within a wider chronological context; it is only from the point of view of such a wider context that any such chronological statements make sense. Whether or not the precise chronologies given in the framework fit with others in the deuteronomistic history in order to harmonize with the summary statement of I Kings 6.1 is of no particular importance; these statements still reflect the intention to portray the deliverers as acting in events which do not stand in isolation but are to be understood in relation to what preceded them and what followed them. It has already been noted, however,[45] that we should distinguish between the statement that the land had rest, on the one hand, and the period of time for which this rest endured, on the other, in view of the fact that statements of rest occur elsewhere without chronological periods accompanying them. If this is so then it is likely that the chronological statements should be treated as later additions to the framework, which have precisely the intention of bringing this otherwise isolated collection into a wider literary and chronological context.

Our conclusions with respect to Judg. 3.7–11 are not very different. There is here a greater stock of formulaic language, but here too there is no indication of an exclusive connection to the deuteronomic-deuteronomistic milieu. The verb 'forget', as in 3.7, finds analogous usages in the original introduction to the deuteronomic law, from which it is then taken up by the later deuteronomistic editor,[46] but its uses in Hos. 2.15; 4.6; 8.14; 13.6, as well as Ps. 44.18,21, point to its being a well established term in this context and familiar long before the deuteronomic-deuteronomistic period. The same is true of the phrase 'the anger of the Lord was kindled against', which appears in Deut. 6.15; 7.4; 18.15,18; 28.36, but is also found in such contexts as Hos. 5.2; II Sam. 6.7; Ps. 78.21,31 and Ex. 22.23. The first of these is prophetic, the second and third belong to the Jerusalemite tradition and the last to pre-deuteronomic law. Neither here nor in any of the other formulae used in this section is there any particular or exclusive connection with Deuteronomy and the deuteronomistic school.[47] It is, therefore, clear that the development of the book of Judges, up to the stage of the addition of 3.7–11, is a process independent of the redactional history of the preceding books of the deuteronomistic history, at least insofar as the last major stages, already seen to be common to Deuteronomy and Joshua, are concerned.

The situation is different with Judg. 2.11–3.6 and 10.6–16. Within these passages it is possible to discern two stages of development which may be directly related to the two deuteronomistic stages of editing in Deuteronomy and Joshua; the relationship is sufficiently close to permit the conclusion that the book of Judges was edited into the deuteronomistic history at the same time and by the same steps as the earlier two books.[48] Our earlier discussion indicated that, apart from isolated later additions in 2.22; 3.3f., and 3.1f., we should distinguish in 2.11–3.6 between a basic layer contained in 2.11,12aa, 13b,14–16 (omitting 15ab), 18abb, 19aab, and a later layer in 2.12abb,13a,17,18aa,19ab,20f.,23;3.5f. Related to these two layers there are to be distinguished two layers within 10.6–16: the basic text lies in 10.6aa, 7–9, and this has been later edited through the addition of the layer contained in 10.6abb,10–16.

The thoroughly deuteronomic and deuteronomistic nature of the vocabulary which appears in the later of these two layers in each case is striking. The phrase 'other gods' (2.12,17,19; 10.13), especially in combination with 'go after' (2.12,19), is typically deuteronomistic,[49] and belongs moreover in the context of the later of the two deuteronomistic layers we have so far identified (cf. Deut. 4.3; 6.14; 8.19; 11.18; 28.14; 29.25; 30.17 and 7.4; 11.16; 28.36,64). 'Bowed down to them' (2.12), especially in combination with 'served them' (2.19), likewise is typical of the later layer (Deut. 4.19; 8.19; 11.16; 29.25; Josh. 23.7,16). However, over and above all this, it is quite clear that we may distinguish these two layers on the very grounds that have already been seen to be effective for the same distinction in Deuteronomy and Joshua. So the deuteronomistic historian in Josh. 21.44 speaks of Yahweh giving Israel rest 'all around' through giving them victory over 'their enemies', and it is then 'into the power of their enemies round about' (Judg. 2.14) that Israel falls as a result of Yahweh's anger. The basic layer in Judg. 2.11ff.; 10.6ff., reflects the concern of the deuteronomistic historian with Israel over against the enemies outside the land, and its focus is on the historical fate of Israel in relationship to the enemies. It assumes that Israel's conquest of the land has been fully accomplished and that the oppression which Israel suffers is at the hands of enemies from outside. By contrast, the later layer reflects the concern of the later deuteronomistic editor at work in Josh. 1.7–9a*a*; 13.1b*b*–6; 23. Israel's conquest of the land is incomplete (Judg. 2.21,23; 3.5f.) and it is so because of Israel's failure to observe the covenant commandments (Judg. 2.17,20). The enemies who threaten Israel are not from outside; they are those who remain unconquered in the land. The connection between Judg. 2.20f. and Josh. 23.5,13,16 is especially close. In both passages the basis for Israel's failure to complete her occupation of the land is transgression of the covenant (Josh. 23.16; Judg. 2.20); in both the consequence of this is that Yahweh does not continue to drive out her enemies (Josh. 23.23; Judg. 2.21), who are in both places described as 'the nations' (Josh. 23.13; Judg. 2.21). What Josh. 23 envisages as a possibility for the future is now in Judg. 2 seen as an actuality. The later deuteronomistic editor in Judg. 2 has taken the deuteronomistic historian's introduction to the period of the judges, which he is here editing, as an account of Israel's failure to fulfil precisely those conditions on which Josh. 23 based Israel's complete conquest of the land; and so the disasters there threatened have now become real.[50]

In one further respect a connection may be established between the work of the later deuteronomist in Deuteronomy and Joshua on the one hand and what is now apparently work from the same hand in Judges. This concerns the common use of the category of the covenant relationship between Yahweh and Israel. As already noted,[51] it is to the later deuteronomist that the introduction of covenant thought and vocabulary is to be credited. Not only in this general way, but also in some detail, the editorial work on Judges resembles that noted earlier. Just as in Joshua there is an apparent step by step progress from the theme of obedience to the law (1.7–9a*a*) through the assertion of incomplete occupation of the land (13.1b*b*–6) to the conclusion that the land will be fully occupied if the covenant is kept (23), so in Judges there is a step by step progression from covenant breaking (2.12a*bb*,13a,17, 18a*a*, 19a*b*, 20f.,23; 3.5f.) through the *Rib* which follows breach of covenant (10.10ff.) to the conclusion that Israel's relationship with Yahweh is restored (10.16). Moreover, just as the later deuteronomist in Deuteronomy (4.29f., 30.1ff.) only hints at Israel's future restoration after punishment for sin and apostasy, without spelling out in detail how this restoration is worked out in history, so also in Judg. 10.16 there is a bare allusion only to Israel's relief from oppression as a result of its renunciation of idolatry ('and he became indignant over the misery of Israel').

It must be concluded, therefore, that the book of Judges exhibits the same process of development as that which lies behind Deuteronomy and Joshua, at least insofar as two deuteronomistic hands may be seen at work here. Basic to Judges there lies the collection of old deliverer stories on the one hand and the list of judges on the other. The former received a framework and introduction in 3.7–11 before it was taken up by the deuteronomistic historian as part of his account of Israel's history. It is to the deuteronomistic historian that we owe, therefore, the most formative influences on the shape of the book and the portrayal of the period of the judges. In combining the deliverers and judges (and in doing so giving the judges a delivering function rather than the deliverers a judging function), in introducing the Jephthah and Samson stories, the deuteronomist aimed to present an account of Israel's history in this period which gave concrete illustration to the inevitable results of Israel's increasing sin.[52] In this work the deuteronomistic historian is continuing where he left off in Josh. 24.29–30.

It is this work which lay before the second deuteronomistic editor who appears in Judg. 2.12a*bb*, 13a,17,18a*a*,19a*b*,20f.,23; 3.5f., 10.6a*bb*, 10–16. As we have seen before in connection with the contribution of this editor in Deuteronomy and Joshua, so here there is a subtle and yet very effective editing of the deuteronomistic history. The significance of the law as a condition of Israel's prosperity is always emphasized, Israel's sin is described in terms of disobedience to the law and going after other gods, and her relationship with Yahweh is described in terms of a covenant, with all the possibilities for breach and restoration, punishment and renewal, which that implies. In this work the later deuteronomistic editor is continuing where he left off in Josh. 23.

We have already seen that the prologue to Judges in Judg. 1.1–2.5 is the probable work of a third editor who has been tentatively identified earlier in Deuteronomy and Joshua. So, in order to complete our sketch of the redactional history of Judges reference must be made to the enigmatic epilogue in Judg. 17–21. Various detailed estimates have been made of the historical background and development of these chapters;[53] these are not of immediate concern. What is important is that the five chapters are held together in one literary unit by their presentation as records of events which took place in a time when 'there was no king in Israel; every man did what was right in his own eyes' (17.6; 21.25; cf.18.1; 19.1).

Deuteronomistic editing has been thought to be present in the chapters.[54] But the indications of this are in fact slight, and, in the light of the discontinuity of the chapters with deuteronomistic editing (at both levels) elsewhere in Judges, insignificant. The nature of the subjects covered by the stories in chapters 17–21 is unparalleled in the central section of the book to which the deuteronomistic contribution substantially belongs; that deuteronomistic contribution, in 10.6a*a*,7–9, provides an interpretative background to the episode of Ammonite oppression in the time of Jephthah and also to Philistine oppression in the times of Samson and Samuel, the connected presentation of which is disrupted by chapters 17–21; the similarities of the birth stories of Samson and Samuel (barren wife, divine intervention, birth of a son, dedication as Nazirite) may indeed reflect the common use of a particular motif, but they also point up the incongruity of chapters 17–21 in the deuteronomistic setting into which they have been abruptly introduced.

It is clear, in fact, that Judg. 17–21 have been brought in later than the two major stages of deuteronomistic editing which have been distinguished in the book. The connections of the chapter are with Judg. 1.1–2.5 rather than with any earlier stage of development. With both prologue and epilogue we have what at first appears to be old tradition, but which also shows unmistakable signs of late formulation and insertion;[55] with both, inner Israelite conditions of moral and spiritual failure are to the fore; Israel's cultic lamentation and sacrifice (at Bethel)[56] are common to both (2.4f.; 20.23,26); if 1.1–2.5 shows contact with an apparent post-deuteronomistic editing of Deuteronomy and Joshua this is no less so with chapters 17–21: the central role of the Levite, the ark and covenant law are concerns which chapters 17–21 share with this stage of development of Deuteronomy and Joshua. Whatever the origin of these stories and whatever their historical value, they belong to the latest stage of the history of the book and are to be linked with its post- rather than its pre-deuteronomistic or deuteronomistic development.

4

Deuteronomistic Editing of
SAMUEL

The history of origins of the book of Judges has been seen to be complex. Basic collections of material existed on the one hand in the Ehud, Deborah-Barak and Gideon stories and in the list of judges in Judg. 10.1–5; 12.7–15 on the other. The former was enriched with a distinctive framework together with an introductory model story in 3.7–11 before any connection was effected between it and the list of judges. That connection we have seen to be the work of the deuteronomistic historian. It was effected through the provision of a new introduction, now to be found in the basic layer of Judg. 2.11ff., which identified judges and deliverers, and was supplemented through the inclusion of stories of Jephthah and Samson, with their introduction in the basic layer of 10.6ff.

The topics of interest to the deuteronomistic historian here conform completely with the work of the first deuteronomistic stage of development of Deuteronomy and Joshua: the history of Israel, Israel's complete occupation of the land, the relationship between Israel in the land and her enemies outside the land; and there is no difficulty in seeing the same deuteronomistic hand at work throughout. Similarly, the hand which edited the work of the deuteronomistic historian, through supplementing the basic layers of Judg. 2.11ff.; 10.6ff., betrays the interests of the later deuteronomistic editor in Deuteronomy and Joshua: Israel's conquest of the land is incomplete because of failure to observe the covenant law; the threat to Israel is from enemies within the land who have not been driven out because of this failure. This editorial continuity between Deuteronomy – Joshua and Judges is finally confirmed by the presence also in Judges, in the prologue and epilogue, of passages which show a close connection with others in the earlier books, which have also been seen to be insertions into the work of the second deuteronomist.

It was argued by von Rad[1] that the relative lack of deuteronomistic editing in Samuel is a sign of the lack of unity in deuteronomistic editing of the books included in the deuteronomistic history; different deuteronomistic hands have been at work in different books. This was said with particular reference to the part of the books of Samuel which follows I Sam. 12, a chapter which, for the deuteronomist, marked the conclusion to the period of the judges and the opening of the monarchic period. However, it should be remembered that in Joshua and Judges at least, the quantity of deuteronomistic editing is perhaps not so much as might at first appear, being found mainly in some introductory passages and in the connecting of already largely formed blocks of tradition. Furthermore, in terms of quantity the deuteronomistic contribution was largely determined by the nature of the sources: thus, an already well developed, coherent presentation of a particular period would offer less opportunity and less need for deuteronomistic literary skills. Quantitative comparisons between the different books of the deuteronomistic history in connection with the deuteronomistic contribution do not yield anything very significant in this regard.

Differences certainly exist between the books of Samuel and earlier parts of the deuteronomistic history. These relate in the first instance most obviously to the sources rather than to the redactional elements. More clearly than in Joshua and Judges, the books of Samuel break down into tradition complexes, fairly loosely strung together; these give the impression of being elaborate, self-contained and almost completed entities before their redactional connection, and do not seem to be affected to the degree apparent in Joshua and Judges by the redactional work carried out to link them. Again, in Samuel we are moving into the area of historical reporting and official source material, and away from the popular tradition which characterizes both Joshua and Judges.[2] In that much of the material of Samuel (especially the succession narrative) is literary creation and does not rest directly on popular tradition, it cannot be derived from short units which have then undergone a long editorial history until their appearance in their present contexts.

It has become clear in recent criticism that the history of origins of the books of Samuel is to be understood in terms of the bringing together of originally unrelated narrative materials or tradition complexes and not in terms of the editorial interweaving of parallel

sources.[3] Particularly since Rost's identification of an ark narrative in
I Sam. 4.1–7.1; II Sam. 6, a history of the rise of David in I Sam. 16 –
II Sam. 5; and an old history of the succession to David in II Sam. 9–
20; I Kings 1–2,[4] it has become widely agreed that the general history
of origins of Samuel is to be followed through within this framework.
Thus, the books are usually divided into the following sections, with
the understanding that these divisions are significant in the history
of origins of the books: the birth of Samuel (I Sam. 1.1–4.1a); the
story of the ark (I Sam. 4.1b–7.1; II Sam. 6); the rise of Saul
(I Sam. 7.2–15.35); the rise of David (I Sam. 16.1 – II Sam. 5.25);
the story of the succession (II Sam. 9–20); and, finally, an appendix
(II Sam. 21–24) containing materials relating the fate of Saul's descendants (21.1–14), war with the Philistines (21.15–22), the Song of
David (22), the last words of David (23.1–7), David's mighty men
(23.8–39), and David's census (24).

Much contained in these complexes derives from old tradition, and
in our following detailed discussion of the stories surrounding the rise
of Saul the complexity of the history of origins of this section will
become apparent: on the other hand, we must also note the story-like
character of such a 'tradition complex' as the succession narrative,
where traditional materials may indeed have been used but whose
character is predominantly that of a historical novel produced as a
deliberate literary composition. The nature of the materials contained
in the books of Samuel is diverse, and there is much in the history of
origins of all the Samuel traditions which, it must be acknowledged,
is still very far from being clear.[5]

Our immediate concern is with neither the earliest nor indeed the
latest stages of the development of Samuel, but rather with its
intermediate stages, and especially with the time when the complexes
were being brought together. This is a period not without its own
difficulties, for it cannot be considered probable that a bare reference
to the deuteronomist will suffice to explain the coming together of all
the complexes of tradition, much less the actual formation of the
complexes themselves. So, it is highly unlikely that the bringing
together of the story of the birth of Samuel, the ark story and the story
of the rise of Saul in I Sam. 1–15 is all simply to be understood as the
result of deuteronomistic editing. The story of the birth of Samuel is
presently separated from its continuation in I Sam. 7 by the ark story
in which Samuel makes no appearance. The ark story is an insertion
between the other two, and the linking of these latter derives from a

pre-deuteronomistic stage of the development of the Saul tradition when it was being transmitted in prophetic circles.[6] The integration of the ark story is effected through the portrayal, in I Sam. 2, of the cultic corruption of the sons of Eli (a theme foreign to the story of Samuel's birth), which here has become the background and reason for the defeat of Israel and loss of the ark related in I Sam. 4. The terminology used in this link and the theological ideas which it expresses – in particular, the historical judgment of Yahweh on Israel for cultic offences – strongly suggest the presence of the deuteronomistic historian.[7]

The conclusion of the first part of the ark story is linked into the beginning of the story of the rise of Saul by I Sam. 7.2, which must also, therefore, be attributed to the deuteronomistic editor, and this verse in turn points to II Sam. 6, the other part of the ark story relating David's bringing of the ark to Jerusalem, as a deuteronomistic insertion at that point. The editor, who must be understood to be the deuteronomistic historian, has used the ark story to illustrate the consequences of cultic corruption, and indeed also to point over the house of Saul (during the rule of which Israel 'lamented after Yahweh') to the Davidic dynasty as the time when Yahweh, through his ark, was again present with his people.[8]

Yet, it is only in the introduction of the ark story into its present contexts that a deuteronomistic hand can be traced in the first coming together of the tradition complexes of which Samuel is composed; otherwise these complexes apparently came together already in pre-deuteronomistic time. In view of the prominence of Samuel at the beginning of the story of the rise of David (I Sam. 16), the association of this complex with the earlier must be set in a similar prophetic context, and, while pre-deuteronomistic links between the story of the rise of David and the succession narrative are more difficult to establish,[9] the deuteronomistic insertion of II Sam. 6 was not necessary to accomplish their connection.

In outline, therefore, it may be suggested that the oldest traditions in Samuel were first brought together into complexes concerned with particular topics, and that only after a fairly developed stage in these complexes had been reached were they linked together.[10] Much of this linking was already done in pre-deuteronomistic time: in particular, the stories of the birth of Samuel, the rise of Saul and the rise of David had already been connected before the deuteronomist, while the same is probably true of the succession narrative. The prophetic circles to which much of this development is to be assigned affirm the role of the prophet in the anointing of the king, but also the legitimacy of the Davidic dynasty over against the house of Saul. It is likely, therefore, that such circles belong to the southern kingdom, and, insofar as they reflect the relation of prophet and king to be found in the northern rather than the southern kingdom, these prophetic circles may represent survivors who came to Judah after the fall of the northern kingdom in 721 BC.[11]

The one area where the hand of the deuteronomistic historian has so far been traced is in the working in of the ark narratives in I Sam. 4.1–7.1; II Sam. 6.[12] In both cases, this editing takes place in close connection with the rise of the monarchy: with the foundation of Saul's monarchy in I Sam. 7ff., and the inauguration of the Davidic dynasty in Jerusalem in II Sam. 5; 7ff. Although the books of Samuel had then already reached a highly advanced form before the work of the deuteronomistic school, that work did make a crucial contribution, particularly to those parts of the existing story where the ark narratives were introduced. While it is not to be denied that incidental deuteronomistic editing is to be found elsewhere in Samuel,[13] it is in fact the case that the really substantial deuteronomistic contribution, in which deuteronomistic stages in the editorial history of the books are most clearly to be traced, is to be found in the introduction of the ark narratives and in the foundation stories of the Saulide and Davidic monarchies which stand in close proximity to the ark narratives.

In the following study of I Sam. 7–12 and II Sam. 7 I hope both to show this deuteronomistic contribution in detail, and also to illustrate, as far as I Sam. 7–12 is concerned, the detailed history of development of at least this part of Samuel, which has already been outlined in general. From this it will be clear that as in Deuteronomy, Joshua and Judges, so here deuteronomistic editing had the effect, first, of bringing the materials into a wider chronological context for the first time, and secondly, of introducing into the deuteronomistic history a series of parenetic texts with a distinctive point of view.

I Samuel (7)8–12 present a clear pattern of arrangement of materials in which a contrast is maintained between two conflicting attitudes towards the monarchy. Through an alternation of critical and favourable passages a tension is created which is then finally resolved. So, in general terms, I Sam. 8 is critical of the monarchy; 9.1–10.16 presents an idyllic picture from which Saul emerges in a very favourable light; 10.17–27 is again critical; 11.1–15 sets the foundation of the monarchy within the context of Saul's defeat of the Ammonite threat and so sees it as making an essential contribution to Israel's security; 12.1–25 rounds off the account of the foundation of the monarchy in a critical way: the monarchy is accepted, the king is the anointed of Yahweh, but his presence will act as no guarantee of Israel's security, for Israel as a whole along with her king still stands under the divine demand enshrined in the covenant law.[14]

This represents a legitimate reading of these chapters and is significant for a literary and theological appreciation of them which is concerned with the intention of the editor responsible for their final organization. But it must still be emphasized that such a presentation is the result of the existence of conflicting traditions and different editorial views on the significance of the event of the institution of the monarchy, and is not to be read simply on one level as an artistic construction designed to project as forcefully as possible the diversity of views on the monarchy and the difficulties in integrating it into Israel's traditional structures and values. The links which connect the different elements of the whole are minimal, and the transitions from one scene to another are very abrupt. Moreover, there are strong links which bind the chapters both to what precedes and to what follows: the beginning of chapter 8 cannot be read without the end of chapter 7 and 9.1–10.16 refers forward to chapter 13 (10.8; 13.8).[15] So the overall creative unity of chapters 8–12 must be set within the context both of its internal detailed disunity, arising from its origins and history, and of its continuity with the preceding and following stories. Our aim in what follows is to examine I Sam. 7–12 (whatever the nature of the links with chapter 13 it is certain that chapter 7 must be included in a consideration of the deuteronomistic presentation of the institution of the monarchy) in all its different sections with a view to determining the history of the tradition and specifically the possibility of more than one deuteronomistic contribution to the formation of the story.

It has been customary since Wellhausen[16] to make a clear distinction between a pro-monarchic and an anti-monarchic 'source' in the account of the institution of the monarchy, and indeed to prefer the former over the latter in terms of historical reliability. The anti-monarchic texts are held to be dependent on the pro-monarchic texts and to reflect the theocratic views of exilic and post-exilic times, and thus to be late and unhistorical. Later proposals that these two 'sources' should be identified with the Pentateuchal sources J and E drastically modified scholarly understanding of them in terms both of establishing the independence of the anti-monarchic texts over against those favourable to the monarchy and of opening the way to a more positive attitude towards the possible historicity of the anti-monarchic source. Although this identification with the Pentateuchal sources has now been widely abandoned, particularly perhaps as a result of the work of Rost and Noth, the view has continued to be strongly projected that it is not satisfactory to consider the anti-monarchic texts simply as the product of late theologizing of the significance of the monarchy, and as reflecting disenchantment with the value of the monarchy for the spiritual and material prosperity of Israel.

Noth's study of the deuteronomistic history marked in crucial respects a re-affirmation of the views put forward by Wellhausen, for he argued that the anti-monarchical parts of the pericope (7.2–8.22; 10.17–27a; 12.1–25) must, on the basis of their language and content, be taken as deuteronomistic and as dependent on the older traditions to be found in 9.1–10.16; 10.27b–11.15. For Noth, however, the deuteronomist was not just editing old materials in order to transform the (historical) pro-monarchic account of the older source; rather, he was bringing together formerly independent traditions in order to provide the first history of the period of the institution of the monarchy: before the work of the deuteronomist no history of the period existed. The old independent traditions in 9.1–10.16 and 10.27b–11.15 are of varying historical reliability. The remaining material is substantially deuteronomistic; but while this historian must be held responsible for much of it (especially in chapters 8 and 12), there are traces in chapters 7 and 10.17–27a of older traditions edited from a deuteronomistic standpoint: these older traditions relate to Samuel's judging activities and the mode of election of Saul as Israel's king. The editing of these older traditions – in order to present Samuel as not only a judge but also a charismatic leader carrying out the task for which Saul was in fact made king – has made them serve an anti-monarchic aim. Such an attitude did not first come into existence with the deuteronomist, but, for Noth, it was only with the deuteronomist that doubts about the monarchy were given their full theological expression.[17]

With what are generally recognized as old traditions contained in 9.1–10.16; 10.27b–11.15, we need not here be much concerned except to note the general editorial history of the traditions and the means by which they came together. The former is a developed form of an old folktale which described how Saul, as a young man in search of his father's asses, was honoured by a seer. The story would have been related in order to illustrate how Saul was from the beginning destined for good things and how his physical attributes commended him to the people as their king. The folktale was modified by the literary form of the call narrative, especially in 9.15ff., 21; 10.1,5–7, which emphasized the role of Samuel in the call and anointing of Saul. This modification betrays the interests and influence of prophetic circles, an influence which appears also in the story of Saul's rejection by Samuel in chapter 13. One may conjecture a pre-deuteronomistic prophetic cycle of traditions relating the call, anointing and rejection of Saul by Samuel and taking up and modifying an old folktale.[18]

In I Sam. 11 we have a quite distinct but parallel tradition of Saul's elevation to the kingship. Saul is here not the object of divine designation by a prophet but rather a charismatic deliverer impelled to action by the spirit of Yahweh. He came forward to meet a particular, limited emergency, and thus stands closely in line with the old charismatic deliverers. In distinction to them, however, Saul's leadership was made permanent and he was elected king. There is no evidence that the story did not always conclude with Saul's elevation to permanent leadership;[19] and indeed the manner in which Saul's elevation is related in v.15 strongly suggests that this is an original component of the story. It is the people who 'went to Gilgal and there they made Saul king before the Lord in Gilgal. There they sacrificed peace offerings before the Lord, and there Saul and all the men of Israel rejoiced greatly.' It is not Samuel who anoints Saul (as in the traditions which have come under prophetic influence), nor is it Yahweh who chooses him (as the deuteronomistic passage in 10.17ff. would have it); Saul's election as king is a spontaneous popular reaction to his military success over the Ammonites, and is, therefore, wholly suitable as an original conclusion to the account of his deliverance of Israel from the Ammonites. To this extent the story remains a parallel account to 9.1–10.16 (23b,24a*b*b).[20]

In order that it might be adapted to its context, however, the story has been edited in two respects. In the first place, a reference to Samuel has been introduced in v.7. The secondary nature of this reference is obvious: Samuel has not hitherto been mentioned in the tradition and he otherwise appears only in the other manifestly secondary passages in vv.12–14. This was a tradition of the rise of Saul as sole inspired leader in battle. Secondly, vv.12–14 have been brought in in order both to connect this tradition with what precedes and also to introduce Samuel as a moving force in a context where he otherwise has no function. The verses conflict with v.15 both in that the role that is assigned to Samuel in vv.12–14 does not feature in v.15, and also in that the latter speaks simply of making Saul king whereas vv.12–14 speak of renewing the kingship. Clearly v.15 would not have been introduced secondarily into a context which already included vv.12–14, and so the latter passage must be judged the later of the two. That it is to a prophetic hand that vv.12–14, along with the reference to Samuel in v.7 are to be ascribed is possible, but unlikely. The prophetic editing of 9.1–10.16 which resulted in a cycle of tradition including chapter 13, did not include the Ammonite story of chapter 11.[21] That story would have unacceptably interrupted a close-knit account in which the links pass directly and immediately from Samuel's direction to Saul in 10.8 to Saul's neglect of that direction in 13.8ff., and from the divine purpose of Saul's anointing, expressed in 9.16, to Saul's victory over the Philistines in chapters 13f. The account of Saul's victory over the Ammonites is not presupposed by the context and is quite extraneous to that context. It is, therefore, to a later stage than that of the prophetic editing that the introduction of the Ammonite story, and therewith the addition of the reference to Samuel in 11.7 and of 11.12–14, belong. Most probably this is deuteronomistic work; there are close links between 11.12–14, and 10.26f.,[22] and the latter is part of a context which, as will be noted below, betrays very strong deuteronomistic influence.

It may be concluded, therefore, that there are two parallel accounts which relate, in a way favourable to the monarchic institution, events leading up to Saul's election as king. These have been, in the one case after editing in prophetic circles, brought together, probably by a deuteronomistic hand, in such a way that they are presented as dealing with events taking place in succession, so that Saul's kingship, once established, is confirmed through his deliverance of Israel from the Ammonites, and so renewed.

These two traditions, whatever their precise historical reliability, are widely accepted as early and as at least reflecting accurately an early positive and favourable attitude towards the monarchy in general and Saul in particular. Apart from the important point that it was as a result of deuteronomistic editing that the two traditions were brought together, there is here nothing of immediate relevance to our present question; but there is, nevertheless, one query thrown up by those traditions and their very existence in the deuteronomistic history in general and in the specific context of the supposed anti-monarchic deuteronomistic texts in particular. If it is true that the deuteronomist is anti-monarchic why has he allowed this opposing viewpoint such forceful and appealing expression, to the extent even that those who oppose the monarchy are described as 'worthless fellows' and deserving of death (10.27; 11.12)? If the answer to this is that the deuteronomist was conservative with regard to handed down tradition, then the question is simply raised in a different form: why did the deuteronomist feel constrained to surround the old pro-monarchic traditions with texts which he himself composed in order completely to subvert the presentation of those old traditions? That form of the question becomes all the more urgent in view of the deuteronomist's clearly positive attitude to David who is not only presented as chosen by Yahweh as a 'man after his own heart' (13.14), but is also constantly used as the standard by which all subsequent kings of Judah are judged. There is clearly a problem here which is not adequately answered by the blanket claim that the so-called anti-monarchic texts in I Sam. 7–12 are deuteronomistic compositions, expressing his revision of the old traditions. It is clearly important, therefore, that the nature and origin of these so-called anti-monarchic texts should be investigated in some detail.

One attempt to resolve the problem without surrendering the basic deuteronomistic thesis of Noth is made by Boecker.[23] Here the deuteronomistic authorship of the later layer is accepted, but the problem is posed in the form of questioning if Noth's description of the deuteronomistic attitude to the monarchy is accurate. Boecker argues that in fact even such an anti-monarchic account as I Sam. 8 leads the introduction of the monarchy back to an express command of Yahweh (8.22), while the account of the choice of Saul by lot in I Sam. 10.17–27 not only has Yahweh taken the initiative in the choice of a king, but also sets forth opposition to the king as contrary to the will of Yahweh. In fact Boecker[24] ascribes pivotal importance to this section: it is only with reserve that the king has hitherto been introduced; from this point he has the approval of Yahweh and it is resistance to him which is contrary to the divine will. The king is indeed not only given by Yahweh, he is the anointed of Yahweh (12.3,5). The existence of texts critical of the monarchy cannot, of course, be denied; but as far as Boecker is concerned, such criticisms are not levelled against the monarchy as such but rather only against particular aspects of it: so chapter 8 (see especially v.20) is particularly concerned that the monarchy might itself become a cause of injustice within Israel because of the burdens it will lay on the people and also that the king, rather than Yahweh, might come to be seen as Israel's deliverer in war.[25] Thus, the problem inherent in Noth's study is resolved simply by the argument that Noth was right in assigning certain texts to the deuteronomist, but wrong in his assessment of what these texts said about the monarchy.

That this is an adequate estimate is, however, doubtful. Boecker has rightly drawn attention to the inevitable implications of the deuteronomist's incorporation of pro-monarchic traditions in his account by drawing out the positive side of the deuteronomistic estimate of the monarchy. But it must be asked if, in doing so, he has not undervalued the negative expressions: the election of a human king is a rejection of Yahweh (8.7; 10.19): the people have acted wickedly in asking for a king (12.17), and effectively the king will make no difference whatever to Israel's welfare. The law and the people's obedience to it remain the only means by which prosperity and security will be achieved (12.24f.). The strength of this negative judgment is not adequately represented if it is treated simply as a warning against certain aspects of the kingship to which, in principle, the deuteronomist remains favourable.

There are two attempts to cope with this situation which are perhaps particularly worthy of note. First, Weiser has been a critic of Noth with respect both to the deuteronomistic history in general and to the background of I Sam. 7–12 in particular.[26] Each of the books within the deuteronomistic history has had its own history of origins, and the nature and extent of the deuteronomistic editing varies widely. As far as I Sam. 7–12 is concerned, such editing is practically absent, being confined to the chronological notice of 7.2b. The most decisive stage in the development of these chapters is pre-deuteronomistic: it belongs to prophetic circles, and because this prophetic stage brought to expression the deuteronomistic view a further deuteronomistic revision was unnecessary. Behind this prophetic editing there is to be found no source as such, but rather a series of traditions, partly contradictory, about the origins of the monarchy; these are sanctuary traditions which developed independently of each other and should be studied traditio-historically rather than by the methods of literary criticism. So in I Sam. 7[27] there is basically a cult tradition rooted in the sanctuary at Mizpah, a historically reliable tradition which presented Samuel as intercessor who proclaimed the judgment of

Yahweh on the Philistines. The desire to demonstrate the actual result of Samuel's intercession led to a secondary development of the tradition, in 7.10–14, in which the military success over the Philistines which in reality belonged to David, is ascribed to Samuel's intercession and the resulting direct intervention of Yahweh. Apart from this, which may be seen also as a polemic against the military successes of David ascribing them to divine rather than human power, the basic tradition here should be treated as a sanctuary tradition going back to the time of Samuel himself.[28]

Similarly, I Sam. 8 is held by Weiser to go back to a historically reliable tradition rather than to a late and unhistorical anti-monarchical source.[29] This time it is a tradition located at Ramah and one which accurately reflects the external and internal difficulties which attended the institution of the monarchy. The chapter has a clear connection with chapter 7, which has already been shown to be early, and further support for the early origin of chapter 8 is provided by the point, established by Mendelsohn,[30] that the 'ways of the king' to which chapter 8 refers, reflect the conditions which existed among the neighbouring Canaanite city-states already in the time of Samuel.

In 10.17–27 there is also old tradition of historical significance concerning Saul's election as king, this time a tradition located at the sanctuary at Mizpah. There are strong associations with the covenant ritual in the speech of Samuel in this passage, especially the recitation of the saving history in v.18. This is a point of contact with the independent, though parallel, tradition of I Sam. 12, a tradition rooted at the sanctuary of Gilgal.[31] I Samuel 12 is not to be judged simply as a valedictory address; here Samuel acts rather as a covenant mediator,[32] and the purpose of the account is to show how Samuel coped with the new conditions which the monarchy introduced. The words used here go back to covenant tradition; they may not indeed have been spoken in this form by Samuel himself, but the whole presentation is, nevertheless, historically correct in putting Samuel forward as the representative of the old covenant tradition responsible for the adoption of the new institution, the monarchy, into that tradition.

Weiser's argument draws attention to and attempts to resolve a weakness in Noth's presentation which is somewhat different from that addressed by Boecker: this is that anti-monarchism was not, according to Noth, new with the deuteronomist (being present in the old speech of Gideon in Judg. 8.22f., for example) but was revived and brought to strong, principled expression by the deuteronomist. The difficulty in this lies at least partly in the fact that Noth offered no context within which one might understand such a view being preserved until the time of the deuteronomist. It has the appearance of a theological attitude plucked out of the air by the deuteronomist with no real roots in Israel though early expressions of it could not be denied. The virtue of Weiser's approach was that it aimed to set the anti-monarchic view within a credible historical context without leaving the long period during which this view would have existed in a vacuum.

Yet, serious weaknesses are clearly apparent in Weiser's argument. The virtual denial of deuteronomistic work in I Sam. 7–12 ignores the strong linguistic and other evidence to which we shall turn shortly; as far as I Sam. 7 is concerned, it also ignores the fact that the combination of judge and deliverer which Samuel represents is a pure reflection of the deuteronomistic book of Judges and a clear expression of the deuteronomistic aim to set Samuel in the succession of pre-monarchic judge-deliverers.[33] Neither the argument that 7.10–14 is a secondary growth referring to the military successes of David, nor the proposed parallel with Deut. 32 are of much avail here, for it is by no means clear that 7.10–14 need to be seen as secondary, and Deut. 32 is itself probably a very late composition.[34] As far as I Sam. 8 is concerned, it is true that there is nothing deuteronomistic about its central section, vv.11–17 – though these customs of the king must surely reflect Israel's own experience of kingship rather than Canaanite practice[35] – but the context shows strong deuteronomistic influence and this must determine the stage at which this material came into its present context. Finally, the covenant thought which comes to expression in 10.17–27; 12.1–25 is a reason not for assigning an early pre-deuteronomistic date to these passages but for linking them most closely to the deuteronomistic context where this theological category achieves definitive expression.[36] In neither case, as we shall note, can the unity of these passages be upheld but this does not affect the existence of a strong deuteronomistic influence in these passages.

Crüsemann's study of the anti-monarchic texts of the Old Testament[37] represents a more thorough and better worked out approach to the problems which they pose, and is concerned specifically to set the anti-monarchic texts within their proper historical and sociological contexts. In fact, it not only provides a credible context of origin and transmission of the anti-monarchic tradition in Israel, but it also goes a long way towards resolving the problem of the conflict (in Noth's study) between the views of the deuteronomist and those of the sources which he took up by shifting that conflict back into the sources themselves. The editorial bringing together of these sources thus represents an attempt to achieve order in the sources available and to present a total picture of the period on their basis rather than a tendentious correction of the sources by setting them within a conflicting editorial framework, a procedure for which there is no analogy and which is inherently unlikely.

Pre-deuteronomistic material unsympathetic to the monarchy is to be found in I Sam. 8.1–3; 8.11–17 and 12.3–5. These three passages betray close connections: the verb *lqḥ*, 'take' as a key term throughout; the use of *mishpāt* in 8.3 ('justice'), 11 ('ways'); the common concern with the question of the relationship of the leader with the people. As a connected series of texts it says in effect: the old order was at times corrupt, but it was better than the new order under the king; the judges may have on occasion taken a bribe, but under the new royal administration it will be a matter of constant taking. There is a clear polemical attitude against the monarchic institution brought to expression in these pre-deuteronomistic texts. The criticism is economic and social, rather than theological, and is to be understood as aimed at, and as having its setting among, those with most to lose: this would have been a wealthy class of landowners; and the period of currency of this criticism, to judge from the nature of the monarchy in Israel presupposed by 8.11–17, is most probably that of the early monarchy, especially the time of Solomon.

While these social and economic anti-monarchic texts can be distinguished by literary means, there are, according to Crüsemann, other texts which express a theological antipathy to the monarchy, which are to be distinguished only traditio-historically. Such texts are now found in deuteronomistic contexts, but express ideas which to some extent conflict with deuteronomistic ideas. The texts in question are 8.7 and 12.12, in both of which human kingship and the kingship of Yahweh are seen as mutually exclusive. The deuteronomist does not otherwise contrast divine and human rule like this, and indeed does not otherwise speak of the kingship of Yahweh. A pre-deuteronomistic traditio-historical context for these ideas of the sole kingship of Yahweh which excludes human kingship is to be found in Num. 23, according to which it is Yahweh alone who is king and brings security to Israel (vv.8,20,21,23), and Deut. 33, according to which (vv.2–

94

5,26–29) at the assembly of the tribes it was neither Saul nor David who became king, but Yahweh; only he is king of Israel and only he is the guarantor of Israel's security. So, besides those contexts in Israel (especially the context of the Jerusalem cult) in which divine and human kingship were fully integrated, a notion taken over from the Canaanite environment, there existed another Israelite context, opposed to the monarchy, in which human kingship was seen as incompatible with the kingship of Yahweh.

The earliest[38] at which such pre-deuteronomistic criticism of the monarchy would have emerged in Israel is the time of David: experience of the monarchy is presupposed; the texts are concerned with its inner workings and effects, and so the time of Saul is probably too early. On the other hand, the time of the eighth-century classical prophets is probably too late, for here, especially with Hosea, there is a clear development of thought. While the anti-monarchic texts lead Israel's social and economic ills back to the monarchy, Hosea sees the monarchy as the product of the evil of the people and so Yahweh's punishing action is not because of the king's own behaviour but because of that of Israel. Insofar as this action involves the removal of the king this is not done as an act of salvation for Israel (which is the sense of the anti-monarchic texts), but in the context of the punishment of the whole people. The radical criticism of the monarchy is best set, therefore, in the time before Hosea who has reinterpreted it to fit his own historical context, in which the monarchy was seen as part of the people and when social conditions were not led back to it in particular.

In fact the anti-monarchic texts are best dated to the time between David's consolidation of the kingdom and the division of the kingdom after the death of Solomon. During this period there was the required freedom from outside threat which would have allowed the growth of opposition to strong, central power. It is in this period that we find prominent individuals able to come forward in opposition to the monarchy on a broad basis of popular support (Absalom, Sheba, Jeroboam I). It is to this time that there belong Old Testament narratives and histories which have as a central concern the relations between king and people, the possible alienation of ruler and ruled, and the object of reconciling alienated Israelites to their ruler. So, the story of the rise of David reflects a concern to justify the Davidic monarchy; the Joseph story sees the rule of Israelite brothers by one of their number as willed by God; Judg. 17–21 seeks to legitimate central state power as the only alternative to anarchy; and the Yahwist sees the monarchy as the fulfilment of divine promise; the succession narrative, like the Yahwist, is also critical of certain monarchic practices and concerned to limit royal power. The root of anti-monarchism is not nomadic or amphictyonic: it lies rather in the fundamentally changed conditions brought about in Israel in the process of change from tribal, loosely associated groups, to centralized state authority. It is as a result of this social change, and as a result also of the passing of those historical factors which made it necessary, that opposition to the Israelite monarchy emerged.

This is a convincing presentation of the historical context of the anti-monarchic texts of the Old Testament, setting them clearly within a credible sociological context which is otherwise lost. It is abundantly clear that it is quite impossible to claim such texts simply as deuteronomistic. This is an important point which should be emphasized, and it leaves us free to examine the texts falling within this context without prejudging the issue of their authorship solely on the basis of the view which they express of the monarchy. We have already followed up the editorial history of the pro-monarchic texts within I Sam. 7–12, and determined the deuteronomistic contribution to that history. The remaining texts, expressing an anti-monarchic view, may now likewise be examined; this can now be done with the recognition of the existence of pre-deuteronomistic texts expressing an anti-monarchic view, and with the aim of determining the nature and the extent of the deuteronomistic contribution to those texts. The texts in question are I Sam. 7.2–17; 8.1–22; 10.17–27a; 12.1–25. Finally, we shall look also at II Sam. 7, where too a strong deuteronomistic influence is to be detected.

In I Sam. 7.2–8.22 the scene is set for the election of Saul as king. The first chapter describes how Samuel acted to deliver Israel from the Philistines, and also performed the duty of judge; the second chapter describes how Samuel's sons, whom he had appointed judges in his old age, did not administer justice, and so the people requested a king. Despite his fundamental objection to this innovation, Samuel followed the command of Yahweh and agreed that the people should have their king. Clearly, in their present form these chapters belong together and have come from an author who intends that they should be taken together. That ultimately it is from deuteronomistic hands that the chapters have come is indicated by a number of points: first, there is a clear connection between 7.3ff. and what have been seen to be deuteronomistic passages in Judges (Judg. 2.11ff.; 3.7ff.: 10.6ff.) –

the reference to Israel as serving the Baals and the Ashtaroth, crying to Yahweh, the presentation of Samuel as deliverer and judge, the acknowledgment 'we have sinned' (I Sam. 7.6; Judg. 10.10). Secondly I Sam. 8.1–3 is clearly connected with Deut. 16.18ff.: in both there is reference to the perversion of justice and the taking of bribes. Thirdly, there is an equally clear relationship between I Sam. 8.4ff., 11ff., and Deut. 17.14ff.: the institution of the monarchy will make Israel 'like all the nations'. That the relationship implied in this and the preceding point is not one in which Deuteronomy is dependent on Samuel, but rather the reverse, is indicated by the deuteronomistic character of the whole account as suggested by the first point.

Yet, 7.2–8.22 is not a unit.[39] In the first chapter there is a repeated introduction to a speech of Samuel in vv.3 and 5, and in fact vv.3–4 quite clearly form a self-contained unit. The verses are not presupposed by what follows, and they themselves require no continuation; in fact, the reference to Israel's acknowledgment of its sin in v.6 is out of place and unexpected after v.4. Chapter 8 likewise betrays a lack of uniformity: the effect of the present organization of the chapter is that Samuel himself appears both petulant and disobedient, for after having been distinctly commanded by Yahweh to accede to the popular demand for a king (v.7), Samuel tried to persuade the people not to have a king and then had to be commanded by Yahweh a second time to do as they ask (v.22). The verbal repetition of the beginning of v.7 at the beginning of v.22 is a further indication of secondary supplementation of the chapter. The most probable resolution is that vv.6b–10 have been subsequently introduced into their present context. The basic story originally ran from v.6 ('. . . give us a king to govern us') to v.11, so that Samuel's recitation of the ways of the king (vv.11–18) was his own reaction to the original request of the people rather than the fulfilment of the divine command to instal a king, a form of fulfilment which is unsuitable to say the least.[40]

There is a strong deuteronomistic influence to be discerned in the language of both the basic layer and its supplement in both chapters. Deuteronomistic terminology abounds, along with quite distinctive deuteronomistic ideas and attitudes.[41] The portrayal of Samuel as exercising the functions of both deliverer and judge in the basic story of chapter 7 presupposes the deuteronomistic combination of these functions in Judges. In 8.5,20 the request for 'a king to govern us like all the nations' makes use of the term *špt* to describe the activities of the king as ruler, in conformity with the deuteronomistic use of this verb to describe the function of the deliverers/judges in Judg. 2.16,18f.

The clear conclusion is that there are here two deuteronomistic layers. The basic one in 7.2,5–8.6a,11–22; and a supplementary deuteronomistic layer in 7.3–4; 8.6b–10. The latter is concerned to be precise about Israel's sinfulness and defines it as turning away from Yahweh and going after the Baals and the Ashtaroth. The connection between this and the later deuteronomistic layer already marked out in Deuteronomy, Joshua and Judges requires no elaboration. Yahweh alone is Israel's deliverer and it is in returning to him that Israel will find her salvation. It is the same deuteronomistic hand at work throughout.

The basic account must then be understood to derive from the deuteronomistic historian; this is the deuteronomistic history taking up and elaborating on old source material. It has an attitude to the monarchy which is not immediately obvious. The reason for this lies not in any ambivalence in the matter in the mind of the deuteronomistic historian himself, but rather in the ambiguity of his sources. In the account of the deuteronomistic historian older traditional material may be recognized primarily within 7.15–8.3 and 8.11–17. That there is any basis in history to the story of the miraculous defeat of the Philistines as a result of Samuel's intercession is exceedingly doubtful. In view of Philistine subjugation of Israel as a result of the defeat of Israel at the battle of Mount Gilboa, the statement that the Philistines 'did not again enter the territory of Israel' (7.13) scarcely represents old traditional material; rather one should judge the story as based on the deuteronomistic desire to present Samuel as a deliverer, in line of succession to the old pre-monarchic deliverers. Its form of presentation may owe much to the earlier account of a meeting of Israelites and Philistines in I Sam. 4. A deliberate contrast with I Sam. 4 (in which the Philistines are the victors) is contrived: the one presents the Philistines as taking the initiative (I Sam. 7) the other Israel (I Sam. 4); the one involves the ark (I Sam. 4) the other not (I Sam. 7). On the other hand, the circumstantial detail of 7.16, in contrast to the generality of v.15 and the redactional purpose of v.17 (Ramah being the setting of chapter 8), encourages confidence in its being older tradition. The same is true of 8.1–3 which, since its subject is the same, must surely derive from the same source as 7.16. It is probable that this traditional material came to the deuteronomistic historian as part of the prophetic tradition, linking the birth story of

Samuel with the folk tale of 9.1ff. Within the remainder of chapter 8, vv.11–17 are clearly pre-deuteronomistic : there is nothing deuteronomistic in their language; some expansions of the text may be recognized (vv.11b,15,16b), and when these are removed the text may be seen to present a clear structure culminating in the threat of slavery in v.17. It has been rightly taken as a pre-deuteronomistic polemical document,[42] best dated to the time of the early monarchy. Its close correspondence with I Kings 9.22 indeed suggests the time of Solomon as the one best suited for its composition.

These traditional texts, taken up by the deuteronomistic historian, did not present a single picture. On the one hand, the pre-monarchic form of leadership exercised by the judges, of whom Samuel's sons were the last representatives, was described as having grown corrupt: justice was perverted and bribes were taken. Thus, the monarchy took on the appearance of an institution essential for the correction of injustice. On the other hand, however, the monarchy itself was a potential source of injustice and oppression in the life of Israel. Both views of the monarchy were strongly represented in tradition and to both of them the deuteronomistic historian had to do justice. As a result of his editing and juxtaposition of materials the institution of the monarchy is seen to have divine permission, though not approval, to be tolerated but certainly not to proceed from a divine provision for Israel's prosperity. It may be that in providing a story of Yahweh's defeat of the Philistines at the intercession of Samuel, the deuteronomistic historian intended not just to portray Samuel as standing in line of succession to the old deliverers, but also to ensure that the reader would not be misled into thinking that the monarchy had its primary basis and chief cause in threats to Israel's survival from outside; for such a basis to the monarchy would have implied that the form of leadership for Israel for which Yahweh had hitherto directly provided, viz. the divinely inspired occasional leaders, was quite inadequate.

Thus, for the deuteronomistic historian, it was first because of corruption and sinfulness within the people that the monarchy came into existence; yet, in itself the monarchy was a form of leadership which carried the possibility of even worse corruption and oppression. The deuteronomist thus allows the reader to see the monarchy as an institution which, necessary though it may have been in human terms, is in fact no guarantee of security and stability; rather, it is a human institution (which can at most claim divine permission) subject to the weaknesses, corruptions, perversions and oppressions which that implies.

I Samuel 10.17–27 presents a rather complex picture. Most obvious is this within v.21, for it is at this point that two methods by which Saul was chosen as king are rather unsatisfactorily combined: on the one hand, he is chosen by lot (vv.20f.), and on the other he is presupposed as already designated because of his physical stature (v.22ff.). The former method presupposes Saul's presence throughout the proceedings, a requirement that v.21b*b* denies in the interests of combining this method of election with another, different one. This is not to say that we find here two old traditions on the election of Saul, for it seems more probable in fact that it is only in the latter part of the section that pre-deuteronomistic material is to be found. The reference to Saul's physical stature in v.23b in particular strongly echoes the old folktale of 9.1–10.16 (cf.9.2), and may well be taken as belonging to the pre-deuteronomistic context from which that folktale derived.[43] At any rate, since Saul's hiding himself in the baggage (vv.21b*b*–24) makes sense only if he had already been designated, it may be assumed that this account of the election of Saul as king was composed with an eye especially to 9.1–10.16, which relates that designation, rather than to 10.17–21b*a*. The latter finds its continuation in vv.25ff., so that this forms a new framework for the older tradition. This framework has introduced the method of election by lot, probably in order to supply a correction to the old tradition. In the latter the element of divine initiative in the election was missing, and it is this that the framework supplies; and in doing so, it uses as prototype the selection process described in Josh. 7.16–18 and again in I Sam. 14.40ff.

Deuteronomistic responsibility for the framework in 10.17–21b*a*,25–27 is certain. The passage is a continuation of the deuteronomistic presentation of chapters 7f.[44] However, 10.17–21b*a*, 25–27 is probably not a single deuteronomistic composition:[45] in a context which is otherwise so manifestly favourable to the monarchy, or at least certainly not ill-disposed towards it, as indicated by the designation of Saul's opponents as 'worthless fellows' (10.27), a jarring note is struck by vv.18f. The anti-monarchic tone of these verses, which is out of place in the context, but otherwise finds its parallel in the late deuteronomistic 8.7, indicates a probable second deuteronomistic contribution, at least to parts of these verses. It is in fact the speech of Yahweh in vv.18a*bb*–19a ('I brought up Israel . . . set a king over us'), which both gives expression to this strong anti-monarchic viewpoint and uses terminology which finds its parallels elsewhere in late deuteronomistic compositions.[46] So here, as also in chapters 7f., a later deuteronomistic editor has incorporated a strong anti-monarchic view into a basic deuteronomistic account which, in taking up older tradition, gives expression to both views of the monarchy while itself remaining not unfavourable.

I Samuel 12 closes the deuteronomistic presentation of the institution of the monarchy with a speech whose deuteronomistic origin has long been recognized.[47] The chapter is probably a single unit,[48] falling into four sections: vv.2–5,6–15,16–19,20–25. Legal forms and ideas predominate: in the first section there is a legal process in which Samuel is exculpated; in the second Yahweh is exculpated in that it is affirmed that he has been faithful to Israel throughout her history whereas Israel has been guilty; in the third scene the people recognize the innocence of Yahweh and their own guilt; the final scene is parenetic rather than legal: Israel is encouraged to obey the law.

There are several factors which indicate not just deuteronomistic origins, but late deuteronomistic authorship, so that the chapter should be seen as an insertion into the deuteronomistic history.[49] In the first instance, its removal restores a direct connection between the end of chapter 11, and the beginning of chapter 13, which records Saul's having become king, his age when he did so, and the years he reigned. This is a regular form for recording royal accessions in the deuteronomistic history. Secondly, the chapter is a speech of Samuel which, as in the late deuteronomistic Josh. 23, is unlocalized, while the occasion is the great age of the speaker. Thirdly, the language of the chapter is consistently late deuteronomistic: 'this day' (vv.2,5); 'this place' (v.8); 'forget' (v.9); 'hearken to the voice of' (vv.14,15); 'rebel against the commandment of' (vv.14,15): 'fear the Lord' (vv.14,24); 'turn aside from following the Lord' (vv.20f.); 'make you a people for himself' (v.22); 'the way' (v.23); 'with all your heart' (v.24); 'faithfully' (v.24). The chapter is clearly a late deuteronomistic creation.

For I Sam. 8–12 it may be concluded, therefore, that the deuteronomistic historian brought together various traditions on the election of Saul, some pro-monarchic and others anti-monarchic. The distinction between a pro-monarchic group of texts, including I Sam. 9.1–10.16 (23b,24abb); 10.27b–11.15, and an anti-monarchic group, including the rest of I Sam. 7–12, a distinction with which we began the study of these chapters, may now be seen to be both inaccurate and misleading: inaccurate because many of the so-called anti-mon-archic texts take their starting point in attitudes not unfavourable towards the monarchy; misleading because it easily leads on to the view that the anti-monarchic texts are later than, and a 'correction' of, the pro-monarchic texts. In fact, the deuteronomistic historian had at his disposal pro-monarchic texts which included not only the folk tale of 9.1–10.16 (in a prophetic edition) and the deliverer story of chapter 11, but also the traditional material contained within 7.15–8.3, telling of the corruption of justice in Israel before the institution of the monarchy. Anti-monarchic tradition available to him is now to be found in 8.11–17. In bringing these diverse traditions together, the deuteronomistic historian reveals his own view; but this certainly cannot be described simply as anti-monarchic: he gives full weight to the pro-monarchic elements which tell of injustice in Israel which prompted the desire for a king, and of the stature and bravery of Saul which recommended him to the people. The anti-monarchic elements too are prominent, so that in general the monarchy is presented as a human institution having divine permission, but having also the potential for corruption and oppression. It is the later deuteronomistic editor who is much more clearly anti-monarchic, emphasizing the desire of the people which prompted the request for a king as sinful and rebellious, and presenting human kingship as an evil alternative to the rule of Yahweh; it carries no guarantee whatever of security but shall be swept away if Israel does not obey the law of Yahweh.

Deuteronomistic responsibility for other contributions to the development of the books of Samuel is certain;[50] but the only other major contribution which is of particular significance for our theme is that to be found in II Sam. 7. The classic study of this passage by Rost[51] began with the observation that the chapter falls into three major sections: the introduction (vv.1–7), the prophecy (vv.8–17) and the prayer of David (vv.18–29). Starting with the last section the kernel of the prayer was seen to lie in v.27a, the promise of a dynasty to David, but the whole prayer, apart from vv.22–24 and possibly also v.26, which were taken to be deuteronomistic, was accepted as old tradition, possibly from the time of David. Within the prophecy, the kernel is formed by vv.11b,16, while vv.8–11a, 12,14,15,17 are later elaboration. But this kernel in vv.11b,16 is not to be set on the same level as the prayer of David, for the latter presupposes an oracle in which the king himself was the immediate recipient of revelation. The introduction to this is in vv.1–4a; but its original continuation has been replaced by vv.4b–7. Rost's view has come in for some serious criticism:[52] in particular, his appeal to a lost original continuation to vv.1–4a and his view that the promise of an eternal dynasty (vv.11b,16) was later edited so that it spoke only of David's immediate successor (vv.12,14f.), have been felt to constitute basic weaknesses. However, these weaknesses concern mainly the detail of the nature of the older materials within the chapter rather than those aspects of Rost's study which are of most significance in the present context. These are, first, the recognition that older sources have been used in the composition of the chapter and so literary criticism must be applied to it; and, secondly, the argument that a deuteronomistic stage of editing may be discovered. On the first of these points the argument of Veijola deserves serious consideration: according to this, two old oracles, one contained in vv.1a,2–7 concerning a prohibition of David's building the temple, and the other in vv.8–10,12,14,15,17, promising David a successor, have been combined by an editor at work in vv.11b,13,16. This editor took the word 'house' or 'temple' from the first oracle, interpreted it in the sense of 'dynasty' (vv.11b,16) and so established a connection with the second oracle, at the same time extending the reference of that oracle so that it no longer referred only to Solomon. The terminology used identifies this editor as the deuteronomistic historian at work at a time of danger to the Davidic dynasty. A later editor, who contributed vv.1b,11a,22–24, is shown from the vocabulary used to be the later deuteronomistic editor extending the promise to the Davidic dynasty to incorporate 'Israel'.

There are certain difficulties in this, again relating especially to the earlier stages of development of the chapter. In addition to those mentioned by Mettinger,[53] it must be questioned if there is a credible context within which the prohibition of David's building the temple would have existed on its own as late as the deuteronomistic stage. In addition, the proposal dispenses completely with the contrast between the prohibition of David building the temple and the promise that Solomon will do so; the latter, in v.13a, is scarcely simply an incidental part of the deuteronomistic redaction otherwise concerned with the permanence of the Davidic dynasty. So it seems better to follow Mettinger in seeing as basic to vv.1–17 the theme of Solomon as builder of the temple (vv.1–7,12–15). On the other hand, the latter's contention that there was a pre-deuteronomistic stage of redaction which introduced the notion of the permanency of the Davidic dynasty is more problematic. This theme appears strongly only in vv.8–9,16, and it is doubtful if it can generally be established as a theme independent of deuteronomistic redaction in the chapter. The designations of David as servant of Yahweh and as prince (*nāgîd*), which characterize this theme, are deuteronomistic terms.[54] If this is so, then the following may be assigned to the pre-deuteronomistic stage of vv.1–17: vv.1a,2–7,12–15. Within what remains vv.1b,8–9,11b,16 use the terminology of the deuteronomistic historian.[55] To that layer there belongs also most of the rest of the chapter, the prayer of David in vv.18–29, a passage which can scarcely be said to have any substantial traditional root. It is concerned with the eternal dynasty of David and its vocabulary marks it as belonging to the deuteronomistic historian: David is the servant of Yahweh (vv.20,21,25,26,27,28,29); it is in deuteronomistic literature that we find parallels to 'confirm the word which thou has spoken concerning thy servant and concerning his house' (v.25; cf. Deut. 9.5; I Sam. 3.12; I Kings 2.4; 6.12; 8.20; 12.15; 29.10), and also to 'and the house of thy servant David will be established for ever before thee' (v.26; cf. I Kings 2.45).

The attitude of the deuteronomistic historian here towards the monarchy marks something of a change compared with earlier expressions on the subject in I Sam. 8–12. There is no doubt of his own view that the Davidic dynasty is a divinely ordained institution, the object of Yahweh's unconditional faithfulness. Whereas he had earlier allowed full expression to anti-monarchic views on the occasion of Saul's election there is now only one view: massive approval for David and his dynasty. This undoubtedly indicates that his earlier opposition, insofar as its existence may be concluded from his permission to let anti-monarchic tradition come to expression, was directed to the monarchy of Saul rather than to the monarchic institution as such,[56] a conclusion which is also indicated by his constant use of David as the ideal against which other kings are measured. Saul was Israel's first king; the institution of monarchy had divine approval; but it was David rather than Saul who was the real object of divine favour.

There remain two passages within II Sam. 7 which are found within the deuteronomistic historian's contribution but do not easily belong: vv.10–11a, 22–24. In both cases the focus shifts from David to the people Israel as the recipient of God's favour and the probability is that these represent a later deuteronomistic addition to the chapter. In addition to the points made by Veijola in favour of this, we must point to the connection which exists between vv.10–11a and

Deut. 4.29f.; 30.1ff., on the one hand, and between vv.22–24 and Deut. 4.7f., 32ff. on the other. The restoration of Israel after punishment ('they shall be disturbed no more'), and the incomparability of the relationship between Yahweh and Israel are significant themes for the later deuteronomistic editor.

With regard to the deuteronomistic editing in Samuel it may be concluded, therefore, that the picture corresponds with what has been established for earlier parts of the deuteronomistic history. The basic editorial work which takes up the older sources and establishes the continuity of the history is the work of a deuteronomistic historian. An earlier prophetic stage of editing had made an important contribution to this work, in that it was then that most of the complexes of tradition within Samuel were first brought together. It was with the deuteronomistic historian, however, that the ark narratives were incorporated, that the prophetic presentation of Samuel as leader, judge and prophet who anointed and ultimately denounced Saul (I Sam. 1–3; 7.15–8.3; 9.1–10.16; 13ff.) was supplemented by the addition of anti-monarchic tradition (8.11–17) and also the tradition of Saul as deliverer (11). In linking this material together the deuteronomistic historian showed himself to be not so much anti-monarchic as rather concerned to present Saul as the last of Israel's judge-deliverers; the monarchic institution, with its divinely designated king, has the full approval of the deuteronomistic historian, but only with David who alone was the recipient of the divine promise of eternal rule.

The later deuteronomistic editor has introduced his own distinctive themes, particularly in I Sam. 12. He is anti-monarchic in principle, and the tension between his own view and that of the deuteronomistic historian is alleviated as far as Saul is concerned only by the fact that the historian was himself fundamentally ambiguous in his attitude to Saul, and, as far as David is concerned, by the fact that, making no distinction between Saul and David and viewing the monarchy as a single institution, the later deuteronomistic editor expressed his view on the occasion of the foundation of the monarchy under Saul. For this editor it is the people, not the king, which is important, and the welfare of this people depends on observance of the covenant law. However, here as elsewhere in his work the later deuteronomistic editor betrays his awareness of Israel's sinfulness and breach of covenant, which must lead to the infliction of punishment, a bleak picture which is yet balanced by the hint of a promise of restoration and renewal.

5

Deuteronomistic Editing of
KINGS

The continuity of the work of two deuteronomistic editors into the books of Samuel has been seen to be probable. A distinction between two deuteronomistic editors is in fact of fundamental importance in the context of Samuel alone, for otherwise it is difficult to discern a coherent deuteronomistic attitude towards the monarchy. When the later deuteronomist's negative attitude, brought to expression within scattered verses through I Sam. 7,8 and 10, but supremely in I Sam. 12, is distinguished from the work of the earlier deuteronomistic historian, and when the latter is recognized as having been concerned to harmonize the conflicting attitudes of his sources, the work of the deuteronomistic historian may then be seen to conform with his contributions in earlier sections, while his successor also stands directly in line with earlier expressions of the later deuteronomistic view.

The deuteronomistic historian has contributed mainly the work of combining given source materials to present a total picture. However, in addition to bringing together older pro-monarchic and anti-monarchic texts, he has also inserted his own compositions (especially in chapter 7), designed primarily to ensure that the reader would understand that while the introduction of the monarchy had divine consent, it was not a necessity arising from any deficiency in divine provision for Israel's welfare. If the sources made it difficult for the deuteronomistic historian to project a uniform attitude to Saul, this is not the case with David: in II Sam. 7 an old pre-deuteronomistic prophetic oracle on Solomon as builder of the temple has been expanded by the historian to include a promise that David, the servant of Yahweh, is the founder of an eternal dynasty.

The later deuteronomistic editor has not only introduced his standard warning about the danger of serving other gods, and his well known theme of obedience to the law as the prerequisite for prosperity; but he has also, in II Sam. 7, significantly modified the promise of an eternal dynasty to David so that now (vv.10–11a,22–24) it is Israel as a whole which is once again, as in Deut. 4.29f.; 30.1ff., the object of the comforting assurance of restoration. A consistent pattern of editing is clear so far through the books of the deuteronomistic history.

After the conclusion of the Succession Narrative in I Kings 2,[1] the story of Solomon begins and continues until I Kings 11. Thereafter, following on the division of the Davidic empire into the kingdoms of Israel and Judah, the histories of both states are concurrently presented, until the fall of Israel (II Kings 17) and the fall of Jerusalem (II Kings 25). An impressive uniformity of presentation pervades the books of Kings: in addition to the marks of unity which characterize these books within the overall context of the deuteronomistic history,[2] one may point especially to the formulaic presentation of the individual kings as the particular unifying element here. This presentation appears in its fullest form in connection with Rehoboam (I Kings 14.21,29–31): 'Rehoboam was forty-one years old when he became king, and he reigned seventeen years in Jerusalem . . . His mother's name was Naamah the Ammonitess . . . Now the rest of the acts of Rehoboam and all that he did, are they not written in the Book of the Chronicles of the Kings of Judah?. . . And Rehoboam slept with his fathers and was buried with his fathers in the city of David. His mother's name was Naamah the Ammonitess. And Abijam his son reigned in his stead.' This type of framework appears from now on for the kings of Israel and Judah, except that for the kings of Israel the age of the king at his accession and the name of the queen mother are not given. With some of the kings the whole or part of the framework is missing; but this is always due to the peculiar circumstances of each case. So the concluding formula is missing for the kings Joram and Ahaziah, who were murdered (II Kings 9.22–28), and the introductory formula is missing for the rebel Jehu who came to the throne on the nomination of a prophet (II Kings 10.34–36). The whole formula is missing for Athaliah because she was regarded as a usurper in Judah (II Kings 11). The concluding formula is missing for those kings who were violently deposed: Hoshea of Israel (II Kings 17.1–6); Jehoahaz of Judah (II Kings 23.31–34); Jehoiachin of Judah (II Kings 24.8–17), and Zedekiah of Judah (II Kings 24.18–25.21).

An additional strong unifying element throughout Kings is the constant explicit use of a single criterion of judgment on the kings of Israel and Judah, viz. whether or not they removed the highplaces. The action of Josiah, whose reform, reflecting the demands of the book of the law which the deuteronomist incorporated in Deuteronomy at the beginning of his work, is taken as the unchanging norm of acceptable behaviour. From the time that the temple was built in Jerusalem by Solomon it was, for the deuteronomist, the worship of Israel at that temple alone which was legitimate. This was 'the city which the Lord had chosen out of all the tribes of Israel to put his name there' (I Kings 14.21; cf. Deut. 12.5,11,14,18,26), and only this sanctuary was permitted. For their failure to dissociate themselves from the sin of Jeroboam who had separated Israel from that sanctuary, all the kings of the northern state are condemned; for their failure to remove the high places and centralize all worship to Jerusalem, most of the Judaean rulers are also condemned.

In Noth's presentation, the unity and uniformity of the books of Kings are strengthened by the consistency of the sources on which they are based, and the way in which these sources are referred to.[3] The sources are mainly official chronicles into the framework of which other materials have been fitted. So, for the Solomonic period, the chief source is clearly 'the book of the acts of Solomon' (I Kings 11.41), which would have provided the deuteronomist with official information on Solomon's court building and commercial operations. The deuteronomist's relationship to the official record is not direct and straightforward: the official record would have covered Solomon's reign in its chronological stages, but the deuteronomist presents his information in a topical rather than a chronological arrangement. That the deuteronomist himself organized the source in this way, or that it came to him already rearranged, is not clear.

The book of the acts of Solomon is the major source; the deuteronomist has supplemented it with traditional stories about Solomon, including the Gibeon tradition of the divine revelation to the king and the story of Solomon's wise decision. Besides composing his own contribution to the portrayal of Solomon,[4] the deuteronomist has also modified his source materials to some extent, particularly in that he has tried to arrange them in order to accommodate the rather contradictory picture of Solomon which history yielded. On the one hand, Solomon was the builder of the temple and so the mediator of divine blessing to the people; on the other hand, it was immediately after Solomon's death that the Davidic empire disintegrated and the unity of the people was destroyed. So the deuteronomist divided his presentation of Solomon into two phases: the first period is one of blessing and prosperity, and on this the emphasis is laid; it is introduced by the divine revelation to Solomon at Gibeon (I Kings 3.4–15), on which then follows the positive account of Solomon extending to the end of chapter 8. The second period, one of apostasy and failure, is presented as if coming towards the end of Solomon's reign; it too is introduced by divine revelation (9.1–9), after which the accounts of Solomon's apostasy and the rebellion of Hadad the Edomite, and Rezon of Damascus (11.14–25), allow the deuteronomist to lead easily into Jeroboam's rebellion and the division of the kingdom (I Kings 11.26–12.33).

For the monarchic period following the death of Solomon the deuteronomist had three major sources. First, there were the Chronicles of the Kings of Israel, from which the deuteronomist derived information on the accession and length of reign of each king; besides this, however, very little historical information was taken from this source. Secondly, there were the Chronicles of the Kings of Judah, again yielding information on the accession and length of reign of each king; additionally, however, this source also yielded information on the temple, especially perhaps the periodic ransacking of it in order to raise money. In the case of both of these sources the deuteronomist is using, according to Noth, not actual official records, but rather unofficial histories of the kings adapted from the official records and written at a time when the period they treated was past. These two sources have yielded the basic framework for the deuteronomist's reconstruction and also some historical detail insofar as this contributed to the deuteronomist's overall aim of relating the steady decline of Israel.[5] His third source, which has not just supplemented this basis in an isolated way but rather has contributed in a major way to its general thrust, yielded stories of prophets: such were the Elijah and Elisha stories, already a collection before the deuteronomist adopted them, and a cycle of stories of prophetic interventions in the succession of Israelite kings in I Kings 11*; 12*; 14*; (20); 22; and II Kings 9–10.[6] Finally, since there would have been no official records dealing with the fall of Jerusalem and the end of the Judaean kingdom, the deuteronomist has completed his presentation in II Kings 25 by using the Baruch story of Jeremiah in Jer.39–41. Insofar as II Kings 25 contains anything not found in Jer. 39–41 it derives from the hand of the deuteronomist himself.[7]

Noth's thoroughly argued presentation was an effective challenge to those who advocated the view that Kings had gone through more than one redaction.[8] His explicit answer to this view, apart from the detailed justification he gave for his own theory of the unity of the deuteronomistic redaction, was simply that the assumption of a pre-exilic deuteronomistic redaction of Kings depended on the attribution to a supposed pre-exilic editor of materials which in fact belong to the sources used by the single, exilic deuteronomistic redactor.[9] Yet although Noth's argument commended itself so strongly, to the extent that his work may rightly be described as 'classic',[10] disagreement with it has now gone beyond the stage simply of criticism to the stage of setting forth a well founded alternative. The nature of this alternative has in broad outline remained fairly consistent, viz. that there was a pre-exilic edition of Kings which was then supplemented during the exile to bring it up to its present proportions. However, the basis on which the alternative has been argued has in recent years been better refined; now it is no longer possible to dismiss it simply as the result of the assignment to a supposed pre-exilic editor of passages which really belong to the sources used by a single exilic deuteronomist.[11]

A major contributor towards the development of this alternative is Cross,[12] whose treatment of the thematic content of the deuteronomistic history takes a comprehensive view rather than one which concentrates on one or two individual passages. He has also provided a credible setting and context within which a pre-exilic edition of the deuteronomistic history could be set, and accounted in a convincing way for the thematic tensions which characterize the deuteronomistic history, especially I and II Kings, in its present form. According to Cross, there are two themes in the deuteronomistic history. The first is the sin of Jeroboam and his successors, the kings of the northern kingdom, and the consequent judgment on the northern kingdom. This theme comes to expression in the following passages: I Kings 13.2–5, 33–34; 15.29 (cf. II Kings 17.7–23); 16:1–4; 21.17–29 (cf. also 20.42f.; 22.8–28 and II Kings 1.2–17); and it reaches its climax in the account of the fall of the northern kingdom and the meditation on this event in II Kings 17.1–23. The second theme is the promise of grace to David and his house. This theme appears in II Sam. 7; I Kings 11.12,13,32,34,36; 15.4; II Kings 8.19; 19.34; 20.6, and reaches its climax in the account of Josiah's reform in II Kings 22.1–23.25. In this climax Josiah is said to have extirpated the cult of Jeroboam in the destruction of the altar of Bethel and the highplaces of 'the cities of Samaria', and to have attempted to restore the kingdom of David. More attention is paid to Josiah and his reform than to any of the other kings who followed David. [13] The deuteronomistic historian deliberately contrasted these two themes, the sinfulness of Jeroboam and the faithfulness of David and Josiah, and in setting them together he provided the platform of Josiah's reform, the means by which the aims of Josiah's reform might be further supported and propagated. Josiah is the new David, and in him, in contrast with Jeroboam and the kings of the north, there is to be found true faithfulness to Yahweh as a result of which the restoration of the Davidic kingdom is taking place. Read in this way, the deuteronomistic history is to be dated to the reign of Josiah; it supports his reform and calls to the north to return to the Judaean fold and acknowledge both Jerusalem as capital and Josiah as king; but it is also a call to Judah, affirming that its restoration depends on the return of the nation to the covenant of Yahweh and a return of her king to the ways of David.

If this is so, then II Kings 23.25 must have been the limit of the Josianic deuteronomistic history. Its extension, to bring the history up to the destruction of Jerusalem and the exile and then finally to the release of king Jehoiachin from prison in exile, is the work of a second deuteronomistic editor. This editor, however, contributed not only II Kings 23.26–25.30; he is also responsible for a subsidiary theme which now runs through the history, and which reflects the Jerusalem catastrophe and wishes to account for it. A major passage from this later editor, apart from the concluding chapters, is II Kings 21.2–15, which functions to portray the coming reform of Josiah as the cause of what was to be only a temporary postponement of the destruction of the kingdom; Josiah's piety delayed the disaster, but because of the sin, especially of Manasseh, the punishment could not be finally averted. In other passages of Kings which also reflect this theme (I Kings 2.4; 6.11–13; 8.25b,46–53; 9.4–9; II Kings 17.19; 20.17f.) we find the late editor's continuation of an edition of the deuteronomistic history which he had already begun in Deuteronomy (4.27–31; 28.36f., 63–68; 29.27; 30.1–20) and continued in Joshua (23.11–13,15f.) and Samuel (I Sam. 12.25). This is a subtheme of the deuteronomistic history, introduced during the exile, updating the original deuteronomistic history from the time of Josiah and addressing it to the new exilic situation.

This is a persuasive treatment of Kings, and one which conforms with much that has been argued here in relation to earlier books of the deuteronomistic history. Those passages in Kings which are argued to reflect a pre-exilic situation are too numerous, too substantial and central to be seen simply as belonging to the sources used by a later editor. Rather, they presuppose the existence in the time of the Davidic monarchy of a definite form of the deuteronomistic history, a form which, far from being just a source for a later editor, was the fundamental work which was later supplemented and adapted. Only in this way can the thematic tensions be satisfactorily explained. Yet, in one respect Cross's proposals remain inadequate: the literary critical basis which could provide a coherent account of the redaction of Kings is incomplete. In particular, a connection must be established between this thematic understanding of the development of Kings and the framework passages which are so characteristic of the total presentation of these books.

In a work which set out consciously to undergird Cross's approach with detailed literary critical argument, Nelson pointed first to a significant characteristic of the regnal formulae which frame the references to each king in Israel and Judah.[14] The pattern is that each king is introduced with the following information: synchronism with his contemporary in north or south (up to Hoshea); age at accession (Judah only); length of reign; capital city; name of queen mother (Judah only); verdict on behaviour. The conclusion of the account of each king's reign refers to the source of information on his activities, his death and burial, and the notice of his successor. There are considerable varieties in the use of this formulaic framework: sometimes these arise from changes in the historian's sources, but at other times the variations are random and reflect simply the freedom with which the historian used the stock phrases and vocabulary at his disposal. It is only with the formulaic framework to the last four kings of Judah: Jehoahaz, Jehoiakim, Jehoiachin and Zedekiah, that there is a difference. Here the formulae are fixed and terse, without any of the elaboration and variation that characterized other usages of the framework. A different and later hand is at work here, imitating the earlier existing forms which embraced the period up to and including Josiah. Thus, the thematic study of Cross may be confirmed by literary critical observation.[15]

Having established that the deuteronomistic history, composed in the time of Josiah, did undergo this late editing, Nelson was then able to mark out, with more or less assurance, those parts of Kings which were with all probability to be assigned to the later editor.[16] There are four groups of such passages. First, there are two passages connected with Solomon: I Kings 8.44–51; 9.6–9. In the first of these there is a clear change between the earlier part of Solomon's prayer of dedication, which presupposes a situation in the land with the temple still standing, and vv.44–51, where the speaker addresses himself *towards* Jerusalem and the description of exile is much more detailed.[17] In I Kings 9.6–9 there is a relationship with other passages secondary to the deuteronomistic history, such as Deut. 29.23–25. The second group of passages relates to the deuteronomistic meditation on the fall of Samaria in II Kings 17.[18] Here vv.7–20,34b–40 may be readily identified as coming from the second edition: the catalogue of sins is at variance with the normal practice of the deuteronomistic historian who usually refers only to the sin of Jeroboam; Judah is included in the accusation (v.13), and, as far as vv.34b–40 are concerned, the vocabulary ('fear the Lord', 'statutes', 'ordinances', 'law', 'commandment', 'other gods' etc.) identifies it as the work of the later editor.[19] The third passage is II Kings 21.3bb–15 where the later editor has expanded on the sins of Manasseh, and so prepared for, and portrayed as inevitable, the destruction of Jerusalem; even Manasseh's successor, the good king Josiah, could not avert this. Finally, the second editor, before adding the concluding chapters to the deuteronomistic history, has supplemented the account of the reign and reform of Josiah in II Kings 22f., through the addition of 22.16–17; 23.4b–5,19–20,24,26–30. Here, the divine determination to destroy Judah and Jerusalem are affirmed despite the royal reform, and the way is prepared for the concluding account of the devastation of the land.

This study represents a significant advance on previous work and refines in a credible way both the redactional history of Kings and the social and historical setting within which the various stages of development are to be located. Two further studies complemented Nelson's results by distinguishing a third stage in the history of redaction.

The first of these to be considered is Dietrich's minutely argued attempt to distinguish a prophetic stage of redaction which followed on the primary deuteronomistic history and preceded the work of the 'nomistic' deuteronomist.[20] Dietrich first categorized four prophetic stories which show remarkable formal and linguistic affinities: I Kings 14.7–11; 16.1–4; 21.20bb–24; II Kings 9.7–10a. The basis of the prophecy is introduced by *ya'an 'ašer*, 'because', and is structured in two parts: one describes what Yahweh has done and the other the human response. The prophecy itself is then introduced by *hinnenni*, 'behold I', followed by a participle. Any variation in this pattern is the result of the different situations in which the prophecies are set and is compensated for by the consistent use of common terminology throughout. Other texts which conform more or less to this established pattern and which share the common stock of language are II Kings 22.16f.; 21.10–15; the basic layer of I Kings 11.29ff. (i.e. vv.29–31,33a,34a,35aba,37abcb); II Kings 22.18–20; I Kings 21.27–29. For each of the prophecies contained in these passages there is a corresponding notice of its fulfilment in a historical event. These fulfilment notices, in I Kings 12.15; 15.29; 16.12; II Kings 10.17; 24.2, have clear connections in terminology among themselves and with the prophecies, so that common authorship may be established. On this basis the prophetic word against Jezebel in I Kings 21.23 and its notice of fulfilment in II Kings 9.36, together with the prophetic word against Ahab in I Kings 21.19b and its notice of fulfilment in I Kings 22.38, may also be allied with the other prophetic passages.

Certain additions to these prophetic passages may be distinguished.[21] There is primarily the second layer of I Kings 11.29ff. (i.e. vv.32,33b,34b,35bb,36,37aa,38aba); and then also I Kings 14.8b,9a; II Kings 23.26f.; 24.3f.; 21.16a; 21.15; 21.4,7b–9; 15.12; 10.30,31a; I Kings 14.15f.; 21.25f.; 15.30; 16.13; II Kings 9.37; 22.17ab. All these passages are both marked off from their contexts and connected among themselves; they are to be ascribed to the late deuteronomistic editor, the 'nomistic' deuteronomist.

A literary critical treatment of II Kings 17, and comparison of its various sections with the layers already discerned, indicates that 17.21–23 are to be assigned to the prophetic layer, while 17.12–19 are from the 'nomistic' editor. The basic composition from the deuteronomistic historian is in vv.7–11,20. It is clear in this case that vv.21–23 are additional to their context; this can also be shown of all the other passages ascribed to the prophetic editor, both prophecies and notices of fulfilment: all may be marked off as expansions or additions to their present contexts, and in some cases stand in conflict with these contexts.[22]

As far as the context of origin of the prophetic layer is concerned, the form in which the prophecies are expressed is, in the historical books, no earlier than the deuteronomistic period; it is a form used in the classical prophets including both Jeremiah and Ezekiel, and of these it is with Jeremiah that contact is closest. Other influence on the formulaic language of the prophetic layer is clear from Jeremiah, Isaiah, Ezekiel, stories and prophetic narratives in the deuteronomistic history, the deuteronomistic history itself, Ex. 32 and Ps. 79; a few other distinctive expressions, if they are not existing technical terms, are perhaps to be ascribed to the author of the prophetic layer.[23] Influence from prophecy is particularly strong, and in general the intention of the author may be described as that of uniting prophecy and the deuteronomistic movement: this editor wished to show the connection of prophecy and history, the role which prophecy plays in history. History is the arena in which the prophetic word works itself out; important events take place in accordance with the prophetic announcement in advance. In order to show this, the prophetic editor may on occasion have 'modified' history to fit the prophetic word; but he also took up older traditional material, including the story of Ahijah in I Kings 14; the story of the unknown prophet in I Kings 13; I Kings 20; 22; 17; II Kings 1, and the Isaiah legends in II Kings 18.17–20.19. None of these has an original connection with the basic work of the deuteronomistic historian.

The stages of redaction of Kings are already clear, but they are confirmed, and their limits and times of composition made precise, by a study of the last chapter of II Kings. The account of the fall of Jerusalem (II Kings 25.1–21a) depends mainly on personal knowledge, with the exception of the catalogue of items plundered from the temple (vv.13–17), which depends on I Kings 7.15ff., a passage which already formed part of the deuteronomistic history. This account is opened and closed by II Kings 24.18f., 20b.; 25.21b, which belong to the deuteronomistic historian and thus can be seen as the close of his account. The second part of the chapter, however, in vv.22–30, is separated from the first by the closing formula of v.21b and is, moreover, different in style and origin. The last paragraph, in vv.27–30, expresses the theme of the permanence of the Davidic dynasty: this has been the constant theme of the 'nomistic' deuteronomist hitherto (cf. I Kings 11.13,32,34,36,38; 14.8; 15.4f.); this editor has emphasized Yahweh's judgment on Jerusalem and Judah because of the sin of Manasseh, but not a judgment on the Davidic dynasty (cf. II Kings 23.26f.; 24.3f.,20a). The story of Gedaliah in 25.22–26 has been excerpted from Jer.40f. by the 'nomistic' editor in order to show that Judah needed Jehoiachin, the surviving Davidic king now brought to honour by the Babylonians.

So it may be concluded that the deuteronomistic historian composed his work just after the fall of Jerusalem, that the 'nomistic' deuteronomist edited the work which came to him just after the rehabilitation of Jehoiachin in *c*.560 BC, before the hopes which this event raised were dashed, and that the prophetic redactor, who followed the historian but preceded the 'nomistic' editor, is to be dated to the early part of the exilic period.

There are several significant points here which distinguish these results from both Noth's classic discussion and the more recent proposals of those who have differed from him. On the one hand, it is affirmed, with Noth, that the deuteronomistic historian worked after the fall of Jerusalem; but, against Noth, that the deuteronomistic history then experienced two stages of redaction. On the other hand, against other views which we have hitherto examined, the idea of a pre-exilic deuteronomistic history composed during the reign of Josiah is not supported, while the more favoured double redaction of the work is supplemented by a further stage. In addition to Dietrich's major contention that a prophetic stage of redaction is to be discerned, there are perhaps two major points to be examined, both of which impinge strongly on the main point: these are, first, that the 'nomistic' deuteronomist has a positive attitude to David, and, secondly, that the work of the deuteronomistic historian extends beyond Josiah up to the destruction of Jerusalem.

That the 'nomistic' deuteronomist expressed himself with regard to the Davidic dynasty in the way proposed by Dietrich[24] is *a priori* unlikely. It is quite out of keeping with this editor's earlier expressed views in I Sam. 12 as well as in Deuteronomy, Joshua and Judges; it is the people Israel, not the king, which, for this editor, is the only significant entity, it is Israel's prosperity in obedience to the law, not the permanence of a royal dynasty as the result of a promise, which is the exclusive concern. One cannot appeal in this connection to the last paragraph of the work, II Kings 25.27–30, for, aside from the fact that the interpretation of this is far from clear,[25] it does not use the distinctive terminology which is said to mark the 'nomistic' deuteronomist's expression of this theme. In order to test Dietrich's view it is not possible to study in detail all the passages which he treats; but one or two fairly crucial ones may be examined.

I Kings 11 is important in this respect. It does not constitute one of the primary passages used by Dietrich, but it is in the context of this passage that the concerns of the 'nomistic' deuteronomist are first established,[26] and, moreover, it is here as much as anywhere else that it may be seen whether or not the prophetic passages are indeed to be taken as a layer additional to the deuteronomistic history. Dietrich proposed[27] that the story of the meeting of Jeroboam and Ahijah is no original part of the deuteronomistic history, but has replaced the historian's account of the rebellion mounted by Jeroboam against Solomon, referred to in 11.26. The account of this meeting is not a unity, however, but is to be divided into two layers: the basic layer, in vv.29–31,33a,34a,35ab*a*,37ab*c*b, has a form which stands alongside the other prophetic stories; the later layer, in vv.32,33b,34b,35b*b*, 36,37a*a*,38ab*a*, is a commentary on this, and is to be assigned to the nomistic deuteronomist. It is in this latter layer that the theme of the permanence of the Davidic dynasty is also expressed.

There is no doubt that vv.29–39 are overfull, repetitious and characterized by changes of emphasis which are occasionally illogical;[28] but the particular solution adopted here is open to serious question. In relation to its two fundamental points an alternative is desirable. These points are (*a*) that the account of the meeting between Jeroboam and Ahijah has replaced the deuteronomistic historian's account of the rebellion mounted by Jeroboam; and (*b*) that the two layers into which the account falls are to be distinguished especially on the basis of the attitude of the later towards the Davidic dynasty.

It is unlikely that the deuteronomistic history ever contained a story of the rebellion of Jeroboam.[29] I Kings 11.26 finds its continuation, not in v.27, but in v.40; taken together these verses constitute an annalistic notice derived from a formal record. Already in v.27a, in the words *wezeh haddābār*, 'and this was the reason', there is the beginning of extraneous material secondarily connected with that notice. This secondary material includes, however, not just the story of Jeroboam's meeting with Ahijah, but also other historical information in vv.27f., concerning Solomon's building operations and Jeroboam's position in command of the corvee, material which is not directly relevant to the prophetic story but which has been brought into this context most likely along with that prophetic story. In other words, there is present in vv.26–40 an account of the rise of Jeroboam which combines a variety of material from official and prophetic sources, but in which there never was to be found any 'original' story of Jeroboam's rebellion. It is surely to the deuteronomistic historian that one must look for the editor responsible for this composite work, including the incorporation of the prophetic story of the meeting between Ahijah and Jeroboam. If this is so, then one must also suspect the validity of a division of this prophetic story in such a way that those parts of it favourable to the Davidic dynasty are assigned to the 'nomistic' deuteronomist, for it has been clear, especially in our treatment of Samuel, that such a view of the Davidic house character-ized the deuteronomistic historian. Moreover it is doubtful that Dietrich's proposed basic text hangs together satisfactorily: v.33, using third person plural form of the verb, cannot have followed originally on v.31; v.34a, which requires a continuation referring to the reservation of one tribe for David, cannot have been followed originally by v.35ab*a*; v.37b is a limitation of v.37a, and cannot come originally from the same hand.

On the assumption that the deuteronomistic historian first adopted the prophetic story into his history, and that this in turn may have been edited by a later nomistic deuteronomist, it seems that the following division of the text best meets the situation: the original prophetic story (contained in vv.29–31,34a,35b*b*,37a) recounted Ahi-jah's prophecy that Yahweh was about to take the kingdom from the hand of Solomon and that Jeroboam would receive, not all of it, but ten tribes. When the deuteronomistic historian incorporated this he edited it through the addition of vv.32,34b*ab*, 35ab*a*,36,37b,38,39. These additions were introduced in order to stress the election of David and Jerusalem (using the distinctive deuteronomistic language: my servant David: Jerusalem the city which I have chosen), the fact (only implied in the original prophecy) that it was after Solomon's death that the division took place,[30] and the fact that the election of David and Jerusalem was not cancelled by the sin of Solomon but only (temporarily) restricted.[31] The material which remains, vv.33,34b*c*,[32] is concerned to emphasize neglect of the commandments as the reason for the disruption of the kingdom and observation of the commandments as the reason for the election of David. It introduces a strong conditional element into a context which, insofar as it concerned the election of David and Jerusalem, was unconditional, and is thus marked out as the work of the nomistic deuteronomist.

Those passages which Dietrich claimed as part of a prophetic edition of the work of the deuteronomistic historian are, therefore, to be seen rather as older source material incorporated by the deutero-nomistic historian. This, however, raises the question of the extent of the work of the deuteronomistic historian, for it seems at first sight that this conclusion is incompatible with the view that the deutero-nomistic history was composed during the reign of Josiah, or in pre-exilic times. A number of these prophetic passages apparently presuppose the fall of the southern kingdom and therefore an exilic date of composition at the earliest. Yet, it is remarkable that it is in relation to just those passages where an exilic date of origin is apparently indicated that it is also questionable if they derive from the same hand as that responsible for the other prophetic passages in the group. Almost all the passages designated by Dietrich as belonging to the prophetic layer are spoken by a named individual prophet to or about a named individual king or queen threatening judgment and punishment on that individual; the passages, both prophecies and fulfilments, are linked to quite clear and definite situations and presuppose only the fate that has overtaken those named individuals. With the exception of the prophecy of Ahijah against Solomon (where, however, it is still a matter of a northern prophet speaking to a designated northern ruler), almost all the prophecies and fulfilments concern only northern rulers and are uttered by northern prophets. Insofar as they are not directed simply against the individual ruler they are directed against that ruler's house. There is presupposed in these prophecies and fulfilments at most the fall of the northern kingdom, within the general framework of the history of which they serve to mark the steady decline towards destruction; but they in fact more probably presuppose only the downfall of the ruling houses at which they are directed. These are prophetic forms which belong authentically within the history of the prophetic movement in northern Israel during the period of existence of the northern kingdom.

The exceptions here, and at the same time the passages which apparently presuppose the end of Judah, are to be found in II Kings 21.10–15; 22.16f., 18ff.; and the fulfilment notice in II Kings 24.2. Judah and Jerusalem with its inhabitants are threatened with destruction, in fulfilment of which it is then recorded that 'bands of the Chaldeans, and bands of the Syrians, and bands of the Moabites, and bands of the Ammonites' were sent against Judah to destroy it. We have in these passages, however, something markedly different from the earlier ones noted. In only one case is the author of a prophecy of destruction named: Huldah the prophetess to whom the threats of 22.16f., 18ff. are ascribed. Otherwise, it is 'his servants the prophets' who have threatened. Although the prophecies are set in the reigns of specified kings (Manasseh and Josiah), they are not uttered against these kings nor against any named individuals: it is the city and the country whose end is promised. It is true that in the case of the prophecy of Huldah there is a specific link to a definite time and place, but this prophecy is distinguished from the others in being quite clearly a late post-Josianic formulation, even if perhaps based on an older prophecy of Huldah promising Josiah success.[33] All these prophecies relating to Judah and Jerusalem, therefore, stand apart from the others in a variety of ways and should most likely be seen as free formulations of prophetic oracles based on an already existing form. In other words, the conclusion that the prophetic passages represent a source taken up into his history by the deuteronomistic historian holds good for those prophecies (and the fulfilments related to them) uttered by northern prophets against specified rulers of the context of the history of the northern kingdom, in which oracles at most the end of the northern kingdom is presupposed; it does not hold for those prophecies uttered against Judah which have no comparable origin in a pre-deuteronomistic source, and these cannot, therefore, be used in order to show that the deuteronomistic historian wrote after the end of Judah.

Dietrich's proposals that the work of the deuteronomistic historian belongs to the exilic period and that it has undergone a prophetic redaction are, then, questionable. His argument for a stage in the redactional history of the deuteronomistic history to be assigned to a nomistic deuteronomist is partially confirmed by our study of I Kings 11.29ff., for this indicated that a layer later than that of the deuteronomistic historian is to be found there. However, the verses here assigned to it and those proposed by Dietrich are quite different; so our understanding of the nature of the work of the nomistic deuteronomist is correspondingly different. Several other parts of the books of Kings may with relative ease be separated off as deriving from the same nomistic hand as that at work in I Kings 11;[34] but fundamental to the credibility of any such procedure there remains the issue of the relationship between such different stages of development and the history of the books of Kings as this may be established by a study of the redactional passages which act as a framework to the references to the individual kings of Israel and Judah. If it can be shown from the latter that the books have undergone a process of development analogous to that suggested by the study of passages such as I Kings 11, the case as a whole will be the stronger. It is in this context that Weippert's study of the judgment formulae in Kings is most helpful.[35]

These judgment formulae ('he did what was good/evil in the sight of Yahweh', etc.) are useful in this connection because their stereo-typed language and their incorporation of comparisons between one king and another show that they derive from an author giving a grand overview of the historical period, who stands at some distance from the period he is describing, and who is not interested in the historical details of the reigns of individual kings for themselves alone; they are thus framework passages into which source materials are incorpor-ated. Moreover, the variations in the judgment formulae permit the discernment of steps in the development of the formula and therewith also of the whole corpus of Kings which it now embraces.

There are three groups of these framework judgment formulae, which are distinguished by style and expression. The groups relate to progressively more extensive or later sections of Kings, which means that they may be set in chronological order, the group covering the smallest section of Kings being the earliest and the group embracing the most extensive section being the latest.

The first and earliest group breaks down into two basic and closely related forms of expression, the one being used when kings of Judah are being judged, the other when kings of Israel are judged. The formula applied to Judaean kings is composed of four elements: he did/did not do what was right in the sight of Yahweh; according to all that his father did; only they did not take away the high places; the people still sacrificed and burned incense on the high places. It is used in I Kings 22.43; II Kings 12.3f.; 14.3f.; 15.3f.; 15.34f.; 16.2b,4. The formula applied to Israelite kings is composed of three elements: he did what was evil in the sight of Yahweh; he did not turn aside from all the sin of Jeroboam; with which he made Israel sin. It is found in II Kings 3.2a,3; 10.29,31; 13.2,6,11; 14.24; 15.9,18,24,28; 17.22. Identity of authorship for both of these forms of expression is indicated by a number of points: the first elements of each formula are contrasting forms of identical structure; there is the common use of the verb *sûr* ('take away', 'turn aside') with the negative; in each case the sin of the individual king is not the reason for the judgment – for Judaean kings it is the people who did not take away the high places, while for the Israelite kings it is the sin of Jeroboam which is the basic fault. That it is a matter here of a distinct stage in the development of Kings, represented by this group of formulae, is finally confirmed by the fact that the formulae are used of contemporary kings of Israel and Judah over a specific period of time, viz. the period of the reigns of the Judaean kings from Jehoshaphat to Ahaz inclusive and their Israelite contemporaries from Jehoram to Hoshea inclusive. This period is the last one hundred and thirty years or so of the northern kingdom until its destruction by the Assyrians in 721 BC.[36]

The latest period covered by this group of formulae, the end of the northern kingdom and the reign of Ahaz in Judah, would indicate that this stage of development of Kings is to be dated to the time of Ahaz's successor Hezekiah. Its purpose should probably be determined in connection with two significant events: the fall of the northern kingdom and the cultic reform which II Kings 18 ascribes to Hezekiah. This reform involved the removal of the high places, and this action is used as the criterion of judgment by the formulae. The aim of this production was to inculcate the right mode of behaviour for Judaean kings to follow, in the light of and in order to avoid the fate that had overtaken Israel.[37]

The formulae of the second group lie outside the block which is covered by the formulae of the first group. Only at the edges of the first block will some overlap be observed; otherwise this first block does not show the formulae of the second group. This indicates that with the second group we have a new stage in the redaction of Kings, taking up existing material and extending it on either side.

The redactor at this stage shows, as is to be expected, clear dependence on the forms used in the first stage, yet at the same time distinctive variation. There are two formulae in this group and they depend on those of the first group; yet, whereas in the first group one formula was used of Judaean kings and the other of Israelite kings, here in the second group that distinction no longer holds. The distinction here is simply between good and evil kings, whether Israelite or Judaean. It is true that all Israelite kings are evil, but the important point is that when a Judaean king too is judged as evil the formula of judgment used on him is the same as that used of the Israelite kings. The two formulae of this group are, first: he did that which was right in the sight of Yahweh; like David his father (used of Judaean kings in I Kings 15.11; II Kings 18.3; 22.2),[38] and, secondly: he did that which was evil in the sight of Yahweh; he walked in the way of his father/Jeroboam; and in his sin which he made Israel to sin (used of Israelite and Judaean kings and also generally of the kingdom of Israel in I Kings 14.16,22; 15.3,26,30,34; 16.2,13,19,25f.,30f,; 21.22; 22.53f.; II Kings 21.2,15,16f.,20f.).[39] There is a clear connection between this group and the first in the phrase 'he did that which was good/evil in the sight of Yahweh', but equally clear deviation in, for example, the reference to David as an ideal figure and in the absence of the verb *sûr*. The relationship between the two groups is best seen as one in which the second is dependent on the first, an understanding confirmed by the fact that the formulae of the second group appear outside the limits of the material embraced by the formulae of the first group.

The period covered by the formulae of the second group begins with Rehoboam;[40] the last king covered by it is Josiah. This would suggest the time of Josiah's successor Jehoahaz as the time of redaction. Since this period lasted only three months (II Kings 23.31), however, it may be that the work was begun in the time of Josiah, that it was prompted by the reform of Josiah, just as the first redactor's work was prompted by the reform of Hezekiah, and that it is on the basis of that reform that Josiah is judged positively. The purpose of this stage of editing was evidently to update the earlier and set it in a wider context. There is no sign that the redactor had a view of history as a time of increasing sin leading to inevitable judgment and punishment; rather, he recognizes the benefits of the monarchy and its potential for good; and in the advent of Josiah with his reform he sees a clear counterpart to David.

The third and last group of formulae has only four examples, and only one formula is used with just very slight variation: he did what was evil in the sight of Yahweh; according to all which his father(s)/Jehoiakim had done. The formula is used only of the last four kings of Judah, in II Kings 23.32,37; 24.9,19. Again, the dependence of the formula on the formulae of the first two groups is obvious; but for two reasons the authorship of this formula must be distinguished as independent: first, had the formula come from the author of the second group it is difficult to see why he did not follow the form there used; secondly, the application of the formula to Josiah's immediate successor Jehoahaz, including the phrase 'according to all that his fathers had done' (II Kings 23.32), is startling in the extreme, in view of the fact that Josiah himself is praised so extravagantly. There is clearly a break here, in which an already existing account of the monarchic history of Israel and Judah has been taken, considered as a whole and updated to the time of the exile.

There is much here of considerable relevance and importance for our purposes. This supplies a clear outline and reliable framework for the redaction of Kings, within which the content must be fitted. In doing this there is, of course, much uncertainty and it is doubtful that it will ever be possible to be perfectly precise on what all stages of redaction contained.[41] Nevertheless, even if difficulties remain, it is possible to draw some conclusions on the general nature of these stages of redaction, and conclusions, moreover, which show a remarkable conformity with earlier arguments concerning the deuteronomistic stages of editing in earlier books. The first stage of redaction is not so important in this connection since it apparently, like older stages of Judges and other books, does not go outside the limits of a restricted part of a particular period; its horizons are considerably more limited than those of the deuteronomistic historian. Yet it is a significant stage in that the basis on which judgment is meted out on the kings – whether or not they removed the highplaces – is a clear deuteronomistic principle, directly linked with Deut. 12, and so must be taken as belonging to an early stage of the deuteronomic-deuteronomistic movement.

The second stage of redaction of Kings is for us, however, most important. With its reference to David as an ideal type and its inclusion of Josiah it clearly represents a major stage in the development of Kings incorporating the earlier in a much wider context, a context which includes at least the monarchic period as far as Josiah. It is a stage in the development of Kings which is most naturally to be linked with the deuteronomistic historian. It sees the monarchy as a divinely ordained institution, and looks with favour on David in particular as its ideal representative. Within the framework of this second stage the bulk of the books of Kings belongs, for there is no doubt but that it is to this stage that the major themes of Kings, as Cross has discerned them, are best suited.[42] The sin of Jeroboam and his successors leading to the destruction of the northern kingdom, and the promise of grace to David are contrasting themes which find their unity within a construction framed by the redactional formulae of the second stage. Here too belong the prophecies of destruction on individual northern kings and the fulfilment notices attached to them; these too function to substantiate the condemnations of the northern kings and implicity to confirm the (conditional) commendation of the kings of Judah. In this the deuteronomistic historian has maintained the attitude to the Davidic dynasty which he first forcefully expressed in the oracle of Nathan in II Sam. 7. The deuteronomistic historian's work has David as its pivotal point: he is another Moses, the one who, like Moses, is addressed as 'my servant'; and to him Josiah is a worthy successor. The work points up the importance of Josiah, whether or not Cross's view that it acted as propaganda for that king's reform measures is correct.[43]

The third stage of redaction in Kings should then be linked with the work of the later deuteronomistic editor. Here too, as in this editor's work in passages such as I Sam. 12, there is a very pessimistic view of the monarchy: none of its representatives had done what was right before Yahweh. This is a presentation quite in conformity with what is otherwise known of this editor's work in earlier parts of the deuteronomistic history: it is in obedience to the law, and only in such obedience, that Israel with her king can stand in covenant with Yahweh. The destruction of Israel and Judah followed by the exile signified breach of that covenant; the conclusion that all Israel's and Judah's kings had done evil was inevitable. And yet, if it is true that it is to this same editor that the final paragraphs of Kings are also due (which must be the case unless we think here simply of a late isolated addition), then it is indeed possible that, as in Deut. 4.25ff.; 30.1ff., so here, the later deuteronomistic editor sees Israel's destruction not as the final word but as the prelude to her repentance which may herald future restoration.

Before closing this chapter we must test this conclusion against two passages which are crucial for any discussion of the deuteronomistic history of Kings, II Kings 17 and II Kings 22f.; here especially deuteronomistic material is to be found in the content rather than simply the framework, and unless it can be shown that the conclusions reached on the redactional framework of Kings correspond with the actual content of Kings, the framework remains insubstantial and difficult to relate to the nature and concerns of the deuteronomistic stages of development as they have been discerned elsewhere in the deuteronomistic history.

II Kings 17 falls into two major parts: vv.1–23 and vv.24–41, each of which consists of a historical section followed by a theological commentary. The first part covers the fall of the northern kingdom, the historical events being recounted in vv.1–6 followed by the theological commentary in vv.7–23; the second part covers the circumstances which resulted on the fall of Israel, with the historical section in vv.24–34a and the theological commentary in vv.34b–41. This balance between the two parts of the chapter is reinforced by the strong impression that there is identity of authorship between the historical sections on the one hand, and the theological sections on the other; that the same author is at work in both historical and theological sections is, however, considerably less clear.

The first six verses of the chapter contain material which basically must reflect the first edition of Kings, in its pre-deuteronomistic stage; that stage embraced the account of the fall of Samaria, as the study of the framework passages has shown. Outside the historical report, it contains the formula 'he did what was evil in the sight of Yahweh' (17.2),[44] which is used of Kings of Israel in the first stage. That the deuteronomistic historian who eventually incorporated the first stage of Kings into his more comprehensive work supplemented the account of the fall of Hoshea, in vv.1–6, is impossible to show; but it does seem likely that the deuteronomistic historian has at least contributed to the present form of 17.24–34a, the historical section of the second part.[45] Here there is a clear continuation of 17.1–6 in which v.24 joins directly to v.6: Israelites have been exiled from their own land and foreigners, from other parts of the Assyrian empire, are brought in to replace them. However, vv.24–34a also include references which go beyond what may be accepted as probable for the first redactional stage. In particular, the reference in v.32 to the appointment of 'all sorts of people as priests of the high places who sacrificed for them in the shrines of the high places' constitutes a link with I Kings 12.32 and II Kings 23.20 which are to be connected with the work of the deuteronomistic historian at the earliest, being passages which lie far outside the limits of the first edition of Kings. Thus, the historical sections of II Kings 17 may be identified as basically part of the first edition of Kings which has been taken up into the work of the deuteronomistic historian.

The relation of the theological commentary in vv.7–23,34b–41 to the historical sections must be discussed, but first it should be established that these two theological commentaries derive from the same hand. In the first place, it is not possible to carry through any literary critical division within either of these sections: they are both consistent units. The separation of vv.19f. from what precedes can be done only on the basis of the theory that vv.7–18 belong to a pre-exilic deuteronomist who could not have referred to the fall of the southern Kingdom. This, however, is an inadequate approach; vv.7–18 are not without threatening reference to Judah (v.13), and it is unreasonable to expect any extensive reference to the fall of Judah, even in an exilic deuteronomist, at this particular stage in his presentation. Verses 19f. are a proleptic reference to what is to be taken up in more detail later at the appropriate point.[46] Similarly, within vv.34b–41 no literary critical division is justified; v.41 is a concluding verse from the hand of the author of vv.34b–40, connecting that section with the history that precedes.

That vv.7–23,34b–41 belong together as the work of a single author is highly likely.[47] The two passages share significant terminology: fear other gods (17.7,35,37,38); bow down to other gods/host of heaven (17.16,36); serve idols/other gods/the Baals (17.12,16,33,35,41); commandment(s), statutes, laws (17.13,34b,37); covenant (17.15,35,38). The second section is quite clearly directed against an existing Samaritan community whose worship is condemned as illegitimate, while the first is a theological comment on a past historical situation; but this difference is no more than the result of the fact that the two passages comment on different historical situations: the first on the historical fall of Samaria, the second on the existing community after the Assyrian conquest; this does not then necessarily show different authorship. It is the same deuteronomistic spirit which informs both passages, with their demand for the exclusive worship of Yahweh who brought Israel up from the land of Egypt.

Just as clearly, neither of these theological commentaries is from the hand of the deuteronomistic historian responsible for the historical accounts to which they are attached. It is the second theological commentary which particularly clearly shows this independence. While vv.24–34a are prepared to acknowledge that the community in Samaria fears Yahweh, while at the same time its people, who are in large part foreigners, worship their own gods, vv.34b–40(41) strongly correct this, to the point of contradiction: 'they do not fear the Lord, and they do not follow the statutes or the ordinances or the law or the commandment which the Lord commanded the children of Jacob, whom he named Israel'. When the worship of Yahweh is combined with the worship of other gods, it cannot be the worship of Yahweh.

There can be no doubt of the origin of this theological commentary. It is the theology of the second deuteronomist which is expressed here. The emphasis on the law and the exclusive worship of Yahweh as its chief element is the hall mark of this and the terminological connection with such passages as Deut. 4.19 and Josh. 23.7,16 confirms the presence here of that deuteronomistic hand. Insofar as the theological passages presuppose at least an exilic date they may be then assigned to the third stage of development of Kings which we have assigned to this second deuteronomistic editor.[48]

The story of Josiah's reform in II Kings 22f. presents problems which are not going to be resolved in the space of a few paragraphs. Nevertheless, it must at least be indicated that these chapters are not inconsistent with the view being presented here.[49]

One of the most incisive analyses of II Kings 22f. has come from Lohfink,[50] who has noted that the part of the story which deals with the finding of the book of the law (22.3–20; 23.1–3,21–23) falls into four sections all of which begin and end with a reference to the king (22.3–11; 22.12–20; 23.1–3; 23.21–23). Also, the sections begin alternately with 'the king sent' (22.3; 23.1) and 'the king commanded' (22.12; 23.21). The concern of each section has been summarily described by Lohfink as repentance, oracle of salvation, covenant renewal, festival; and these are taken to be the four acts which comprise a covenant renewal ceremony. Covenant renewal is central to the story, and the whole world of the story is the world of covenant making. As Lohfink notes, this may well be described as a unit within the Josiah story; that it is a unit deriving from the time of Josiah himself, however, and reflecting a historical event which took place under Josiah is a rather different question.[51] Outside general theoretical considerations dealing with the history of covenant in Israel,[52] the real support for locating this unit in the time of Josiah himself is that it apparently shows no knowledge of the violent death which Josiah in fact suffered (23.29f.), but instead records the prophetic promise that Josiah would be gathered to his grave 'in peace' (22.20).

Over against this possible, but by no means essential, connection with the time of Josiah, one must set the fact that the book of the law/ covenant story is closely connected with the concerns of the later deuteronomist, and that its present setting is probably the work of the deuteronomistic historian. The first scene of the story, 22.3–11, contains strong indications of disunity. Thus, v.10 constitutes a new beginning over against v.9 and cannot be its original continuation. In fact, v.10 continues v.8, leaving v.9 as the interruption. That verse, however, continues the matter of the repairs being carried out on the temple in vv.3–7; this story of temple repair is the basic account here into which the story of the finding of the book of the law has been fitted.[53] That story continues unbroken to 23.3, describing the validating of the book by Huldah the prophetess and the consequent covenant festival.

Much attention has been devoted in recent years to the oracles of Huldah. The first oracle, in 22.16–17, is generally recognized as a deuteronomistic composition.[54] The language of the oracle is late: the formula 'behold I will bring evil on' is found in late layers of Jeremiah (19.3,15; 32.42), as is also the expression 'that they might provoke me to anger' (Jer. 7.18; 25.7; 32.29); there is nothing concrete and specific in the oracle; it is general and formulaic. By contrast, the second oracle in 22.18–20, which is directed to Josiah personally, has been widely thought to be based on a historical oracle from Huldah promising Josiah a peaceful death, an old oracle from the time of Josiah which only here and there has some deuteronomistic elements.[55] In fact, however, the two oracles belong closely together, and it is doubtful that any pre-deuteronomistic material may be detected in either.[56] In form, they are held together by the pattern proclamation-foundation-proclamation-foundation-proclamation. In language there is deuteronomistic material ('humbled yourself before Yahweh', 'rent your clothes' (as a ritual act of repentance) 'wept before me'), while there is no particularly pre-deuteronomistic language. In content the two oracles being closely together: the first, with its declaration that general judgment is inevitable, forms the basis of the second, in which Josiah is exempted from that judgment; in addition, the second oracle is best understood as making reference back to the first (the words of Yahweh referred to in vv.18,19, being those spoken in vv.16f.).

If both oracles are deuteronomistic compositions with no older historical basis, what then of the promise to Josiah of a peaceful death? First, in the light of the prophecy-fulfilment scheme which dominates the deuteronomistic books of Kings, it is unlikely that in just this one place the deuteronomist felt forced to preserve an original prophetic oracle in spite of its apparent lack of fulfilment. It is, therefore, questionable that an oracle to be judged old because of discrepancy with the historical course of events is to be found here. Secondly, the form of the promise to Josiah shows that its intention is different from what is presupposed in the view that it is old and genuine. It falls into three parts and reaches its climax in the last: 'your eyes shall not see all the evil which I will bring upon this place'. The first two parts refer to death and burial, understood as separate items (as also in Gen. 15.15), and it is to the second that the words 'in peace' are attached. Josiah will be buried 'in peace' because the conditions of war will not yet exist so as to prevent his burial, and he will, moreover, be buried in his own grave and not, like the last three kings of Judah, in a foreign land. So, this is a salvation oracle to Josiah only in the context of the general proclamation of doom; it is to be understood only within that overall setting. It is, therefore, not to be distinguished from the general deuteronomistic presentation as an original oracle.

By contrast, 23.4–20 stands out from the context of the deuteronomistic lawbook story. There is here no, or very little, narrative account; it is instead a catalogue of reform measures; there is no reference to a book of the law or book of the covenant on which the reform measures are ostensibly based; stylistically, there is a notable frequency of use of the *waw*-conjunction, rather than the expected *waw*-consecutive of the context. It is by no means clear that it is possible to carry through a successful literary criticism of these verses, along the lines suggested by Hollenstein,[57] in order to reconstruct a redactional history for the passage, for it is difficult to see why a redactor would have created the chaotic order of subjects dealt with in the passage which such a critical approach presupposes. Rather, there is here a catalogue of reforms, in which all possible reforms are mentioned, and in which first the south (vv.4–14) and then the north (vv.15–20) are covered, so that a complete and all-inclusive reform can be presented.[58] However, the passage altogether stands clearly apart from the context of covenant making on the basis of a law book, into which it has now been incorporated.

It is thus evident that within these chapters there is a layer constituted by the temple repair story in 22.3–7,9 and Josiah's reform measures in 23.4–20,[59] to which has been added a story setting the events recounted in the first layer within the context of the finding of a lawbook and the making of a covenant. The concern of this lawbook story with a lawbook, covenant making and obedience to the commandments immediately connects it with the second deuteronomistic editor; but this identification can be assured only when the layer on which it is based has also been identified. That the latter is the work of the deuteronomistic historian is suggested by a number of factors. In the first instance, the account of repairs to the temple cannot be seen as deriving from any official annal; it is a story created for its present context and directly based on II Kings 12.9–16.[60] Secondly, the reform measures of 23.4–20 also do not give the impression of being a transcription from an official annal with historical and chronological concerns;[61] rather, here too it is a story, in which the intention is to emphasize the complete thoroughness with which Josiah carried out his destruction of pagan cult objects. Furthermore, the verbs which are favoured in the passage to describe the actions of

Josiah, especially 'burn', but also 'break down', 'break' and 'cut down', are precisely those used in the deuteronomic demands for the carrying through of such reforms (especially Deut. 7.5;12.2f.); in addition, the very objects of these reform measures: the Asherim, the altars, the pillars, the cult prostitutes, the high places etc., are precisely those which feature in the demands of the deuteronomic law.[62] Of the strongly deuteronomic/deuteronomistic character of this story there can be no doubt. In it, Josiah is being deliberately presented as acting in conformity with the demands of the law of Moses.

The history of the material within II Kings 22f. can thus be seen to conform not only with II Kings 17, but also both with conclusions already drawn on the development of the framework passages in Kings and conclusions drawn earlier on the concerns of the two deuteronomistic editors. The deuteronomistic historian has presented Josiah as a reformer of the cult unequalled in Israel's monarchic history, as the one who above all led Israel in obedience to the law of Moses. His account comes to expression in 22.1–7,9; 23.4–20, and to a fitting conclusion in 23.25. The later deuteronomistic editor, at work not only in the updating of Kings beyond the time of Josiah, but also in casting the whole history in a new light, has set the story of Josiah in a quite new context,[63] so that the benefits of his reforming acts accrue to him alone, while the nation pursues its course towards inevitable destruction. The dominant concern of this later deuteronomistic editor with the law and covenant is maintained throughout.

It is thus evident that the redactional history of Kings conforms with that of the earlier parts of the deuteronomistic history. The thematic approach of Cross has persuasively indicated the existence of a pre-exilic stage of the deuteronomistic history and has suggested a plausible setting for it within the context of Josiah's reform. This approach has been seen to harmonize well with other redactional studies, directed to the framework formulae in Kings. Of the three stages of development which these formulae presuppose, the second and third are particularly relevant to our purpose, for the second, being aware of the particlar benefits of the monarchy, fits well into the approach of the deuteronomistic historian (as seen especially in II Sam. 7), while the third, being thoroughly pessimistic with regard to the monarchy as an institution, fits equally well with the understanding of the later deuteronomistic editor (as seen especially in I Sam. 12).

The deuteronomistic historian in Kings used official material and other sources, especially prophetic oracles directed to northern kings and dynasties, to bring his account up to Josiah: Josiah is not only a second David (II Kings 22.2), he also stands as a supreme example of the faithful one, obedient to all the law of Moses (23.25) with which the deuteronomistic historian had opened his account. Moses, David and Josiah are the key figures in the deuteronomistic history, and in the activities of the last of these the authentic expression of the will of Yahweh for his people is to be found.

The later deuteronomistic editor has brought this work to a very different conclusion, for a very different audience. Events had proved the accuracy of his programmatic statement in I Sam. 12 on the monarchy: it had not guaranteed Israel's prosperity. The obedience to the law which is the only way has not marked the lives of any of Israel's kings, and so the people has suffered destruction. Yet the glimmer of hope for possible restoration is not lost but perhaps, as elsewhere in his work, is to be found here again, in the closing paragraphs of II Kings 25.

to the law and avoidance of the worship of other gods as the preconditions of security, but also to his theme, already introduced in Joshua: Israel's conquest of the land was incomplete and the danger to her came from those within the land whom she has been unable to conquer.

Again, as in Deuteronomy and Joshua, so in Judges there is significant post-deuteronomistic material. Both the prologue and epilogue of Judges stand outside the deuteronomistic presentation as late additions. These passages have the appearance of having originated, with the others to which they are linked in Deuteronomy and Joshua, at a post-deuteronomistic stage of development. The authorship and background of this stage are very enigmatic, but its constant ritualistic and levitical concerns perhaps suggest a time and place of origin in priestly circles from which the combination of deuteronomistic history and Tetrateuch ultimately derives.

The picture in the books of Samuel conforms to that so far established for the deuteronomistic history. Although a pre-deuteronomistic, prophetic stage of editing is probably responsible for a first significant arrangement of much of the material here, the contributions of the deuteronomistic historian and of the later deuteronomistic editor follow a familiar pattern. Through the incorporation of the ark narrative and the tradition of Saul as deliverer, the deuteronomistic historian effected a close link with the pre-monarchic period presented in the book of Judges; through his editing of the oracle of Nathan in order to emphasize the permanence of the Davidic dynasty, he established a link with subsequent parts of the deuteronomistic history. Thus, the deuteronomistic historian incorporated the existing traditions on the period of Saul and David into a wider chronological context. His editing went further than this, however; his view of the Davidic dynasty as the divinely instituted monarchy led to a corresponding depreciation of Saul whom the deuteronomistic historian prefers to see as standing in succession to the pre-monarchic leaders rather than as a king of Israel appointed by Yahweh. It is David and his dynasty who receive the full approval of divine designation and promise.

The later deuteronomistic editor in Samuel too has decisively modified the story which lay before him. The sinfulness of Israel is once again emphasized and is seen to be expressed in the demand for a king, a demand which this editor condemns on principle: it is incompatible with the kingship of Yahweh. Yet again, however, the glimmer of a new beginning is seen beyond the punishment which must follow Israel's sin, a hope which in II Sam. 7 as in Deut. 4, is only hinted at and receives little concrete content.

In the books of Kings a similar lack of redactional unity is apparent. An early stage of Kings, composed in the context of the reform of Hezekiah and in the light of the fall of the northern kingdom, is indicated by a particular form of the judgment formula used of Israel's rulers. This was a limited presentation of the royal history, in which, however, the main lines of subsequent editions were already laid down: the histories of Israel and Judah are integrated so that the people is effectively a single entity; the kings of the northern kingdom are all condemned; and the judgment is expressed in general terms of doing evil in the sight of Yahweh.

At the second stage the monarchic history was extended to the time of Josiah. Distinctive of this stage is the presentation of David as an ideal figure against whom subsequent kings of Judah are measured. Clearly the horizons are now much broader, and there is much in favour of taking this stage as the work of the deuteronomistic historian already identified in earlier books. The attitude of the judgment formulae of this stage towards the Davidic dynasty is that of one of the two themes which Cross has distinguished as a major element of the content of Kings, and it is thus to this stage of redactional development that the bulk of the books should be assigned. The approval of the Davidic dynasty which is thus such a fundamental feature of this stage conforms well with the deuteronomistic historian's attitude as expressed especially in II Sam. 7. That part of the deuteronomistic history requires a continuation such as that represented by this second stage of the redactional history of Kings. The deuteronomistic historian, therefore, concluded his work with the account of the reign and reform of Josiah.

The third and final stage of the redaction of Kings is then clearly to be seen as the work of the later deuteronomist. The negative attitude towards the monarchy which the formulae of this stage express supports this conclusion, for it is the same attitude as that found in I Sam. 12. Similarly, the theological judgments expressed in II Kings 17, which so emphasize the law and the need for the exclusive worship of Yahweh, which we have linked with this stage of redaction, also reflect the interests of the later deuteronomist. It is to this final stage of the history of Kings, too, that out of the pessimistic gloom a ray of hope for the future displays the basic belief of this later deuteronomist that the purposes of Yahweh for Israel were not fulfilled in the destruction of 587 BC.

Over against these positive results, it must also be emphasized that very much more work is necessary both on the deuteronomistic history in general and on specific parts of it. In general, there is room for a great deal more refinement in the detailed distinguishing of the contributions of the deuteronomistic editors. In particular, further study is required on the post-deuteronomistic passages to be found especially in Deuteronomy, Joshua and Judges, for the background and authorship of these remain highly uncertain. In fact, the setting within which the work of the deuteronomistic school in general took place must be a significant area for future research.

At present there exists little agreement on even most fundamental points in this connection. The setting within which the work of the deuteronomic-deuteronomistic school is to be set, throughout the whole history of its existence, is unclear. The fundamentally north Israelite origins of Deuteronomy have been repeatedly advocated,[1] but its close associations with Judah must also be noted.[2] The solution, that the 'original Deuteronomy' derived from survivors of the northern disaster in 721 BC who subsequently fled south and in Judah sought to inaugurate a reform so that a similar catastrophe might be avoided there, is probably basically correct; but the precise context of origin of this original Deuteronomy, whether levitical, prophetic or wisdom, remains unsettled.[3] When we go on from Deuteronomy to the deuteronomistic history, it is doubtful if any more is agreed than that the first, pre-exilic edition of this was, like Deuteronomy itself, composed in Palestine. As far as the second edition is concerned arguments are raised for both Palestinian and exilic origin,[4] and in each case, of course, different views are put forward on the purposes for which the work was compiled. It is the lack of clarity on this very issue which is probably the root problem.

This question of purpose should be considered first of all not in terms of whether the work is ultimately negative or positive, whether it views the history of Israel as completed or sees the possibility of renewal and restoration; rather, it is a question of the relationship of the work and its authors to the mainstream of Israelite life. Whatever precise understanding has been projected it is usually taken for granted that the work has an official stance, that it represents a proclamation within the mainstream of the ongoing life of the people; so, in more precise terms than are usually used in this connection, it has been presented as the deposit of preaching and teaching activity in the Babylonian synagogue.[5] Some such public and official context is that normally accepted for the setting of the work of the deuteronomistic school. It is perhaps here, however, that the first questions should be raised.

Given that prophetic attitudes and themes are so strong in the work of the deuteronomistic school,[6] it is not unlikely that as the prophets so the deuteronomistic movement represents a fringe element within Israelite society, having no official position as such within cult or society as a whole.[7] It is clear that the work of the deuteronomistic school, based on the deuteronomic law, is directed against the popular piety of the late monarchic and exilic periods; it follows the historical fiction of the deuteronomic law's self-presentation as the law of Moses proclaimed before the entry into the land, in describing deviation from its norms as apostasy to the Canaanite cults; but what is at the heart of its concern is ordinary popular religion practised by those who considered themselves good Yahwists, some aspects of which are held by the deuteronomistic school to be incompatible with Yahwism.[8] In this there is conformity with several prophetic passages (Ezek. 8; Jer. 7.1–15,16–20; 44.15–19), where the basic prophetic material is directed against popular religious practices and uses the polemic of idolatry to combat those practices.

The answer of the prophets to such practices is not that of the deuteronomists: so the popular and naive idea of Yahweh's presence at the sanctuary is countered by the deuteronomic-deuteronomistic school with a theology of Yahweh's name, but by the prophets with an affirmation of the conditional presence of Yahweh, dependent on the people's right ethical behaviour. However, the object of deuteronomic-deuteronomistic concern was the object also of prophetic concern, and the prophetic answer was by no means unacceptable to the deuteronomists. In the deuteronomistic editing of those prophetic passages the prophetic complaint about particular popular practices and beliefs (baking bread for the Queen of Heaven; adherence to a magical conception of the temple as guarantee of the presence of Yahweh) is usually simply extended and generalized in order to present it as a complaint about the worship of other gods, and the purpose of such expansion is to draw an even sharper contrast between what is done and what should be done and so to justify a condemnation no less strong than that of the prophets themselves.

If the deuteronomistic school thus continues the work of the prophets it does not reflect the main stream of Israelite faith and practice, but rather stands opposed to it with the same critical attitude that characterized the prophets. The deuteronomists are different from the prophets, especially in that they deal with existing texts, but they are no more central to Israelite society than were the prophets; they apply that pre-exilic critical message of the prophets to the popular piety of exilic and post-exilic times, a piety which, as Jer. 44.15–19 indicates, had much in common with its pre-exilic antecedents. It is in the closer determination of the place of the deuteronomistic school or circle within its social context that it will perhaps be possible to arrive at more secure conclusions on the purposes for which the deuteronomistic history was composed.

B. *The Deuteronomistic History and the Pentateuch*

The problem of the relationship between these two literary blocks is not central to our present discussion, but it is closely enough associated with it to require a sketch of the way in which the problem might best be approached. It is a problem which arises primarily from the fact that the deuteronomistic history, however many editions it may have gone through, is a composition independent of what precedes and apparently not composed as the literary continuation of what precedes. It has its own beginning and can be understood on its own terms. It is an account of the history of Israel from the point of its entry into the land until its expulsion from the land, a history considered as a totality standing under the law of Moses received at Sinai.

The problem of the extent of the Pentateuchal sources and so also the question of a literary relationship between the Pentateuch and the following books, has usually been approached by the method of applying to the successive books the approaches and the results already accepted as appropriate for those which have preceded. Thus, it is largely on the basis of results achieved in Genesis and Exodus[9] in this respect, that the book of Numbers has also been seen to be based on continuous sources. So, for example, Noth[10] can write that 'if one was to take the book of Numbers on its own, then one would think not so much of "continuous sources" as of an unsystematic collection of innumerable pieces of tradition of very varied content, age and character ("Fragment Hypothesis"). But it would be contrary to the facts of the matter, as will already be clear from the account of the contents of the book, to treat Numbers in isolation. From the first, the book has belonged, in the Old Testament canon, to the larger whole of the Pentateuch, and scholarly work on the book has consistently maintained that it must be seen in this wider context. It is, therefore, justifiable to approach the book of Numbers with the results of Pentateuchal analysis achieved elsewhere and to expect the continuing Pentateuchal "sources" here too, even if, as we have said, the situation in Numbers, of itself, does not exactly lead us to these results.'

Within the framework of this approach, it is also generally presupposed that there once existed an original, independent literary entity, whether one chooses to call this a Tetrateuch, Pentateuch, or Hexateuch, whose intention was to trace the history of Israel up to a given point within the context of a universal or cosmological setting. This literary work is understood to have existed first of all independently of the deuteronomistic history, with which it was then secondarily connected.

The difficulties involved in this understanding have already become clearly apparent: it is especially troublesome to give a satisfactory account of the fact that the supposed J and E sources, insofar as they do not give an account of the settlement of the land, are truncated. The theory that their original endings were discarded either in the interests of fitting this material into the framework of a Priestly document whose focus of concern was such that the conquest lay outside its limits,[11] or of making a smooth connection with the deuteronomistic history, which included an account of the settlement of west Jordan, is a theory born of desperation, and is in principle inconsistent with the nature of the processes whereby materials were brought together as this is otherwise known to us. If the editing of JE to fit it into the context of P was to be so drastic as to remove the whole point and purpose from these sources, why could it not have been equally drastic in the revision of those parts of JE which were retained even though they pointed so strongly towards the settlement of the land as their conclusion; if the bringing together of this Tetrateuch/Pentateuch/Hexateuch with the deuteronomistic history could have the effect that the supposed JE conquest story was omitted in favour of that contained in the deuteronomistic history, why then was that part of JE in Numbers relating the fortunes of Israel in its wanderings from Sinai to the border of the promised land not omitted in favour of the account in Deut. 1–3?[12]

These difficulties suggest that the solution to the problem of the relationship between the Tetrateuch/Pentateuch/Hexateuch and the deuteronomistic history is not to be sought along these lines. In other words, there is little hope of success in attempts to explain the relationship between the two either on the basis that they each once had independent existence, or from the point of view suggested by Freedman,[13] that the deuteronomistic history never existed completely independently of the JE sources. It is, therefore, *a priori* likely that the quite opposite approach, viz. that which takes its starting point with the deuteronomistic history and then works backwards, should hold open better possibilities. That is to say, the *Tetrateuch* should be approached in the first instance as a literary entity which had no independent existence but which was composed primarily as an introduction to the already existing deuteronomistic history. Of course, that does not mean that the content of the Tetrateuch is generally later than the content of the deuteronomistic history, any more than the late dating of the deuteronomistic history involves a similar dating for its content, but what it does mean is that the present arrangement of the materials with Genesis – Numbers standing before Deuteronomy – II Kings is the result of an editorial process which had the purpose of providing a preface or introduction to the deuteronomistic history. The effect of this is that we should see the Tetrateuch as comprising traditional materials, the collection and arrangement of which was largely carried out under the impetus of the already existing deuteronomistic history.

A preliminary study of the relationship between the deuteronomistic history and the Tetrateuch/Pentateuch along these lines is opened up by Friedman, who follows Cross in the distinction between a pre-exilic deuteronomist from the time of Josiah and an exilic deuteronomist which supplemented this. Friedman proposes that we should also distinguish between a pre-exilic and a later priestly writer, the first being a response to the first edition of the deuteronomistic history and the second being exilic.[14] The first 'edition' of the priestly writing was more a collection of priestly compositions than a continuous, coherent narrative; it comprised materials composed as an alternative both to JE and D texts, which were not to the priestly author's liking. The work of the priestly writer in the exile consisted of binding these materials into the existing JE by means of a new framework, so effecting a new creation holding together in some tension the originally separate JE and P.

This work has the merit of keeping to the fore the problem of the relationship between the Pentateuch and the deuteronomistic history, and especially the question of the relationship of priestly and deutero-nomistic materials in the light of the close parallels and connections which may be established between them. On the other hand, however, it is in many respects not radical enough in the approach which it proposes; traditional Pentateuchal criticism with its distinction between an early JE and a later (pre-exilic, exilic or post-exilic) P is simply presupposed with the modification that one is to think of two stages of development of P. On the latter point, however, insofar as the earlier P is understood to be composed of fairly isolated materials not connected into a coherent 'document', there is little difference between the proposal here and the current widespread assumption that P, while a late document, contains older materials.

It is in the light of present radical questioning of the adequacy of traditional Pentateuchal criticism that the difficulties in Friedman's account become clearest. This questioning emanates especially from van Seters, Schmid and Rendtorff,[15] and is concerned with both the notion of coherent Pentateuchal sources and the periods of Israel's history to which the so-called JE material is usually dated.

We need not get involved here in the basic questions raised by van Seters[16] against the traditio-historical method, except to note that it is undoubtedly true that more emphasis should be placed than has hitherto been done on the literary composition of the texts and the literary influence of one text on another. The significant issue for our purposes is the fact that there is agreement among all three on the general point that a connected presentation of the story of Israel's origins from patriarchs to entry into the land is a late phenomenon which has at least close connection with the work of the deuteronomic-deuteronomistic school. Whether or not the term 'Yah-wist' is used to describe the stage of first bringing together of traditions to form a connected account, this editorial activity is to be regarded as exilic. Traditional source criticism is, therefore, abandoned, and replaced by a view of the 'Yahwist' as the late redactor of older tradition.

Schmid's chief interest is religio-historical: the time of Solomon, usually regarded as a period of cultural enlightenment and therefore as an appropriate context for the production of the Yahwist's work, was in fact a time of strong Canaanizing tendencies in state, monarchy, temple and religion, and so quite unsuitable for the development of the historico-theological thought represented by J. The exilic period as the time of origin of J is suggested not only on general grounds but also by a detailed study of particular passages usually assigned to J: so the story of the call of Moses in Ex. 3f. uses a literary form known from classical prophecy and is comprehensible only against the background of classical prophecy; the plague stories of J show prophetic and deuteronomistic forms; the vocabulary and the theme of many of the wilderness wandering stories are deuteronomistic. This conforms with general traditio-historical considerations relating to the Sinai pericope (which, as a covenant story, is to be seen with Perlitt as deuteronomistic), the patriarchal traditions (in which, for example, the promise of a son may be old patriarchal material, but the promise of many descendants is deuteronomistic and reflects a late time of decline and threat), the apparent deuteronomic-deuteronomistic connection of the exodus and Sinai themes, the silence or near silence of pre-exilic prophecy on much that is fundamental and constitutive to the Pentateuch (patriarchs, Moses, exodus and Sinai covenant). It is therefore concluded that the historical theology of J (which is to be understood as a redactional and interpretative process rather than as a school or individual) is relatively late in Israel's history, presupposing prophecy and coming to expression in a time of crisis, a time of threat to the national religion of Israel and to its own very identity and existence.

Rendtorff's proposals bear some similarities to those of Schmid,[17] especially in that Rendtorff too assigns to a late date any stage at which a continuous presentation of the Pentateuchal story came into existence. However, Rendtorff also draws particular attention to the present difficulties in Pentateuchal criticism with regard to the nature and contribution of J, the distinguishing of J and E, the reconstruction of an independent priestly source, and the usually overlooked impossibility of taking literary criticism and form criticism simply as two stages in the one continuum of Pentateuchal criticism. Literary criticism and form criticism are too different in their approaches and presuppositions to be easily combined, a point well illustrated by the fact that the stages of growth between the short units discerned by form criticism and the longer narratives treated by literary criticism receive so little attention.

Apart from these criticisms, Rendtorff also points to the relative isolation of the larger units (patriarchs, exodus, Sinai, wilderness wandering, settlement) within the Pentateuch. Thus, the covenant and promise which are determinative for the patriarchal tradition are largely absent from the exodus tradition: Ex. 1.7 refers to the multiplying of Israel but without reference to the promise to the patriarchs; Ex. 3.8 refers to the land to be occupied as a strange land in the hands of foreigners, and with no reference to the fact that the patriarchs had long lived there and had been promised possession of it by God. The Sinai pericope makes only sporadic reference to the exodus and to the patriarchal promises; such references are always in marginal parts of the complex, never at its centre. The wilderness wandering tradition, in connection with the murmuring of the people, makes reference to Egypt, but never in such a way as to presuppose the foregoing tradition of the exodus as a saving act of Yahweh. Finally, the settlement tradition of Numbers has only slight reference to the exodus and the patriarchs.

There are links between these units: thus, the promise to the patriarchs in Gen. 50.24; Ex. 13.5; 32.13; 33.1–3; Num.14.23; 32.11, relates the units together; but these compositional links have no firm connection to their narrative contexts, but are to be classified as belonging to an editorial layer closely connected to the ideas and vocabulary of Deuteronomy. This editing was succeeded by a priestly editorial layer: in view of its gaps, the priestly work cannot be considered an independent source, but represents a further stage in the development of the Pentateuch, introducing chronological notices and theological interpretations. It is, however, the earlier deuteronomic redaction which is of primary significance, being that which first brought together the independent longer units within the Pentateuch.

An implication of this, to which Rendtorff briefly alludes,[18] is that the Pentateuch probably never existed without Deuteronomy and the deuteronomistic history. The existence of a unit, the Pentateuch, is based on the understanding of these five books as Torah, not necessarily on their existence as a single, independent literary unit. This brings immediately to the forefront the issue of the relationship of the Pentateuch and the deuteronomistic history, and in particular the question of their relative priority. For if a connected presentation of the Pentateuchal story is not to be found before the deuteronomic-deuteronomistic period, and if it is the case that it is deuteronomic-deuteronomistic editing which first brought this presentation into existence, then it may also follow that the very basis on which the 'Pentateuch' or, in the first instance, the Tetrateuch, came to be formed was the deuteronomistic history as an existing literary entity; thus, the Tetrateuch would have come into being as the prologue to the deuteronomistic history and would never have had independent literary existence.

Immediately pertinent to this question is the recent work of Rose, directed specifically to the question of the literary, theological and chronological relationship of the works of the Yahwist and the Deuteronomist.[19] Three groups of texts are here investigated: first, texts from Josh. 2–6 and related texts in Genesis–Numbers; secondly, Josh. 9–10 with Gen. 34; and, thirdly, Deut. 1–3 with related texts in Exodus and Numbers, in Josh. 14 and Judg. 1. Throughout, the purpose is to determine whether relationships may be established between the texts in each group, in terms of their deriving from a particular literary source (J), and also in general to comment on the question of the existence of a J source which may be dated to the early monarchic period. In view of the specific question being addressed, viz., the relationship of Yahwist and Deuteronomist, the form that the approach takes is specifically that of testing the possibility that texts from the deuteronomistic history presuppose texts from Genesis–Numbers and constitute their direct continuation.

In the first group, Josh. 5.10–12 and Ex. 16.35 are selected as linked texts. The former of these is, as a text, basically deuteronomistic, though it has received further precision at the hand of the priestly writer. It should perhaps be seen as fulfilling the command of Deut. 26.1ff.; but, in any case, it stands with II Kings 23.21–23 as a theological framework to the whole monarchic period on which the deuteronomist is passing judgment. In the vocabulary used (*ḥānāh*, 'encamp'; *'abûr hā'āreṣ*, 'produce of the land') there is an indication of older tradition, which stood within the context of war story, according to which an army when besieging a city (*ḥānāh* means 'lay siege to' as well as 'encamp') ate of the produce of the land. The deuteronomistic reinterpretation of this, however, has been carried through in the interests of drawing a contrast between the wilderness wandering period (when manna was eaten) and the time of living in the land (when the produce of the land was eaten) In Ex. 16.35 the structure of the text is not parallel. Here a basic P account has been given a post-P interpretation in the addition of v.35b. So, while a priestly redaction may be identified in Josh. 5.10–12, it is a priestly author at work in Ex. 16.35. Where the two texts share a real literary connection is not until the post-priestly stage in that the precise geographical information of Ex. 16.35b is intended to remove any ambiguity from Josh. 5.10–12, while the phrase 'in that year' in

Josh. 5.12b is a reference back to the period of forty years referred to in Ex. 16.35. This is a late common literary layer.

Joshua 5.13–15; Num. 22.22–35 and Ex. 3.1–5 are also related in some way. Traditio-historically, it may be established that the oldest form of the story of the vision of (the angel of) Yahweh is to be found in Josh. 5.13–15. The well known extra-biblical form of the vision followed by the war oracle, belonging originally to the context of seeking a divine assurance before a decisive battle, is here adapted, through the replacing of the war oracle by the story of Josh. 6, in the interests of presenting the settlement as carried out miraculously. Numbers 22.22–35 has close ties with Josh. 5.13–15, but also with the later I Chron. 21.16 (where the angel is likewise a punishing angel), while Ex. 3.1–5 is a literary creation in which the traditional ideas and themes are generalized and, loosed from their old contexts, brought together to provide that element of the call which relates the vision. On a literary level Ex. 3.1–5 should be held to come from the hand responsible for the secondary adaptation of Josh. 5.13–15, for it was that which turned this tradition into something like a sanctuary legend, with which Ex. 3.1–5 may be compared. The author/redactor at work here stands close to deuteronomic and deuteronomistic ideas.

In Ex. 3.20; 34.10; Num. 14.11 and Josh. 3.5 a link has been established in the use of the phrase 'do wonders'. However, this cannot be claimed to be a fixed usage, belonging to only one literary work; it is a formula belonging to different literary works. Moreover, since Ex. 3.20; 34.10 apply it comprehensively without any specific reference, while Josh. 3.5 uses it with reference to the specific event of crossing the Jordan, one must claim Josh. 3.5 as reflecting the oldest usage. This in turn may suggest the possibility that rather than that the exodus story has affected the form of Josh. 3f., it is the latter which affected the form of presentation of the exodus story, a possibility which, on the literary level, is supported by the evidence of post-deuteronomistic redactional activity in Ex. 3.20; 34.10.[20]

In general, it may be affirmed of the conquest story of Josh. 2ff. that it goes back to a Benjaminite tradition, expressing a claim to its territory, a tradition taken over first by Ephraim and then by Judah, likewise in the interests of expressing territorial claims in the interests of all Israel. The redactional stage which changed the old war story into an account of Israel's settlement under the leadership of Yahweh is to be associated with deuteronomic/deuteronomistic time (rather than with Noth's older 'collector'), and to be distinguished from a later priestly redaction. It is with the latter stage that one must associate the work of an author or redactor on the related texts from Genesis–Numbers.

The second group of texts, Josh. 9–10 and Gen. 34, have in common the question of the relationship between Israel and the Canaanites. The results of a close literary and theological study here are not inconsistent with the picture already presented. The treatment of the Gibeonites as Canaanites and their subordinate status, as shown in Josh. 9, is the result of a long development with a political background, a development which was not completed in the time of David. The 'Canaanite problem' was not primarily national and theological; it was social. It was a conflict between urban and non-urban, international and national, a conflict which comes to a head in the time of Jehu, in the context of which 'Canaanite' came to stand as a term of abuse, with both international and inner-Israelite overtones, a term standing for all that was non-Israelite in the sight of Israelite nationalism. The term lost its social roots with the destruction of the northern kingdom; it now got a theological sense, as in the deuteronomic movement, when it came to refer to non-Yahwistic theology. It is the developed understanding of the term 'Canaanite' which lies behind the treatment of the topic in Gen. 34 and Josh. 9 (to which Josh. 10 is closely connected), and in no case is it possible to see early monarchic material which may be assigned to a J source.

The third group of texts includes those on the basis of which it has been thought possible to set forth the work of the deuteronomist as a new literary entity taking up and summarizing, in order to mark a new beginning, the latter part of the Tetrateuch. These texts are those in Deut. 1–3 and their parallels in Genesis–Numbers. So Ex. 18 and Num. 11 have been understood as the E and J material respectively on which Deut. 1.9–18 based its account of the institution of a judicial system to assist Moses. In traditio-historical terms Ex. 18 presents the oldest story of the institution of a judicial and leadership organization incompatible with and so earlier than the monarchy. The task for which those elected are instituted is referred to in more generalized terms in Deut. 1 and Num. 11, which are therefore later presentations, and in the latter of them especially there is a new interpretation of Ex. 18 insofar as it is as the founder of a prophetic office that Moses is now presented. In the question of the literary relationships of the texts, a literary dependence of Num. 11 on Ex. 18 and Deut. 1 may be demonstrated, but it is only from a traditio-historical point of view that Ex. 18 may be dated earlier than Deut. 1. In literary terms they are all late compositions, so that in no case can one speak of Pentateuchal documents from early monarchic time.

Numbers 13f.; Deut. 1.19–46 and Josh. 14.6–15 relate the military prowess of Caleb and also his faithfulness to Yahweh. In origin the tradition about him was originally concerned with legitimating settlement in the face of those who rejected it: the compatibility of settlement and faithfulness to Yahweh is affirmed. In time, the tradition was modified to express a claim to the land, as the gift of Yahweh to Caleb, over against territorial pressure exerted by Judah. This stage of the development of the tradition is reflected in Josh. 14.6–15. In Deut. 1, on the other hand, the story is largely demilitarized, and Moses is pushed to the forefront, with the outcome of the battle now dependent not on human strength and weapons but on belief in Yahweh. The theologizing tendency is continued in Num. 13f., where, even before the priestly redaction, it is no longer a Caleb story, as in Josh. 14, nor a story of the disobedience of the people, as in Deut. 1, but a theological spy story in which, despite all human preparations, it is Yahweh who gives the victory and where the spies function not as seekers of information but as propagandists for the faithfulness of Yahweh. The three accounts cannot be set on a single line of progression; their differences reflect rather different uses at different times of a common tradition. In this way Josh. 14 reflects most closely of the three the Caleb tradition.[21]

In general, it may be affirmed, therefore, that the deuteronomistic presentation of the wanderings of Israel from Sinai/Horeb to the border of the promised land was the first such presentation, and that the material in Numbers is in part directly dependent on this and in part the later formulation of a common tradition in order to meet different and later concerns. In this there is conformity with what has already been established with regard to the relationship between texts of Josh. 2ff. and their related passages in Genesis–Numbers, viz., that general priority is to be assigned to the deuteronomistic history which is then either an earlier formulation of traditions finding a later literary deposit in Genesis–Numbers, or indeed the literary source on which such Tetrateuchal texts are directly dependent.

The implications of this for our understanding of the process of formation of the Tetrateuch are significant. That the stories of the wanderings of the patriarchs and of Israel from Egypt to Sinai/Horeb are likewise post-deuteronomistic in their formulation may not be shown by the same method, since parallel texts in the deuteronomistic history do not exist. Yet, it is an inevitable consequence of the results so far produced that the Tetrateuch should be seen as a later introduction to the deuteronomistic history. In this way, as Rose notes, one comes back to something like von Rad's contention that the historical credo is the basis of the Hexateuch – not in the sense that the Hexateuch is the baroque elaboration of such an ancient historical creed, but rather in the sense that the Tetrateuch originated on the basis of a conception of Israel's history deriving from the deuteronomic/deuteronomistic context and finding its first expression in the historical summaries to be found there.

Notes

Introduction

1. Noth, *Überlieferungsgeschichtliche Studien*; reference here is also made to the English translation of that part of the German original (pp. 1–110) which is concerned with the deuteronomistic history.

2. Cf. Kraus, *Erforschung des Alten Testaments*, 411ff. For detailed studies see also Jenni, *ThR* NF 27, 1961, 1–32, 97–146; Radjawane, *ThR* NF 38, 1973, 177–216; Nelson, *Deuteronomistic History*, 13ff.

3. Wellhausen, *Die Composition des Hexateuchs und der historischen Bücher des Alten Testaments*, 238. Wellhausen's doubts related to the possibility of uncovering these sources with any certainty, rather than to the possibility that the sources did not in fact exist.

4. Cf. Eissfeldt, *Hexateuch Synopse;* id., *Die Quellen des Richterbuches*; id., *Die Komposition der Samuelisbücher*. See also Benzinger, *Jahvist und Elohist in den Königsbüchern*.

5. Cf. Gressmann, *Die Anfänge Israels*, 13.

6. Cf. Hölscher, *Die Anfänge der hebräischen Geschichtsschreibung*, 99.

7. So Benzinger (cf. n.4), and also Caspari, *Die Samuelbücher*.

8. Even as early as de Wette, *Lehrbuch der historisch-kritischen Einleitung in die kanonischen und apokryphischen Bücher des Alten Testamentes*, 233, deuteronomistic editing was recognized in Joshua; for other details, cf. Radjawane, *ThR* NF 38, 1973, 178f.

9. Kuenen, *Historisch-kritischen Onderzoek naar het antstaan en de verzemeling van de Boeken des Ouden Verband*; German translation: *Historisch-kritischen Einleitung in die Bücher des Alten Testaments*; see also de Vries, *JBL* LXII, 1963, 31–57; Nelson, *Deuteronomistic History*, 14ff. For similar views, cf. Eissfeldt, *Introduction*, 242ff.,246f.,255f.,266f.,280f.,299ff.

10. Gressman (cf. n.5); Alt, *Kleine Schriften* I, 176ff.

11. Noth, *Josua*.

12. Noth, *Josua*, 16, denied the possibility of the pre-deuteronomistic material in Joshua being a continuation of the Pentateuchal sources. In *Theologische Studien und Kritiken* 65, 1892, 44ff., Kittel denied that the basic material of Judges and Samuel is a combination of J and E; he argued that the books consist rather of a variety of complexes: hero stories, royal stories, ark

150

stories, prophet stories, which could not be divided into two continuous literary sources. For the view that the form critical method of Gunkel, aimed at discerning pre-literary traditional units, is in fact incompatible with literary critical source criticism, cf. Rendtorff, *Das überlieferungsgeschichtliche Problem des Pentateuch*, 6ff.,96ff.,142ff. Here the important point is made that the methods of source criticism presuppose what form criticism tends to deny, viz. individuality of style allowing the critical discernment of different authors. On Rendtorff see further below.

13. Noth, *Überlieferungsgeschichtliche Studien*, 4 (ET, 5).

14. For some more detailed treatment of deuteronomistic language, cf. Wright, IB 2, 318f.; Minette de Tillesse, *VT* 12, 1962, 29ff.; Nicholson, *Deuteronomy and Tradition*, 30.

15. Noth, *Überlieferungsgeschichtliche Studien*, 5f. (ET, 5f.).

16. Ibid., 18ff. (ET,18ff.).

17. For other discussions of the chronology, cf. Rowley, *From Jospeh to Joshua*, 86–98; Boling, *Judges*, 23.

18. Ibid., 100ff. (ET, 89ff.).

19. Ibid., 103 (ET, 91f.).

20. Ibid, 100 (ET, 88). For details of Noth's view of the deuteronomist's treatment of his sources, a treatment which involved selectivity and editing of what was chosen, cf. *Überlieferungsgeschichtliche Studien*, 95ff. (ET, 84ff.).

21. Soggin, *Introduction*, 161. Soggin, while noting that the existence of the deuteronomistic history is generally recognized, remarks, however, that it may still be questioned if the work of the deuteronomist is 'a matter of scattered interpolations and revisions which only assume a certain organic character here and there (in Judges and Kings), or do we have a history which is unified in scope and ideology'. The question asked here has implications of a more serious nature than is apparently recognized.

22. Cf. Engnell, *Critical Essays*, 58ff. See further, North, in *The Old Testament and Modern Study*, 63ff. Engnell's work in this connection began to appear from 1945 onwards.

23. Jepsen, *Die Quellen des Königbuches*. Jepsen's evaluation of the theology of the deuteronomist differs from that of Noth, however, in that for Jepsen it is a work of reflection which summons its readers to repentance and hope for the future. See further Radjawane, *ThR* NF 38, 1973, 187f.

24. Boecker, *Die Beurteilung der Anfänge des Königtums in den deuteronomistischen Abschnitten des 1. Samuelbuches*. Cf. Radjawane, *ThR* NF 38, 1973, 190ff.

25. For some more detailed treatment of this, and for further bibliography, cf. my article in *ZAW* 90, 1978, 3ff.

26. Noth, *Überlieferungsgeschichtliche Studien*, 54ff. (ET, 47ff.).

27. Cf. also McCarthy, *Interp* 27, 1973, 401ff.

28. Hoffman, *Reform und Reformen*.

29. Eissfeldt, *Introduction*, 241ff.; Freedman, *IDB* 3, 711ff. For a fuller account, including the work of Hölscher, cf. Radjawane, *ThR* NF 38, 1973, 192ff.

30. Eissfeldt, *Introduction*, 247.

31. So in the analysis of Judg. 7 in particular the first narrative marked out contains certain repetitions in vv.19,20,22 of a type which is otherwise used

to justify the separation of sources, as with the reference to the flight of the enemy in vv.21f.

32. Quite apart from the question of gaps in the material, which might be explained as the result of omission on the occasion of the combination of documents, it must be pointed out that a source consisting of such folkloristic material as we find in I Sam. 9, on the one hand, and the court history of David in II Sam. 9–20; I Kings 1–2, on the other hand (both of which Eissfeldt assigns to J) can hardly be called coherent.

33. von Rad, *The Problem of the Hexateuch*, 1ff.; id., *Old Testament Theology* I, 327ff. See also Radjawane, *ThR* NF 38, 1973, 200ff.

34. See the review of discussion by Hyatt, in *Translating and Understanding the Old Testament*, 152ff.

35. Bright, IB 2, 544.

36. Cf. *Überlieferungsgeschichtliche Studien*, 206ff. (not included in the English translation).

37. So also Bright, IB 2, 543f. It is, therefore, with more consistency that von Rad, Weiser and Fohrer, for example, who believe JE to be present in Joshua, also argue for the presence of P there.

38. von Rad, *Old Testament Theology* I, 327ff.

39. Ibid., 347

40. As Fohrer, *Introduction*, 194f.

41. Cf. below, Ch.3, n.52.

42. Cross, *Canaanite Myth and Hebrew Epic*, 276ff.

43. Cf. also Gray, *I & II Kings*, 6ff.,753ff., who argues that references to the exile of Judah within the books of Kings (for example, II Kings 17.19f.) give the impression of being exilic additions to an already existing work which did not know of the exile of Judah. The following study stands in the line of approach suggested by Cross and Nelson. Unlike the work of these, however, which is based on Kings, from which approaches are then made to earlier passages in the deuteronomistic history, the attempt is made here to work systematically through the books of the deuteronomistic history, to plot out at least in outline their stages of redaction, and, in attempting to establish links between stages in different books, to portray the growth of the deutero-nomistic history in at least two major stages of its comprehensive development.

44. Polzin, *Moses and the Deuteronomist*.

45. Cf. also below, on Joshua, p. 43.

1. Deuteronomistic Editing of Deuteronomy

1. For the deuteronomistic account of the institution of Joshua by Moses as his successor, cf. below, p. 45.

2. Cf. Noth, *Überlieferungsgeschichtliche Studien*, 14ff. (ET, 14ff.).

3. Cf. especially Levenson, *HTR* 68, 1975, 203–33. See also the references to Baltzer, Wolff and Plöger in this context given by Boecker, *Die Beurteilung der Anfänge des Königtums in den deuteronomistischen Abschnitten des 1. Samuelbuches*, 9. Smend, *Die Entstehung des Alten Testaments*, 73, also reckons with the later

incorporation of the deuteronomic law into the deuteronomistic history as a serious possibility.

4. Cf. my article in *Proceedings of the Irish Biblical Association* 4, 1980, 68–83. See also further below.

5. For the detail of what follows see especially my article in *JBL* 100, 1981, 23ff.

6. Cf. Wright, IB 2, 351; Baltzer, *Das Bundesformular*, 41ff. (ET, 31ff.); Kline, *Treaty of the Great King*, 28ff. The proposals made by these scholars are not identical: Wright finds 4.1–40 as necessary to give point and meaning to chapters 1–3; Baltzer finds a covenant or treaty form in 1.1–4.40, with the historical prologue of that form in 1.6–3.17 and both laws and sanctions in 4.1–40; Kline sees 1.6–4.49 (cf. also Weinfeld, *Deuteronomy and the Deuteronomic School*, 69ff., with reference to 1.1–4.40) as a whole as the historical prologue to Deuteronomy, the latter being understood as a covenant renewal document; but all are unanimous in seeing the first three chapters (at least) in terms of the historical prologue of the covenant formulary. Other criticisms of this parallel may be made besides the (in this context) chief point made in the text on the nature of the history in chapters 1–3. Polzin, *Moses and the Deuteronomist*, 39f., 56f., adopts a literary approach to the question of the relationship of the chapters. In chapters 1–3 Moses reports the past and then in chapter 4 he analyses and interprets it in relation to present and future. The relation of chapters 1–3 and 4 is that of Deuteronomy to Joshua–Kings, for there too the latter interprets and applies the former. This view is to be seen within the context of Polzin's overall literary approach, which concentrates on discerning the tendency of the work which now stands before us and hesitates to discern layers of redaction; cf. above, pp. 19ff. Even within the terms of Polzin's approach, however, there are difficulties in his interpretation: the discontinuity between chapters 1–3 and chapter 4, referred to below, weakens his view of chapter 4 as an analysis and interpretation of the history of chapters 1–3.

7. For a recent example of this kind of literary critical approach, cf. Mittmann, *Deuteronomium 1.1–6.3*. The latter's rather cavalier dismissal of the literary and stylistic studies of Lohfink in particular as arbitrary and subjective has been subjected in turn to a searching criticism by Braulik, *Bib* 59, 1978, 351–83.

8. Cf. Lohfink, *Bib* 41, 1960, 105–134.

9. For the alternative view that Deut. 1.9–18 is rather a late insertion from the hand of a later deuteronomist, cf. Rose, *Deuteronomist und Jahwist*, 231ff. Rose understands that pre-deuteronomic tradition is reflected here, but that it is a tradition which had no significance for either Deuteronomy or the early deuteronomist, as comparison with Deut. 16.18f.;17.8–13 shows (these passages assign to the levitical priests the functions assigned to Moses in 1.9–18). Rose provides a rather different picture of the composition of chapters 1–3 in his earlier work, *Der Ausschliesslichkeitsanspruch Jahwes*, 146ff.: without detailed literary argument he proposes for chapters 1–3 a deuteronomistic basis which has throughout been supplemented by occasional additions from a later deuteronomistic hand, the latter being that of the author of (the basis of) chapter 4.

10. For this pattern (movement of Israel, Yahweh's instruction, pre-history of settlement of the area, provision of food, departure of Israel or occupation of the land), cf. Sumner, *VT* 18, 1968, 216–28. There is a strong possibility that in two cases, the encounters with Moab and Ammon in Deut. 2.9a*b*–12,18–23, we have late post-deuteronomistic additions modelled on the account of the encounter with Edom in 2.4–6; cf. my *Deuteronomy*, 133ff. This, however, does not substantially affect the point at issue here. These are isolated expansions which do not disrupt the essential unity of chapters 1–3 and do not constitute a recognizable uniform redaction of these chapters.

11. In general cf. Noth, *Überlieferungsgeschichtliche Studien*, 95–100 (ET, 84–8). On Deut. 1–3 in particular cf. Lohfink, *Bib* 41, 1960, 108ff.

12. For slightly different explanations of the distinction between the accounts given in Num. 20 and Deut. 2 of Israel's encounter with Edom, cf. Noth, *Überlieferungsgeschichtliche Studien*, 33f. (ET, 30f.), and Lohfink, *Bib* 41, 1960, 130f. See also Rose, *Deuteronomist und Jahwist* (cf. below, p. 148), where it is proposed that in Num. 13f.; Deut. 1.19–46 (and Josh. 14.6–15) no literary dependence of one text on another can be demonstrated, but that all represent adaptations of a common tradition at different times. For our purposes here the fundamental point (serving to distinguish Deut. 1–3 from Deut. 4.1–40) is that an older tradition is taken up by Deut. 1.19–46, whatever the precise relationship of that tradition to Num. 13f. may be.

13. Braulik, *Die Mittel deuteronomischer Rhetorik*; Lohfink, *Höre Israel*; see also my study of Deut. 4 in *JBL* 100, 1981, 23ff.

14. Cf. McCarthy, *Treaty and Covenant*, 169f., on the parenetic use of history in the treaties.

15. Cf. my *Deuteronomy*, 166f.

16. Lohfink, *Höre Israel*, 93–96.

17. Nelson's argument, *Deuteronomistic History*, 90ff., for a complex history of origin of chapter 4 cannot be refuted in detail at this point. It adds little to the literary critical arguments of Noth and others, and takes inadequate account of the points raised by Lohfink and Braulik. Nelson's chief reason for separating out vv.19f. seems to be that the author here has illicit worship in general in view rather than the worship of images in particular. The force of this is somewhat diminished by the point that for the author of 4.1–40 the worship of images is the worship of other gods.

18. Cf. my article in *JBL* 100, 1981, 27f., n.17, for references in this connection.

19. For the justification for this cf. my *Deuteronomy*, 34ff.

20. Cf. Smend, *Die Entstehung des Alten Testaments*, 73, who suggests that the effect of the later deuteronomistic editing was to make even clearer the already existing connection of history and law.

21. The stylistic explanation, which is advocated especially by Lohfink, *Das Hauptgebot*, 30f.,239ff.; and Braulik, *Die Mittel deuteronomischer Rhetorik*, 149f., is certainly difficult and uncertain to apply in detail. For an attempt in the context of 4.1–40, cf. my article in *JBL* 100, 1981, 27ff.

22. Noth's way of referring to Deut. 1–3(4) suggests that he thinks in the latter terms rather than the former; cf. his *Überlieferungsgeschichtliche Studien*,

13f.,38f. (ET,13f.,33f.), where he questions if chapter 4 is to be assigned to the deuteronomist or to a later editor.

23. While the author of 4.1–40 understands the prohibition of making images as the chief commandment of the decalogue, the form of the decalogue in Deut. 5 suggests that its intention is to emphasize the significance of the Sabbath commandment; cf. Lohfink, *BZ* 9, 1965, 17ff. For this and other problems in connection with Deut. 5.1–6.3, a passage from which the hand also of the author of 4.1–40 is by no means absent, cf. my article in *Proceedings of the Irish Biblical Association* 4, 1980, 68ff.

24. For the details of the criticism of Deuteronomy which are presupposed here reference should be made to my commentary *Deuteronomy*, 159f., 161f., 194ff. See also Garcia Lopez, *Analyse litteraire de Deuteronome V–XI*, 68ff. (= *RB* 85, 1978, 30ff.), who finds the distinction between the historical and the parenetic basic to distinguishing different literary contributions in those chapters.

25. Cf. my article on Deut. 5 in *Proceedings of the Irish Biblical Association* 4, 1980, 71f.

26. It is certainly by no means excluded that both the deuteronomistic historian and this later editor also contributed to the present form of the deuteronomic law. Perhaps most clearly, but by no means exclusively, this is the case in Deut. 12, where the fundamental deuteronomic law of centralization appears three times. For a treatment of this chapter, suggesting that the original deuteronomic law lies in 12.13–19, which later received 12.8–12 from the deuteronomistic historian, and 12.1–7 from the later editor, cf. my *Deuteronomy*, 221f. For further studies cf., for example, Merendino, *Das deuteronomische Gesetz*; and Rose, *Der Ausschliesslichkeitsanspruch Jahwes*, 17ff.

27. For the detailed justification for marking out the later editor's work in Deuteronomy, reference should be made especially to my article in *JBL* 100, 1981, 35ff. On the deuteronomic origin of 6.4f. and its relation with the deuteronomic centralization law, cf. Rose, *Der Ausschliesslichkeitsanspruch Jahwes*, 134ff.

28. One notable exception to this is 11.29–30, for which see further below.

29. Deut. 10.19 is very probably a late addition; cf. also Lohfink, *Das Hauptgebot*, 223. The treatment of 10.12–22 by Rose, *Der Ausschliesslichkeitsanspruch Jahwes*, 124ff., results in a division between a deuteronomic layer (vv. 12*,17,18,20ab*b*,21ab*a*), a first deuteronomistic layer (vv.12b*,13,14,19, 21b*b*) and a second deuteronomistic layer (vv.15,16,20b*a*,22). Little literary critical justification for this division is provided, and it neither resolves any more satisfactorily the question of the place of v.19 (cf. ibid., 130, n.4), nor takes adequate account of the unity of the whole section in 10.12–11.32.

30. Probably 26.1–15 is an addition to the deuteronomic law from a later hand; cf. my *Deuteronomy*, 331f.

31. It is probably an error in principle to start from the assumption that the original Deuteronomy is the lawbook found in the temple in the time of Josiah's reform, and from that point to attempt to determine the content of the original book. Rather, the subject must be approached within the limits of Deuteronomy itself; and here it seems likely that we should set a broad framework only: the original book of Deuteronomy is the book which lay

before the deuteronomistic historian and was incorporated (and supplemented) by him; on the other hand, this book was the result of the bringing together of older bodies of law into a collection characterized by the deuteronomic concern with centralization, and provided with a parenetic introduction using characteristic deuteronomic terminology. For a fuller consideration, cf. my *Deuteronomy*, 47ff., 348ff.

32. Rose, *Der Ausschliesslichkeitsanspruch Jahwes*, 101ff., distinguishes in 26.16–19 three layers: a basic deuteronomic layer (vv.17ab*a*,18a*a*), containing the 'covenant formula'; a first deuteronomistic layer (vv.17b*b*,18b,19b*a*), which, wishing to obviate the interpretation of that formula in terms of a possible claim of Israel on Yahweh, emphasized Israel's obligation to obey the law; and a second deuteronomistic layer (vv.16,18a*b*,19ab*b*), which no longer thinks in terms of a covenant relationship between Yahweh and Israel, but exalts Yahweh as God of all the nations. There is some good possibility that an older deuteronomic layer is present in these verses, not only in the formula of vv.17ab*a*,18a*a*, but also in v.19b*a*, in view of the conformity in language and thought between these verses and the basic layer of Deut. 7. However, the distinction between two deuteronomistic layers within the verses is unlikely: the emphasis of what Rose takes as the first of these is a major concern also of what he takes as the second: the obligation on Israel to obey the law, and there seems little pressing reason to separate them. Deut. 27.1–8 is a later insertion which, along with its closely related passage in 27.11–26, comes from a hand even later than that of the editor at work in 4.1–40; see further below.

33. On 29.1 cf. especially Kutsch, *Verheissung und Gesetz*, 140f.; and on Deut. 31.1 cf. Seitz, *Redaktionsgeschichtliche Studien zum Deuteronomium*, 33f.

34. Cf. also McCarthy, *Treaty and Covenant*, 199ff.; Perlitt, *Bundestheologie im Alten Testament*, 27ff.

35. On the reason for this see further below.

36. On Deut. 27.1–8,11–26 see n.32. Deut. 11.29–30 (cf. above n.28) stand out from their context by their particular geographical concern, disrupting the continuity of the context which culminates in the general warning to obey the law in the land. Deut. 10.8–9 gives information on the Levites which conforms with that in 31.9ff.,25f., and these verses too should probably be added to this list of passages.

37. Cf. below, p. 51.

38. Cf. above n.31.

39. On Deuteronomy as covenant law and law of Moses, cf. my article in *Proceedings of the Irish Biblical Association* 5, 1981, 36ff. For the general use and modification of covenant or treaty categories in Deuteronomy see especially Lohfink in *Gott in Welt*, 423–44.

40. Cf. my article in *JBL* 100, 1981, 50.

2. Deuteronomistic Editing of Joshua

1. Cf. Wenham, *JBL* 90, 1971, 140ff.
2. It might be argued in most cases that conformity between the practices

presupposed in the stories of Joshua and the prescriptions of the deuteronomic law is to be explained not from the dependence of Joshua on Deuteronomy but rather from their common basis in traditional practice. This could certainly be true of the stories of Achan and the five kings at Makkedah; but with the Gibeonite story at least there is apparently a direct link to specifically deuteronomic legislation. The traditional practice relating to warfare is reflected in Deut. 20.10–14; but this has been modified by the peculiarly deuteronomic provisions in Deut. 20.15–18 which distinguish between warfare against enemies outside the land and warfare against enemies within the land (cf. my *Deuteronomy*, 293f.). It is the deuteronomic modification of the law which is presupposed in the present form of the Gibeonite story. For a consideration of this story, cf. Gottwald, *The Tribes of Yahweh*, 521ff.

3. It is now clear that von Rad's original presentation of the holy war as an old Israelite institution, which in the period of the judges never came to full historical expression, must be modified. Israel, like other nations, thought of the gods as participating in war (cf. Weippert, *ZAW* 84, 1977, 460ff.); however, it is not until the time of Deuteronomy and later that a holy war ideology as such begins to emerge. Holy war theory represents a deuteronomic interpretation and schematization of past events, though founded on existing tradition of Yahweh's participation in the old wars of Israel; see especially Stolz, *Jahwes und Israels Kriege*; Jones, *VT* 25, 1975, 642ff.

4. On the theme of Israel having rest in the land, cf. also Deut. 3.20; 12.10; Josh. 1.15; 23.1, and, further, von Rad, *The Problem of the Hexateuch*, 94ff.

5. Polzin, *Moses and the Deuteronomist*, 75ff.

6. On the distinction made by Polzin between reporting and reported word, between word of Moses and the narrator's application of this in the presentation of the history, cf. above, p. 20.

7. So it is difficult to bring Josh. 8.2 into relation to the holy war laws of Deut. 20 by saying that the commands of Yahweh in the deuteronomic law are being interpreted through suspension in the story of Josh. 8; and it seems forced to take the record of Joshua's setting up stones in the middle of the Jordan (Josh. 4.9), for which there is no divine command, as a testament to the necessity for change and mobility in the understanding, interpretation and application of God's word.

8. Noth, *Überlieferungsgeschichtliche Studien*, 40ff. (ET, 36ff.).

9. For what follows cf. Lohfink, *Scholastik* 37, 1962, 32ff.

10. The verbs *'br*, 'cross over', and *bw'* 'enter', introduce the conquest story in Josh. 1.2,11, while it is in connection with the division of the land in chapters 13–21 that *naḥªlâ*, 'possession', becomes the characteristic term. For other pre-deuteronomistic and deuteronomistic passages associating these tasks, cf. Num. 27.17; 34.17; Deut. 1.38; 3.21; 31.3.

11. The problem of the relationship of Josh. 23 and 24 is perhaps well illustrated by the ambivalence of Noth; see below, p. 49.

12. Smend, in *Probleme biblischer Theologie*, 494ff. Smend's very acute observations cannot, however, be followed in relation to Josh. 24.1–28 which he ascribes to the deuteronomistic historian; see further below.

13. Verse 8 is not to be taken as later than v.7, as Smend suggests may be the case. Its relationship to v.7 is certainly not that of v.7 to v.6.

14. That Yahweh is referred to in the third person in the closing part of this formula constitutes a problem whether the last part of v.9 is joined directly to v.6 or to the first part of v.9. In fact, it is probably easier to understand it in conjunction with v.6, for then we may see the use of the third person of Yahweh in connection with the appearance of the institution formula in Deut. 31.7f. (where Yahweh is referred to in the third person), with which section in particular there is a close vocabulary link.

15. 'According to all the law', cf. Deut. 4.8; 'this book of the law', cf. Deut. 29.30; 30.10; 31.26; 'keep' and 'do' in relation to the law, cf. Deut. 4.6; 5.1,29; 6.3; 7.12; 11.32; 26.16; 28.1,15 etc.

16. That the basic text is from the hand of the deuteronomistic historian is further confirmed by the point that just as Josh. 1.2 supplements the formula of institution in relation to the occupation of the land, so 13.1aba, 7 supplements it in relation to the division of the land among the tribes. So Josh. 1.2; 13.1aba, 7 complement each other in relation to the formula of institution; cf. Lohfink, *Scholastik* 37, 1962, 40f.

17. On Israel's 'rest', cf. above n.4.

18. Cf. Noth, *Überlieferungsgeschichtliche Studien*, 45 (ET, 40), who sees chapters 13–19 as closely reflecting the view of the deuteronomistic historian and as having been inserted in that work soon after its completion.

19. Cf. Baltzer, *Das Bundesformular*, 71ff. (ET, 63ff.); McCarthy, *Treaty and Covenant*, 203f.,221ff. Baltzer sees the common use of the covenant formulary in both chapters as sufficient explanation for their common features; McCarthy, while recognizing the background and influence of the covenant tradition, emphasizes, at least for Josh. 24.1–28, the differences from the covenant formulary and the contribution of the prophetic tradition.

20. Cf. Noth, *Überlieferungsgeschichtliche Studien*, 9 n.1 (ET, 102f., n.15); id., *Josua*, 10,15f.,137ff.

21. Smend, in *Probleme biblischer Theologie*, 503f. Smend does not explicitly state that 24.1–28 comes from the deuteronomistic historian, but since he sees the relationship between chapters 23 and 24 as analogous to that between the later deuteronomistic editor and his basic text in Josh. 1 and 13, it is apparently intended that 24.1–28 should be understood to share with that basic text the authorship of the deuteronomistic historian. The objections of Nelson, *Deuteronomistic History*, 20f., to Smend's general treatment of Joshua rest mainly on this assignment of Josh. 24.1–28 to the deuteronomistic historian. Nelson's own proposal, ibid., 94ff., to assign Josh. 24.1–28 to the second deuteronomistic editor, is no more convincing. See also Rösel, *VT* 30, 1980, 342ff., who sees Josh. 24 (with Judg. 1) as constituting a transition between Joshua and Judges which has been edited by the deuteronomist, but which is older than the pure deuteronomistic transition in Josh. 23 (and Judg. 2.6ff.).

22. It is not possible to agree with the recent work of Mölle, *Der sogenannte Landtag zu Sichem*, who has found it possible to trace a deuteronomistic stage of editing in Josh. 24 which took place in two phases: one pre-exilic and the other exilic or post-exilic, the second showing close connection with the deuteronomistic history. Mölle proposes that Josh. 24 has gone through four stages: the original story is a Shechemite tradition of a particular event; the

second is a stage which interpreted this as a covenant on analogy with the Sinai covenant and may be assigned to E; the third is from the JE redactor and is intended as a warning to Judah in the light of the fall of Samaria; and the fourth is the two-phase deuteronomistic stage. It is by no means improbable that old tradition is to be found in Josh. 24 (see further below), but Mölle's proposals suffer from the relative isolation within which he treats Josh. 24, particularly as far as its relation to the deuteronomistic history as a whole is concerned; moreover, he shows no acquaintance with the work of Smend referred to above nn.12,21.

23. This difference arises from the fact that Josh. 8.30–35 stands as a link between Deuteronomy and Josh. 24. The law of the covenant ceremony, the law of God, is thereby affirmed to be the law which Moses commanded Israel to obey on the border of the promised land (Deut. 27.1–8).

24. The reason for the placing of these passages in their present contexts is not altogether clear. It may be that Josh. 8.30–35 comes at the conclusion of the story of the defeat of Ai because the editor responsible for its introduction considered that now the way to Shechem was open and so the fulfilment of the command given by Moses in Deut. 27.1–8 could be narrated at its earliest point (cf. Noth, *Josua*, 52). In the case of Josh. 24.1–28 it may be simply that the editor wished to present this covenant making ceremony as the concluding act of Joshua in order to strengthen the parallel with Moses (Deut. 29.1) and to throw into stark relief the behaviour of Israel following the death of the generation of Joshua, as recounted in Judges.

25. Cf. also Soggin, *Joshua*, 242f., on the discrepancy between the two passages in relation to the stones on which the law was written: were these different from, or identical to, the stones of which the altar was constructed? For a discussion of the relationship between many of these passages, especially Deut. 11.29–30; 27; Josh. 8.30–35; 24.1–28, cf. L'Hour, *RB* 69, 1962, 161ff.

26. Cf. my *Deuteronomy*, 218f., 340f.

27. Cf. Noth, *Josua*, 12f. For a description of the process of coming together of the originally separate aetiological stories, first as a Benjaminite tradition of settlement and then as a national tradition, within the context of the recognition of Gilgal as a national sanctuary, especially in the time shortly before the foundation of the monarchy, cf. Alt, *Kleine Schriften* I, 176ff.; for a recent significant contribution, cf. Rose, *Deuteronomist und Jahwist*, 147ff.

28. On the deuteronomistic view of the task of Joshua as a twofold one, involving not just conquest but also division of the land, cf. above. This suggests that at least chapters 13–19 (or a substantial part of them) formed part of the deuteronomistic book. Chapter 20 is more difficult. It is probably a deuteronomistic passage which has had some later priestly editing introducing the reference to the high priest in v.6. In the deuteronomistic context it functions to fulfil the command of Moses given in Deut. 19, for which cf. my *Deuteronomy*, 284ff. The list of levitical cities in chapter 21 has often been assigned to P; but it is probable that in fact the list formed part of the deuteronomistic book of Joshua. It is presupposed here by Num. 35, which forms part of the Tetrateuchal redaction connecting Genesis–Numbers with the deuteronomistic work, and it is likely that the deuteronomistic historian

would have wished to ensure that in the scheme of the latter half of Joshua no tribe was left unmentioned; cf. Noth, *Numbers*, 252f.; Soggin, *Joshua*, 202f.

29. One must emphasize with Aharoni, *The Land of the Bible*, 251, 254, however, that the original border descriptions would have been more detailed and precise in making clear, for example, to which tribes the towns mentioned in the delineation of the borders belonged. For further studies, both of the history of the border descriptions and of their relationship to the reality of the Israelite settlement, see especially Alt, *Kleine Schriften* I, 196ff.; Noth, *Aufsätze* I, 229ff.

30. Cf. Alt, *Kleine Schriften* II, 276ff. For a different account, however, cf. Aharoni, *The Land of the Bible*, 260ff.

31. Cf. my *Deuteronomy*, 284f.

32. Cf. the discussion in Noth, *Josua*, 131f,; Soggin, *Josua*, 202ff.

33. Cf. especially Alt, *Kleine Schriften* I, 187ff., who sees Joshua at home both in Josh. 10.1–5 and in Josh. 17.14ff.

34. If this is so, then it would affect the date assigned to the collector, for if he was responsible for the inclusion within the total border descriptions of the city lists which have their background in the period of Josiah – and there is no reason for going later than the collector for the inclusion of this material – then it is to the end of the seventh century rather than to *c*.900 BC that one should date him. This is not out of keeping with the language of the collector, which brings him close to the deuteronomic circle. Also in support is the strong reflection of deuteronomic law in the story of the Gibeonites. Noth takes Josh. 11.16–20 as from the hand of the collector. The deuteronomic theory of *ḥērem* is strongly expressed here, as also the notion of the hardening of the heart, an idea which cannot be placed earlier than Isaiah.

35. For these, cf. especially Noth, *Josua*, 9. These additions, some of which are quite substantial, relate especially to the Levites and their function with regard to the ark.

36. Josh. 22.1–6 is a deuteronomistic epilogue recounting the return home of the transjordanian tribes, who, following the command of Moses, had helped their brethren in the conquest of west Jordan (Deut. 3.18ff.; Josh. 1.12ff.). For the remainder of chapter 22 as priestly tradition, cf. Kloppenborg, *Bib* 62, 1981, 347ff. The deuteronomistic historian will also have had a note on the death of Joshua. This is now found in Josh. 24.29–30(31), which thus forms the conclusion to the deuteronomistic historian's portrayal of this vital period of Israel's history. On the relation between these verses and Judg. 2.6–10, cf. below pp. 59f. The last two verses of chapter 24 must be seen as a very late addition, deriving from the time of the connection of the deuteronomistic history with the Tetrateuch and providing a link with Gen. 50.24–25; Ex. 13.19; Num. 20.23–29.

3. *Deuteronomistic Editing of Judges*

1. For literary appreciation of Judges, cf. Gros Louis, in *Literary Interpretations of Biblical Narratives*, 141ff. See further Polzin, *Moses and the Deuteronomist*, 146ff. It is maintained here that the interpretative process begun in Deuter-

onomy and Joshua (cf. above p. 43) is continued with a concentration on the question of why Israel has been unable completely to drive out the former inhabitants of the land. No single answer is possible to this, for the framework to the stories which emphasizes the apostasy of Israel, in its turn, cannot explain why then Israel continues to exist. The limitations of any ideology to explain or predict is seen by Polzin as the general theme of the book of Judges.

2. Cf Childs' characterization of the introduction in Judg. 1.1–2.5, 'A theological judgment is made by its characterization of the period. No leader after Joshua has arisen. The unity of the nation has been fractured. The successes from the divine blessing have given way to a failure to repel the enemy', *Introduction*, 259.

3. See also Soggin, *Judges*, 41. The precise nature of the relationship between Josh. 24.29–30 (31) and Judg. 2.6–9(10) has been the subject of some discussion. Noth, *Überlieferungsgeschichtliche Studien*, 8, n.3 (ET, 102, n.14), believes that Josh. 24.29–31 is a secondary repetition based on Judg. 2.6–10; it was introduced when Joshua was constituted as an independent literary unit and thus had to contain a concluding note on the death of Joshua. However, in general, it is more likely that the longer, fuller and more theologically expressed account (Judg. 2.6–10) is later than and built on the shorter and simply historically informative account (Josh. 24.29–30). Josh. 24.31 can be easily seen as a theological supplement to the historical note of Joshua, deriving from the author of Judg. 2.6–10 and intended to make the transition smoother. This view of the relationship of the passages is supported by the observation that Judg. 2.6 refers to Joshua dismissing the people, which presupposes the late Josh. 24.1–28. So Judg. 2.6–10 is from the hand of the editor responsible for Josh. 24.1–28 and other passages, or from a later hand.

4. Cf. Smend, in *Probleme biblischer Theologie*, 506ff.

5. It is not the case that Judg. 2.2 sees the sin of Israel as its failure to expel the inhabitants, over against Josh. 23 which sees the non-expulsion of the inhabitants as punishment for sin, as Smend (following Weinfeld, *VT* 17, 1967, 93ff.) suggests. In both cases, forbidden alliances with the inhabitants of the land are the reason for Israel's incomplete conquest.

6. Judg. 1 is usually treated with very high esteem from a historical point of view, since it contradicts the picture given by Josh. 1–12 of a conquest consisting of a single, united campaign. This is not a problem for detailed treatment at this point, but it is relevant to note, and indeed to some extent supportive of the view of the late insertion of the material which is put forward here, that some recent study has cast doubt on the propriety of taking Judg. 1 too easily as genuinely historical, especially since there is little in the chapter which is not derived from isolated passages within the book of Joshua; cf. Auld, *VT* 25, 1975, 261ff.; de Geus, *Vox Theologica* XXXVI, 1966, 32ff.

7. This pattern of presentation has been emphasized particularly by von Rad, *Old Testament Theology* I, 327ff.

8. The figure of Samuel is quite clearly closely associated with this overall presentation; on this see further below.

9. It is especially Richter who has discussed the nature and structure of this framework; cf. his *Die Bearbeitungen des 'Retterbuches' in der deuteronomischen*

Epoche. For a summary treatment of Richter's work, cf. Schlauri, *Bib* 54, 1973, 367ff.

10. On the dependent nature of this element, cf. Richter, *Bearbeitungen*, 64.

11. The rest formula in Josh. 11.23; 14.15 contains no reference to a period of time; such references in the formula in Judges may be later additions inserted in the interests of building the deliverer stories into wider chronological contexts; cf. Richter, *Bearbeitungen*, 65. Beyerlin, in *Tradition und Situation*, 11f.,26, apparently takes the complete rest formula as having been added later in the interests of contributing to the total deuteronomistic chronological system. However, the lack of any numerical reference in Josh. 11.23; 14.15, would support rather the simple omission of the periods of years as secondary.

12. On the old collection, or deliverer book, as it is called by Richter, cf. Richter, *Traditionsgeschichtliche Untersuchungen zum Richterbuch*, 336ff. One should include also in the collection the story of Abimelech in Judg. 9. Abimelech is linked closely with the Gideon story through the identification of Jerubbaal, Abimelech's father according to Judg. 9, with Gideon, in Judg. 6.25–32; 7.1; 8.29–32,33–35; and even if Gideon and Jerubbaal are in fact the names of two originally quite independent individuals (see the review of this problem by Emerton, *JTS* 27, 1976, 289ff.), their identification is certainly older than the stage of collection of the deliverer stories. The framework is inappropriate to the figure of Abimelech, who is presented in the deliverer book as a concrete example of the faithlessness of Israel (cf. Richter, *Bearbeitungen*, 113, who assigns Judg. 9.16b–19a,22,55, to the author of the framework).

13. The isolated verse 3.31 recounting Israel's deliverance from the Philistines by Shamgar bears a relation only to element *(iv)* of the framework. The verse is, however, an addition; it breaks the connection between 3.30 and 4.1. The name is taken from Judg. 5.6 and the notice has been composed on the analogy of II Sam, 23.11f. Cf. Richter, *Bearbeitungen*, 6,65,92ff.

14. On the list of judges, cf. especially Noth, *Gesammelte Studien* II, 71ff.; Richter, *ZAW* 77, 1965, 40ff.; Schunck, SVT 15, 1966, 252ff.

15. A further constant element in the list of judges is probably the use of 'and . . . judged' in the introduction to the judges (12.8,11,13). The use of 'and . . . arose' in 10.1,3, and of the verb 'deliver' in 10.1 must certainly be seen as a secondary assimilation of the literary form proper to this list to the forms of presentation of the deliverers into the context of which the list is now set.

16. This is the case with those deliverer stories already seen to constitute an original collection: the stories of Ehud, Deborah-Barak, and Gideon. On the term 'judge' in connection with Othniel and Samson see further below.

17. That the judge Jephthah and the deliverer Jephthah were the same individual is not an issue at this point.

18. Cf. Richter, *Bearbeitungen*, 13ff.; id, *Bib* 47, 1966, 485ff.

19. With the exception of element *(v)* to be found in 11.33.

20. On Judg. 3.7–11 see especially Richter, *Bearbeitungen*, 23ff.,52ff.

21. Cf. Richter, *Bearbeitungen*, 24f.,61.

22. Cf. also Noth, *Überlieferungsgeschichtliche Studien*, 7 (ET, 7), who believes

that there are three parallel sentences in vv.11b,12,13, all of which have been secondarily introduced.

23. Cf. also Smend, in *Probleme biblischer Theologie*, 505.

24. Cf. Noth, *Überlieferungsgeschichtliche Studien*, 7 (ET, 7f.); Richter, *Bearbeitungen*, 35ff.; for the following see, however, especially Smend, in *Probleme biblischer Theologie*, 505f.

25. Cf. Smend, ibid.; Richter, *Bearbeitungen*, 37. Yahweh is spoken of in the third person in the latter part of v. 22, which does not fit with the first person used in v.21.

26. Cf. Richter, *Bearbeitungen*, 35ff.

27. There is probably a late gloss in 2.15ab ('as the Lord had warned and as the Lord had sworn to them'). Richter, *Bearbeitungen*, 30, sees the reference to an oath of Yahweh here as quite unsuitable; Beyerlin, in *Tradition und Situation*, 25f., sees it as a reference back to Deut. 31.14–22.

28. Richter, *Bearbeitungen*, 35, sees within vv.11–19 only vv.13,15ab,17, 18aa as additions which have come in on a catchword basis, and have really nothing to do with each other. However, in the light especially of 2.20f. they do show a consistency of concern which justifies our thinking of a single editor at work here.

29. This understanding of the nature of Israel's subjugation as enslavement to the worship of other gods seems to be present also in Josh. 23 (vv.6f.,12f.); as we shall later see, it is probable that the editor at work in Judg. 2.12abb,13a,17,18aa,19ab,20f.,23; 3.5f. is the author of Josh. 23.

30. Cf. also Veijola, *Das Königtum*, 45f., who finds the deuteronomistic historian in 10.6aa,7b (without 'into the hand of the Philistines and'), 8a (without 'the Israelites'), 8b (without 'eighteen years'). The remainder is understood to be from the later deuteronomistic editor, to whom the whole of the continuation in vv.9–16 is also to be ascribed.

31. *Tradition und Situation*, 18ff. Beyerlin sees the same form also in Judg. 6.7–10 (for the hand of the later deuteronomistic editor in the latter passage, cf. Veijola, *Das Königtum* 43ff.; Nelson, *Deuteronomistic History*, 72ff.). The literature on this subject is extensive; for a treatment of Deut. 32 where the form is also to be found, and for some bibliography, cf. my *Deuteronomy*, 380ff. The connections between the passages are clear: compare, for example, Deut. 32.37f. and Judg. 10.14.

32. It is unnecessary here to enter into the question of the background and setting of the *Rib* and the associated problem of the history and setting of covenant thought in Israel. Whether or not the *Rib* form had the early origin that Beyerlin describes, it is clear that in Judg. 10.13–16 there is a literary adaptation of the form, the age of which is to be determined by the age of the context in which it appears.

33. See especially the table in Richter, *Bearbeitungen*, 51. This will have to be modified to take account of what is here proposed relating to the development of 2.11–3.6; 10.6–16, which differs in some essential respects from the proposals of Richter.

34. On the secondary application of the verb 'judge' to Othniel in 3.10, cf. above. p. 66.

35. See above p. 61, on the fourth element of the framework passages.

36. For conjectures see my study in *Israelite and Judaean History*, 320ff. The proposal of Richter, *ZAW* 77, 1965, 40ff., that the form of the list reflects the monarchic state of Israel and the royal annals listing its successive rulers, remains most probable; for a criticism, cf. Thiel, *Die soziale Entwicklung Israels in vorstaatlicher Zeit*, 134ff.

37. The view of Fohrer, *Introduction*, 212f.; and de Vaux, *The Early History of Israel*, 688f., that it is wrong to separate Jephthah from the other deliverers, a view which I followed in *Israelite and Judaean History*, 291f., depends on an inadequate treatment of the redactional history of the Jephthah story.

38. Noth, *Überlieferungsgeschichtliche Studien*, 61 (ET, 52), however, argues that the Samson story is a later addition to the deuteronomistic history; there is no reference to Samson in I Sam. 12.11 in the series of those who delivered Israel. That series, however, is incomplete even apart from its lack of reference to Samson.

39. That these two references to Samson as having judged Israel reflect different stages in the development of the Samson story is unlikely. Judg. 15.20 provides no conclusion to the Samson story and must be a secondary repetition from 16.31.

30. The death notices on Othniel in 3.11 and Ehud in 4.1 also reflect the literary form proper to the judges rather than that proper to the deliverers, and so should be seen to derive from this same period of redaction of the book; cf. Richter, *Bearbeitungen*, 61,74.

41. Possibly 6.7–10 belongs at this final stage; cf. above n.31.

42. Cf. Fohrer, *Introduction*, 194.

43. Cf. Deut. 4.25; 9.18; 17.2; 31.29; I Kings 11.6,14,22; 15.26,34, etc.

44. Cf. Beyerlin, in *Tradition und Situation*, 12. On the connection with Deut. 17.2, cf. also Richter, *Bearbeitungen*, 83f.,85f.

45 Cf. above n.11.

46. Cf. above p. 34 on Deut. 8.

47. The settings and contexts within which the collection of deliverer stories, the collection with its framework, and the collection, framework and Judg. 3.7–11 are to be set are very difficult to determine. Richter, *Traditionsgeschichtliche Untersuchungen zum Richterbuch*, 336ff., very plausibly relates the old collection of deliverer stories to prophetic circles in the northern kingdom in the time of Jehu; and the editing of this collection, providing the framework and the introduction in 3.7–11, he connects with the time of Josiah and the restoration of the popular army, the edited collection being intended to provide a stimulus and support for the traditional holy war ideal; cf. also his *Bearbeitungen*, 91.

48. Cf. also Richter, *Bearbeitungen*, 75ff.; in *Tradition und Situation*, 13ff. In that the literary criticism of these passages which is adopted here differs from that of Richter and Beyerlin, so also the conclusions with regard to deuteronomistic stages of editing are different. Neither Richter nor Beyerlin distinguish two stages of deuteronomistic editing within these passages.

49. Cf. Beyerlin, in *Tradition und Situation*, 13ff.

50. Cf. Smend, in *Probleme biblischer Theologie*, 504f.

51. Cf. above p. 39.

52. The actual contribution of the deuteronomistic historian in terms of

material introduced by himself is not so great as sometimes imagined. In particular, the framework of the deliverer stories, and 3.7–11, are not to be traced to his hand. This observation will have an effect on the account of the work of the deuteronomist given by von Rad, *Old Testament Theology* I, 327ff., especially insofar as he contrasts the 'cycles of apostasy, enemy oppression, repentance and deliverance which Israel passes through in Judges' with the deuteronomistic presentation of Kings, where 'the Deuteronomist lets the sin mount up throughout whole generations so as to allow Jahweh to react in judgment only at a later day' (347). In this context von Rad then questioned the connection between the work of the deuteronomist in Judges and that in Kings. However, in the light of what has been argued here, it seems that the cyclic view of Israel's history presented in the book of Judges derives from the sources which the deuteronomistic historian incorporated and is not his own composition; moreover, one should set against this presentation the express statement of the deuteronomistic historian himself in Judg. 2.19, that succeeding generations 'behaved worse than their fathers'. The deuteronomistic historian clearly has in mind not a regularly repeated cycle of sin, punishment and repentance, but rather a mounting burden of sin and guilt; this is quite in conformity with the picture of Kings. Cf. also Trompf, SVT 30, 1979, 219ff., who emphasizes the consistency throughout the deuteronomistic history of the deuteronomist's teaching of the operation of principles of retributive justice in Israel's history. That is the theology of history into the framework of which the deuteronomist has incorporated his sources.

53. Judg. 17–18, a story of the migration of the tribe of Dan within Palestine, relates the origin of the sanctuary of Dan; it has been edited to discredit that sanctuary. For a treatment of its history, cf. Noth, in *Israel's Prophetic Heritage*, 68ff. Judg. 19–21 tell of Israel's punishment of the tribe of Benjamin for its failure to punish the city of Gibeah for a crime committed against the concubine of a Levite; for an interpretation in the context of an Israelite amphictyony, cf. Noth, *Das System der zwölf Stämme Israels*, 100ff.; for a critical treatment of this and an alternative, cf. my *Israel in the Period of the Judges*, 42ff., 79ff. See further Crüsemann, *Der Widerstand gegen das Königtum*, 155ff.

54. Cf. Soggin, *Judges*, 5,265,281.

55. On Judg. 1.1–2.5 cf. above p. 60; on the priestly elements of chapters 19–21, cf. for example, Wellhausen, *Prolegomena*, 237, and the discussion in Noth, *Das System*, 102f., n.2.

56. On the possible identification of Bochim in Judg. 2.1–5 as Bethel, cf. Gray, *Joshua, Judges and Ruth*, 253f.

4. Deuteronomistic Editing of Samuel

1. von Rad, *Old Testament Theology* I, 346.

2. See especially Rendtorff, in *Probleme biblischer Theologie*, 428ff.

3. Cf. above p. 16.

4. Rost, *Das kleine Credo*, 119ff. For a discussion of the problem of the succession narrative and its continuation into I Kings 1–2, cf. Flanagan, *JBL* 91, 1972, 172ff.

5. A good recent general account, with bibliography, is provided by Hayes, *Introduction to Old Testament Study*, 229ff. For some detailed treatments of various topics, cf. (in addition to Rost, above n.4) Miller and Roberts, *The Hand of the Lord* (on the ark narrative); Mettinger, *King and Messiah*, 33ff. (on the history of David's rise); ibid., 27ff., and Crüsemann, *Der Widerstand gegen das Königtum*, 180ff. (on the succession narrative); McCarter, *I Samuel*, 23ff. (on the ark narrative, the rise of Saul and the rise of David).

6. The different presentations of Samuel in I Sam. 1–3 and 7–12, and the time gap presupposed between them, make it unlikely that they are an original unit; it is possible, however, that I Sam. 1–3 was composed in prophetic circles as an introduction to an already existing story of the rise of Saul at the stage at which that story was being transmitted in prophetic circles. On this as one context of transmission of the tradition cf. below pp. 84f.

7. McCarter, *I Samuel*, 16,18f., finds deuteronomistic responsibility only in the oracle against the house of Eli in I Sam. 2.27–36 (3.11–14) which expresses 'the Deuteronomistic polemic against the non-Jerusalemite priesthood – the priests of the "high places" ', while the incorporation of the ark story is held to belong to a pre-deuteronomistic prophetic stage. However, the oracle against the house of Eli is a part of the deuteronomistic basis for introducing the ark story, and that story has no essential link to a pre-deuteronomistic prophetic stage.

8. In view of the lack of continuity between I Sam. 4.1–7.1 and II Sam. 6 (the ark is left at Kiriathjearim at the end of the first section, but is retrieved from Baalejudah at the beginning of the second; Eleazar is priest in charge of the ark in I Sam. 7.1, but in II Sam. 6 it is Uzzah and Ahio who have the charge of it), it is unlikely that there is an old connection between these stories so that they formed a single ark narrative; for a full discussion, cf. Miller and Roberts, *The Hand of the Lord*, 22ff. There is only one reference to the ark between I Sam. 7 and II Sam. 6, to be found in I Sam. 14.18. This is a doubtful reference, however, and the text should probably be emended, with LXX, to read 'ephod'; cf. McCarter, *I Samuel*, 237.

9. See, however, Rendtorff, in *Probleme biblischer Theologie*, 439, who, on stylistic grounds, suggests the possibility that these two complexes derive from the same circle.

10. The relative ease with which the complexes may be separated suggests this.

11. Cf. also McCarter, *I Samuel*, 21ff., who describes this prophetic stage (to which, however, he also assigns the integration of the ark narrative) as proto-deuteronomic.

12. It is widely supposed that II Sam. 21–24, an appendix comprising heterogeneous materials and interrupting the continuity within the succession narrative between II Sam. 9–20 and I Kings 1–2, came in at a post-deutero-nomistic stage; for a review of discussion cf. Childs, *Introduction*, 273ff.

13. The determination of such deuteronomistic passages is difficult, and the proposals of Veijola, *Die ewige Dynastie*, seem at times somewhat overconfident; see also the criticism by Mettinger, *King and Messiah*, 21ff.

14. Cf. Childs, *Introduction*, 277f. See also McCarthy, *Interp* 27, 1973, 401ff. The latter is more precise in describing chapters 8–12 as consisting of an

alternation of reports and stories: criticism of the monarchy is found in Samuel's speeches, contained in the reports, while the stories are positive and favourable. See also my article in *ZAW* 90, 1978, 1ff. The latter is here modified in some critical respects, especially with regard to the presence of more than one deuteronomistic hand in these chapters.

15. For these points of contact, cf. Weiser, *Samuel*, 27ff.; Miller, *CBQ* 36, 1974, 157ff. The level of growth of the tradition to which these links belong is an important question; it is certainly pre-deuteronomistic, and to that extent the unity and isolation from its context of chapters 8–12 from the deuteronomistic period on becomes all the more significant.

16. Several good and readily accessible accounts are available dealing with the history of research in this context. See particularly, Langlamet, *RB* 77, 1970, 161ff., which contains an excellent bibliography. For the wider deuteronomistic context, cf. Jenni, *ThR* NF 27, 1961, 104ff.; Radjawane, *ThR* NF 38, 1973, 192ff. For more recent summaries, see Veijola, *Das Königtum*, 5ff.; and Crüsemann, *Der Widerstand gegen das Königtum*, 3ff. The latter makes some interesting points on the effect of their own historical background on the historical estimate of the anti-monarchic texts held by Wellhausen, Budde, Alt and Noth in particular.

17. Cf. also Noth, *History*, 172f.

18. To the stage of prophetic development of the old folktale, which shifted the emphasis from Saul to Samuel, there would also belong the introduction of the story of the birth of Samuel now in I Sam. 1–3. For some recent study of I Sam. 9.1–10.16, see especially Schmidt, *Menschlicher Erfolg und Jahwes Initiative*, 58ff.; Birch, *JBL* 90, 1971, 55f.; Miller, *CBQ* 36, 1974, 157ff. Since it is in prophetic circles in the northern kingdom that one finds the emphasis on the prophetic role in anointing the king (cf. II Kings 9.1–10), it is probably to such a circle that the modification of the old folktale on Saul should be assigned. The conclusion to the old folktale is no longer clearly preserved. It is probably to be found in 10.23b and possibly 10.24abb; these fragments, which account for Saul's designation as king by his physical attributes, stand out from their present strongly deuteronomistic context. See further below, and also my article in *ZAW* 90, 1978, 13.

19. The argument (for which cf. Macholz, *Untersuchungen zur Geschichte der Samuel-Überlieferungen*, 152ff.; Wildberger, *ThZ* 13, 1957, 466ff.; Boecker, *Die Beurteilung der Anfänge des Königtums*, 59f., n.2) that the original tradition is preserved in vv.1–11 only and related simply a charistmatic deliverance carried out by Saul, which did not culminate in his election to the monarchy, has little in its favour: it presupposes that it is only secondarily (through the work of the deuteronomist?) that the story has then been brought into the kingship context to act as public confirmation of Samuel's secret anointing of Saul in 9.1–10.16; it demands the supposition of a complex tradition history, particularly since 11.12–14 (which, especially because of the different view of Samuel which it puts over, cannot be from the same hand as v.15) are to be seen as deriving from a deuteronomistic hand connecting the story of chapter 11 with that of 9.1–10.16 (23b,24abb); see further below.

20. See my article in *ZAW* 90, 1978, 15f.

21. Cf. also Veijola, *Das Königtum*, 48f.

22. I Sam. 10.27b (emended) is the introduction to 11.1ff. (cf. Driver, *Notes on the Hebrew Text of the Books of Samuel*, 85); on 10.26–27a see further my article in *ZAW* 90, 1978, 3, n.6.

23. Boecker, *Die Beurteilung der Anfänge des Königtums*.

24. Ibid., 59f.

25. Ibid., 30ff. Cf. also Clements, *VT* 24, 1974, 403f., who sees 8.11–17 as a fragment of tradition reflecting conditions in the time of Solomon, here introduced by the deuteronomist as a criticism of Saul, rather than of the Davidic monarchy of which he approved.

26. Weiser, *Samuel*; id., *Introduction*, 161ff.,166ff.

27. Weiser, *Samuel*, 13ff.

28. Weiser, *Samuel*, 18ff., reinforces this by arguing for a parallel between Samuel's cultic proclamation of judgment on the Philistines in vv.2–9 and the Song of Moses in Deut. 32 which, following Eissfeldt and others, he dates to the pre-monarchic period.

29. Weiser, *Samuel*, 27ff.

30. Mendelsohn, *BASOR* 143, 1956, 17ff.

31. Weiser, *Samuel*, 62ff.,79ff.

32. Weiser relies here on Muilenburg, *VT* 9, 1959, 347ff.

33. This point cannot be countered by the argument (Weiser, *Samuel*, 22) that Samuel is intercessor rather than deliverer in chapter 7 and that it is Yahweh who directly intervenes to effect the victory over the Philistines. Just as with the old pre-monarchic deliverers so here it is through Yahweh and Samuel that deliverance comes to Israel; cf. Judg. 2.18, and Veijola, *Das Königtum*, 33f, n.30.

34. Cf. my *Deuteronomy*, 380ff.

35. Cf. Clements, *VT* 24, 1974, 403f.; Veijola, *Das Königtum*, 65f.; Crüsemann, *Der Widerstand gegen das Königtum*, 66ff.

36. This subject is too vast to elaborate at this point; suffice it then to say that the nature of pre-deuteronomistic covenant thought in Israel is obscure to say the least, while in deuteronomic-deuteronomistic writings it is the significant religious category; cf. ch.5, n.52, and, for a summary, cf. my *Deuteronomy*, 64ff.

37. Crüsemann, *Der Widerstand gegen das Königtum*. For his treatment of I Sam. 8–12, cf. ibid., 54ff.

38. Cf. Crüsemann, *Der Widerstand gegen das Königtum*, 85ff.

39. Cf. also Veijola, *Das Königtum*, 30ff.,53ff.

40. Verse 9b is clearly the later supplementer's attempt to alleviate this awkwardness. The proposal of Veijola, *Das Königtum*, 53ff., that vv.6–22a have all been subsequently inserted in the context does not get rid of the difficulty of the double command of Yahweh to Samuel; moreover, it is primarily based on the uncertain foundation that there is a caesura between vv.5 and 6, in vv.1–5 the request for a king deriving from the perfectly laudable desire to remove judicial corruption, and in vv.6ff. the request reflecting evil on the part of the people. No such clear demarcation exists, for the statement that in having a king Israel will be 'like all the nations' (v.5) must surely, despite Veijola, be taken as pejorative.

41. See especially Veijola, *Das Königtum*, 30ff.,56f. The language men-

tioned is not always found only in deuteronomistic passages, but is characteristic of such passages. For the deuteronomistic character of the supplementary sections within these chapters, reference may be made especially to the following: 'with all your heart' (7.3, cf. I Sam. 12.20,24; I Kings 8.23); 'put away the foreign gods' (7.3, cf. Judg. 10.16 and Josh. 24.23); 'he will deliver you out of the hand of the Philistines' (7.3, cf. Josh. 24.10; Judg. 6.9; 8.34; I Sam. 12.10,11); 'the Baals and the Ashtaroth' (7.4, cf. Judg. 2.13; 10.6; I Sam. 12.10); 'I brought them up out of the land of Egypt' (8.8, cf. Deut. 9.7; II Sam. 7.6; I Kings 8.16); 'forsaking me' (8.8, cf. Deut. 28.20; 31.16; Josh. 24.16,20; Judg. 2.12,13 etc.); 'serve other gods' (8.8, cf. Deut. 7.4; 11.16; 28.36; Josh. 23.16; 24.2,16 etc.); 'solemnly warn' (8.9, cf. Deut.8.19; II Kings 17.13,15). For the deuteronomistic character of the basic story, reference may be made to the following: 'we have sinned against the Lord' (7.6, cf. Deut. 1.41; Judg. 10.10,15; I Sam. 12.10); 'cry . . . save' (7.8, cf. Judg. 3.9; 10.12,14); 'were subdued' (7.13, cf. Judg. 3.30; 8.28; 11.33); 'the hand of the Lord was against the Philistines' (7.9, cf. Deut. 2.15; Judg. 2.15; I Sam. 12.15).

42. On this cf. Crüsemann, *Der Widerstand gegen das Königtum*, 61ff.,66ff.; cf. also Veijola, *Das Königtum*, 53ff., who prefers a date somewhat later and a setting in the northern kingdom.

43. Cf. above n.18.

44. Cf. Boecker, *Die Beurteilung der Anfänge des Königtums*, 35ff.

45. Cf. Veijola, *Das Königtum*, 39ff.

46. 'This day', cf. Deut. 4.4,8,20 etc.; 'calamities and distresses', cf. Deut. 31.17, where the same phrase is translated by RSV 'evils and troubles'; as in I Sam. 8.8 so again here the saving history appears.

47. Cf. Noth, *Überlieferungsgeschichtliche Studien*, 5,10,47 (ET, 5,9,42).

48. Cf., however, Crüsemann, *Der Widerstand gegen das Königtum*, 62ff., who finds pre-deuteronomistic material in vv.3–5. In view of the structure of the chapter, however (cf. Veijola, *Das Königtum*, 83ff., and below), this seems unlikely. On the other hand, it is not improbable that the references to the king in vv.3 and 5 ('his anointed') are additions; the end of v.5 presupposes only one witness, Yahweh, and not Yahweh and the king.

49. Cf. Veijola, *Das Königtum*, 83ff.

50. These have been pointed to particularly by Veijola, *Die ewige Dynastie* (though, cf. above n.13).

51. Rost, *Das kleine Credo*, 159ff.

52. Cf. especially Veijola, *Die ewige Dynastie*, 69f.; Mettinger, *King and Messiah*, 48f. Veijola and Mettinger also provide short histories of the study of this chapter since Rost, with special reference to Mowinckel, Herrmann and Görg.

53. Mettinger, *King and Messiah*, 50.

54. Cf. Veijola, *Die ewige Dynastie*, 76f.; McCarthy, *JBL* 84, 1965, 131ff.

55. For the giving of rest from all the enemies round about (vv.1b,11b) cf. Josh. 21.44.

56. Cf. Clements, *VT* 24, 1974, 405ff.

5. Deuteronomistic Editing of Kings

1. Cf. above chapter 4 n.4 for the limits of the succession narrative.
2. For the general characteristics which Kings shares with other parts of the deuteronomistic history, cf. above pp. 4ff.
3. For the sources, cf. Noth, *Überlieferungsgeschichtliche Studien*, 67ff. (ET, 57ff.), on Solomon; and 72ff. (ET, 63ff.), on the later monarchic period.
4. For Noth the deuteronomist composed I Kings 5.15–32, the prayer of dedication of the temple in chapter 8, the account of the vision of God in 9.1–9, and the story of Solomon's apostasy in 11.1–13.
5. That this was the deuteronomist's aim was argued by Noth. It is a reading which is not generally accepted and, as indicated below, must be seriously modified. This in turn, of course, will have implications for our understanding of the nature of the material which the deuteronomist derived from his sources.
6. The story of Jehu's accession in II Kings 9–10 probably did not originally belong to the Elijah-Elisha cycle; cf. Noth, *Überlieferungsgeschichtliche Studien*, 80 (ET, 69).
7. This would be the case with, for example, the account in II Kings 25.13–17 of the temple items destroyed or taken by the Babylonians, an account composed by the deuteronomist on the basis of I Kings 7.15ff., part of the account of Solomon's building works.
8. Cf. Hölscher, in *Eucharisterion*, 158–213; Begrich, *Die Chronologie der Könige von Israel und Juda und die Quellen des Rahmens der Königsbücher*; Jepsen, *Die Quellen des Königsbuches*. For other references in this connection, cf. Nelson, *Deuteronomistic History*, 13ff.
9. Cf. Noth, *Überlieferungsgeschichtliche Studien*, 91, n.1 (ET, 139, n.1).
10. Cf. Nicholson's foreword to Noth, *Deuteronomistic History*, viiif.
11. This criticism must apply to the arguments in favour of a pre-exilic edition of the deuteronomistic history put forward by Eissfeldt, *Introduction*, 281ff., and Gray, *I & II Kings*, 7f.,753f. Eissfeldt's proposal that Huldah's promise that Josiah would go to his grave in peace presupposes a time before Josiah's violent death and so also a pre-exilic edition of the deuteronomistic history is (apart from its doubtful interpretation of that oracle, for which see below), open to the objection that Huldah's oracle is a pre-exilic source used by an exilic deuteronomist; Gray's view is in principle little different. In neither case has it been shown that definable redactional stages in the development of Kings belong to specified periods.
12. Cross, *Canaanite Myth and Hebrew Epic*, 274ff.
13. For a discussion of the account of Josiah's reform, cf. below pp. 128ff.
14. Nelson, *Deuteronomistic History*, 31ff.
15. Cross, *Canaanite Myth and Hebrew Epic*, 287f., noted that the absence of a concluding speech or peroration on the fall of Jerusalem is remarkable, given the deuteronomistic historian's custom of appending such compositions at appropriate points; this lack marks off the concluding section of Kings from the earlier work of the deuteronomistic historian, which included such speeches or reviews.
16. Nelson, *Deuteronomistic History*, 53ff.

17. Linguistic usage confirms this, since there is clear connection between vv.44–51 and, for example, Deut. 4; 30. Compare I Kings 8.47f. and Deut. 4.29–31; 30.1–10.

18. The deuteronomistic historian's comment on the fall of Samaria is to be found in II Kings 18.9–12, a passage based on the chronicles of the kings of Judah. The deuteronomistic historian anticipated this report in his earlier reference to Hoshea king of Israel in II Kings 17.1–6; cf. Noth, *Überlieferungsgeschichtliche Studien*, 78ff. (ET, 67ff.).

19. Nelson, *Deuteronomistic History*, 99ff., makes the point that the conditional promises in I Kings 2.4; 8.25; 9.4f., have commonly been regarded as exilic changes of the unconditional promises of I Kings 11.36; 15.4; II Kings 8.19, which go back to Nathan's oracle (II Sam. 7). However, Nelson argues (cf. also Friedman, *The Exile and Biblical Narrative*, 12f.), the conditional promises all refer to Solomon, and they suggest that with Solomon's obedience his throne will be established over northern Israel. They are independent of the unconditional promise relating to the Davidic rule in Judah and Jerusalem and so are not necessarily part of the exilic edition of Kings.

20. Dietrich, *Prophetie und Geschichte*.

21. Dietrich, *Prophetie und Geschichte*, 28ff. The passages are noted in the order in which Dietrich deals with them.

22. So, for example, II Kings 9.7–10a expands on v.3 (cf. v.12); I Kings 14.7–11 are not presupposed by vv.17–18a; I Kings 22.38 stands in conflict with v.40 which implies Ahab's peaceful death.

23. These last include 'both bond and free in Israel' (I Kings 14.10; 21.21; II Kings 9.8); 'I will utterly consume . . . as a man burns up dung until it is all gone' (I Kings 14.10; cf. 16.3; 21.21); 'I will wipe Jerusalem as one wipes a dish, wiping it and turning it upside down' (II Kings 21.13); 'until the Lord removed Israel out of his sight' (II Kings 17.23).

24. For similar views, cf. Veijola, *Die ewige Dynastie*, 141f.

25. Does it express a hope for the continuation of the Davidic dynasty after the catastrophe of 587 BC (so von Rad, *Old Testament Theology* I, 343; Zimmerli, *Grundriss der alttestamentliche Theologie*, 159, ET, 179f.), or is it simply a closing historical note with no deeper theological meaning (so Noth, *Überlieferungsgeschichtliche Studien*, 108, ET 98)?

26. So Dietrich, *Prophetie und Geschichte*, 28f., takes I Kings 14.8b,9a as coming from the hand of the nomistic deuteronomist mainly because of its connection with the nomistic layer in I Kings 11.

27. Dietrich, *Prophetie und Geschichte*, 15ff.

28. So v.33 provides the foundation of v.31 and not for v.32; v.34b should surely, following on v.34a, refer to the retention of one tribe for the house of David, not to the deferment of the taking away of the kingdom until the time of Solomon's successor.

29. Cf. also Debus, *Die Sünde Jeroboams*, 4f.

30. These concerns are brought together also earlier in the chapter, in vv.12f. It is most probable that the one tribe which was reserved is a reference to the state of Judah, rather than strictly to one of the twelve tribes (cf. Debus, *Die Sünde Jeroboams*, 10,13ff.); so too it is the deuteronomistic historian who

uses the expression 'you shall be king over Israel' in v.37b, with reference to the northern kingdom.

31. On this reading it is then unnecessary to take vv.38b*b*,39 as a gloss (as frequently proposed); in the light of the understanding of the deuteronomistic historian followed here, it can be seen as expressing his conviction that the northern kingdom held no divine approval, but that the empire of David would (under Josiah) be eventually restored.

32. For vocabulary reasons the phrase 'by keeping my statutes and my commandments' in v.38 probably also belongs here.

33. Cf. my *Deuteronomy*, 92ff. I would now modify the conclusions there presented, in the light of the work of Hoffmann; cf. further below p. 129.

34. See further below pp. 125ff.

35. For the following, cf. Weippert, *Bib* 53, 1972, 301ff; and also Barrick, *Bib* 55, 1974, 257ff.

36. There are some deviations from these two forms within these limits, as in the formulae used of the Judaean kings Jehoram and Ahaziah (II Kings 8.18,27). Yet these two cases are ones, and the only ones, where Judah was ruled by a direct relation or descendant of the royal house of Israel, Athaliah the daughter of Ahab having married Jehoram. So the judgment on these two Judaean kings uses the formula of condemnation found otherwise with the Israelite kings ('he did what was evil in the sight of Yahweh'). Yet there is a close relationship also to the formula used of the Judaean kings in that the father-in-law/son-in-law relationship mentioned corresponds to the father-son comparison drawn in the formula used of the Judaean kings. Thus the deviation from the normal formula is open to explanation and identical authorship may then be accepted also for II Kings 8.18,27. For other minor deviations from the forms in this group, cf. Weippert, *Bib* 53, 1972, 313ff.

37. It is difficult to understand, on the other hand, why the history covered by the formulae of this group should have begun with Jehoshaphat king of Judah and Jehoram king of Israel, rather than, say, with the beginning of the divided kingdom. Weippert, *Bib* 53, 1972, 320, n.2, suggests the possibility that the beginning with Jehoshaphat and Jehoram is connected with the fact that these two kings made common cause and did not continue the old hostility between the two states.

38. Cf. also I Kings 15.5 (with reference to David) and I Kings 11.33 (with reference to the conditions under Solomon). The basic formula here may sometimes be extended or modified: David may be referred to as 'my servant' rather than 'his father'; the formulaic language 'walk in the way of/after' may also be found.

39. The basic structure of the second formula of this group is acknowledged by Weippert, *Bib* 53, 1972, 327f., to be difficult to plot out since the elements indicated are frequent rather than absolutely constant. Moreover, additional material, such as 'provoking the Lord to anger', 'more than all his father(s) had done (before him)', also appears on several occasions.

40. This cannot be taken to mean that the account of the history embraced by this group of formulae begins only with the division of the kingdom. The reference to David as an ideal figure would indicate that the history being recounted probably included an account of this king.

41. Cf. Ackroyd, *IDB Suppl*, 517: 'We may need to recognize that the text, in any of the forms known to us, represents a certain element of accident, of fixation at a point which is not neat and well rounded, but leaves unevenness and inconsistency.'

42. Cf. above p. 110.

43. For an extended treatment of the link between Moses and Josiah in the first edition of the deuteronomistic history, cf. Friedman, *The Exile and Biblical Narrative*, 7ff. Those parts of Kings already assigned by Cross and Nelson to the work of the deuteronomistic historian are undoubtedly to be taken as representing the bulk of his distinctive work; they should be supplemented with the prophetic passages directed against individual kings which Dietrich has marked out; see above pp. 113ff.

44. On the judgment expressed on Hoshea as the work of the first stage redactor, cf. Weippert, *Bib* 53, 1972, 320f.

45. On the unity of this section, with no older source discernible, cf. Hoffmann, *Reform und Reformen*, 134ff.

46. On Noth's view that vv.21f. are non-deuteronomistic because they no longer see the primary sin of Israel as the sin of Jeroboam, cf. Hoffmann, *Reform und Reformen*, 128f.n.4. Hoffmann also further reinforces the unity of vv.7–23 by an analysis of the structure, language and content of the verses, and by the observation that it is only in v.23 that the real conclusion, suggested by the starting point of the section (v.6), is reached.

47. It is a fundamental error in Hoffmann's treatment of the chapter (*Reform und Reformen*, 127ff.,137ff.) that he marks off vv.34b–41 alone from the rest of the chapter, and identifies only the latter as deuteronomistic. There is no linguistic or theological support for this, and it glosses over all the points which the section has in common with vv.7–23. It is only in vv.34–41 that Hoffmann is prepared to see the hand of a second deuteronomistic editor.

48. Hoffmann, *Reform und Reformen*, 132f., has rightly drawn attention to the close parallels between II Kings 17.7–23 and the account of the sins of Manasseh in II Kings 21 (cf. 17.16f. and 21.3,6). The two passages function to provide theological justification for the political destructions brought on Israel and Judah respectively; both derive from the same (exilic) deuteronomistic hand.

49. These chapters have been the subject of many studies; for a recent approach, with bibliography, cf. my *Deuteronomy*, 85ff. What follows here represents a considerable modification of some details in my earlier view, resulting especially from the work of Hoffmann.

50. Lohfink, *Bib* 44, 1963, 261–88,461–98.

51. Cf. also Noth, *Überlieferungsgeschichtliche Studien*, 92 (ET, 80), who sees 22.3–23.3 as a record incorporated into his history by the deuteronomist.

52. A consideration of this subject is impossible at this point. It should, however, be pointed out that the theory of an old covenant festival in Israel is finding less and less favour. 'Covenant' is a deuteronomic-deuteronomistic keyword whose pre-deuteronomic roots are very difficult to discern; for a study, cf. my *Deuteronomy*, 64ff.

53. Dietrich, *VT* 27, 1977, 18ff., has suggested this literary criticism of 22.3–11, but thinks that the conclusion to be drawn from it is that the

deuteronomist combined two existing stories: one dealing with repairs to the temple, the other with the finding of the lawbook. To this Hoffmann rightly objects that the story of the finding of the lawbook is too thin to be a credible independent account (*Reform und Reformen*, 192, n.5). When, however, the lawbook material is seen as (late) deuteronomistic material added in to supplement an already existing (deuteronomistic) story of repairs to the temple (see below), then Hoffmann's general objections to any literary critical division of this passage largely lose their force.

54. Cf. Wurthwein, *ZThK* 73, 1976, 404ff.; Rose, *ZAW* 89, 1977, 52ff.

55. Cf. my *Deuteronomy*, 93f., where I followed Rose, *ZAW* 89, 1977, 54ff., who refers only to 'a desolation and a curse' and 'the evil which I shall bring' as deuteronomistic elements.

56. Cf. especially Hoffmann, *Reform und Reformen*, 170ff., for the following.

57. Hollenstein, *VT* 27, 1977, 326ff., distinguishes three stages of development of vv.4ff.: a basic text, a deuteronomistic redaction of this text, and a post-deuteronomistic redaction.

58. Cf. Hoffmann, *Reform und Reformen*, 208ff. Hoffmann, it should be noted, both argues for the unity of vv.4–20 and also holds that the verses belong inseparably to their context. In this he has undervalued the significance of the stylistic differences between the verses and their context and also the lack of reference to the lawbook in vv.4–20. This is not to say that vv.4–20 are pre-deuteronomistic. As will be noted below, they are the work of the deuteronomistic historian, not that of the later deuteronomistic editor responsible for the context. For Hoffmann's general argument for a single deuteronomistic author of the deuteronomistic history, cf. above pp. 10ff.

59. That these two passages belong to the same layer is probable (cf. further below), and indeed *a priori* suggested by the fact that the story of Hezekiah's reform in II Kings 18 has a similar series of reform measures directly attached to the deuteronomistic introduction of Hezekiah in 18.1–3.

60. Cf. Dietrich, *VT* 27, 1977, 18ff.

61. Cf. Hoffmann, *Reform und Reformen*, 220ff., for this and what follows on the deuteronomistic character of 23.4–20.

62. The detailed lists and references have been comprehensively set out by Hoffmann, *Reform und Reformen*, 224ff.,341ff.

63. To this later editor are to be assigned, therefore, 22.8,10–20; 23.1–3,21–24.

Conclusion

1. For a review and bibliography, cf. Nicholson, *Deuteronomy and Tradition*, 58ff.

2. Cf. especially Clements, *VT* 15, 1965, 300ff.

3. For a discussion, cf. my *Deuteronomy*, 103ff.

4. Noth, *Überlieferungsgeschichtliche Studien*, 97 and n.6 (ET, 85, 141, n.9), thought that the deuteronomistic history was composed in Palestine; for the argument that it is addressed to the Babylonian exiles, cf. Nicholson, *Preaching to the Exiles*, 116ff.; Soggin, *ThLZ* 100, 1975, 3–8.

5. Nicholson, *Preaching to the Exiles*, 134.
6. This much at least must be granted; cf. Nicholson, *Deuteronomy and Tradition*, 69ff.,76f.,117f.
7. For a discussion of the social role of the prophets, cf. Wilson, *Prophecy and Society in Ancient Israel*, especially 135ff., on north Israelite prophecy and its functioning on the periphery of society, particularly after the rise of the monarchy. For a recent and wide-ranging assessment, cf. Culley and Overholt (eds), *Semeia* 21, 1981.
8. For this and what follows see especially Rose, *Der Ausschliesslichkeitsanspruch Jahwes*, 171ff. On several occasions we have disagreed with Rose's detailed analysis of passages in Deuteronomy, but these do not affect the present more general issue.
9. One might also query if the source division of Exodus depends to a large extent on what has been found in Genesis; cf. for example Schmidt, *Exodus*, 8, who acknowledges the greater difficulty of source division in Exodus over against Genesis.
10. Noth, *Numbers*, 4f.
11. Cf. above p. 18.
12. One of the merits of Fohrer, *Introduction*, 195,205, and Weiser, *Introduction*, 147 (cf. also Eissfeldt, *Introduction*, 257), is the attempt to relate the literary critical processes to the life of the community in which they took place. So, the existence of a Pentateuch (which, since it does not include the account of the settlement of west Jordan, is substantially the truncated JE to which we have referred) is explained against the background of the political conditions in the restored community; here, it is argued, a programmatic claim to independent disposal of the land, as the theoretical basis of the life of the community (which is what a Hexateuch would have constituted), would not have been tolerated by the ruling power. This, it should be noted, provides a (partial) explanation for the fact that it was the Pentateuch which eventually came to be accepted as normative; it does not, nor does it pretend to, presuppose a certain literary critical view of the origin and content of the J, E and P documents nor of the developing and changing relationship between the Tetrateuch/Pentateuch and the deuteronomistic history.
13. Cf. Freedman, *IDB* 3, 711ff.; id., *IDB Suppl.*, 226ff.
14. Friedman, *The Exile and Biblical Narrative*.
15. The treatment here cannot be elaborate. For more extensive discussion and reviews of the problems under discussion, cf. especially the articles and reviews by Rendtorff, Whybray, van Seters, Wagner, Coats, Schmid, Clements and Wenham, in *JSOT* 3, 1977; the three major works which lie at the heart of the discussion are: van Seters, *Abraham in History and Tradition*; Schmid, *Der sogennante Jahwist*; and Rendtorff, *Das überlieferungsgeschichtliche Problem des Pentateuch*. Among critics of these new proposals, particular attention should be paid to Clements, in *JSOT* 3, 1977, 46ff.; and Otto, *Verkündigung und Forschung: Theologischer Jahresbericht* 22, 1977, 82ff.
16. van Seters, *Abraham in History and Tradition*, 139ff.
17. See the discussion between Rendtorff and Schmid in *JSOT* 3, 1977, 33ff.,43ff.
18. Cf. Rendtorff, *Das überlieferungsgeschichtliche Prolem des Pentateuch*, 167f.

19. Rose, *Deuteronomist und Jahwist*.

20. Other texts investigated by Rose include Ex. 13.20; 16.35 and Josh. 4.19, which have been linked because of their common interest in providing place notices; and Gen. 24.8; Josh. 2.17,20 which have been linked because they are all concerned with release from a sworn obligation. In the case of neither group can it be established that a single author or (J) source lies behind these usages.

21. Rose completes his study with references to Num. 21; Deut. 2f. and Judg. 1; 11. Throughout, it is clear that Num. 21 is the work of an author using a lot of oral and also written sources, among which Deut. 1–3 is to be included, in order to create a story of the transition from wilderness to settlement. So there is asserted for the whole of Num. 21 what has been generally accepted as the case for Num. 21.33–35, viz., a direct dependence on the corresponding account in Deuteronomy.

Abbreviations

AB	Anchor Bible, New York
AnBib	Analecta Biblica, Rome
ATANT	Abhandlungen zur Theologie des Alten und Neuen Testaments, München
BASOR	*Bulletin of the American Schools of Oriental Research*, New Haven, Conn.
BBB	Bonner Biblische Beiträge, Bonn
Bib	*Biblica*, Rome
BK	Biblischer Kommentar, Neukirchen-Vluyn
BWANT	Beiträge zur Wissenschaft vom Alten und Neuen Testament, Stuttgart
BWAT	Beiträge zur Wissenschaft vom Alten Testament, Stuttgart
BZ	*Biblische Zeitschrift*, Freiburg, Paderborn
BZAW	Beihefte zur *Zeitschrift für die alttestamentliche Wissenschaft*, Geissen, Berlin
CBQ	*Catholic Biblical Quarterly*, Washington
ET	English Translation
FRLANT	Forschungen zur Religion und Literatur des Alten und Neuen Testaments, Göttingen
HAT	Handbuch zum Alten Testament, Tübingen
HTR	*Harvard Theological Review*, Cambridge, Mass.
IB	The Interpreter's Bible, 12 vols, Nashville 1951–57
IDB	*The Interpreter's Dictionary of the Bible*, Nashville 1962
IDBSuppl	*The Interpreter's Dictionary of the Bible, Supplementary Volume*, Nashville 1976
Interp	*Interpretation*, Richmond, Va.
JBL	*Journal of Biblical Literature*, Philadelphia, Missoula
JSOT	*Journal for the Study of the Old Testament*, Sheffield
JTS	*Journal of Theological Studies*, Oxford
KAT	Kommentar zum Alten Testament, Leipzig, Gütersloh

NF	Neue Folge
RB	*Revue Biblique*, Paris
RSV	Revised Standard Version, London and New York 1962
SBT	Studies in Biblical Theology, London and Nashville
SVT	Supplements to *Vetus Testamentum*, Leiden
ThLZ	*Theologische Literaturzeitung*, Leipzig
ThR	*Theologische Rundschau*, Tübingen
ThZ	*Theologische Zeitschrift*, Basel
VT	*Vetus Testamentum*, Leiden
WMANT	Wissenschaftliche Monographien zum Alten und Neuen Testament, Neukirchen-Vluyn
ZAW	*Zeitschrift für die alttestamentliche Wissenschaft*, Geissen, Berlin
ZDPV	*Zeitschrift des deutschen Palästinavereins*, Wiesbaden
ZThK	*Zeitschrift für Theologie und Kirche*, Tübingen

Bibliography

Ackroyd, P. R., 'Kings, I and II', *IDBSuppl*, 516–19.

Aharoni, A., *The Land of the Bible*,[2] London 1979.

Alt, A., 'Josua', *Kleine Schriften zur Geschichte des Volkes Israel* I, München 1953, 176–92.

— 'Das System der Stammesgrenzen im Buch Josua', *Kleine Schriften* I, 193–202.

— 'Judas Gaue unter Josia', *Kleine Schriften* II, München 1953, 276–88.

Auld, A. G., 'Judges 1 and History: a reconsideration', *VT* 25, 1975, 261–85.

Baltzer, K., *Das Bundesformular*, WMANT 4, [2]1964 (ET: *The Covenant Formulary in Old Testament, Jewish and Early Christian Writings*, Oxford 1971.

Barrick, W., 'On the Removal of the High Places in 1–2 Kings', *Bib* 55, 1974, 257–59.

Begrich, J., *Die Chronologie der Könige von Israel und Juda und die Quellen des Rahmens der Königsbücher*, Beiträge zur historischen Theologie 3, Tübingen 1929.

Benzinger, I., *Jahvist und Elohist in den Königsbüchern*, BWAT NF 2, 1921.

Beyerlin, W., 'Gattung und Herkunft des Rahmens im Richterbuch', *Tradition und Situation: Studien zur alttestamentlichen Prophetie* (A. Weiser Festschrift, ed. E. Würthwein and O. Kaiser), Göttingen 1963, 1–29.

Birch, B. C., 'The Development of the Tradition on the Anointing of Saul in I Sam. 9.1–10.16', *JBL* 90, 1971, 55–68.

Boecker, H. J., *Die Beurteilung der Anfänge des Königtums in den deuteronomistischen Abschnitten des 1. Samuelbuches*, WMANT 31, 1969.

Boling, R., *Judges*, AB, New York 1975.

Braulik, G., 'Literarkritisch und archaeologisch Stratigraphie. Zu S. Mittmanns Analyse von Deuteronomium 4,1–40', *Bib* 59, 1978, 351–83.

— *Die Mittel deuteronomischer Rhetorik*, AnBib 68, Rome 1978.

Bright, J., 'Joshua', IB 2, 541–673.

Caspari, W., *Die Samuelbücher*, KAT 1926.

Childs, B. S., *Introduction to the Old Testament as Scripture*, London 1979.

Clements, R. E., 'The Deuteronomistic Interpretation of the Founding of the Monarchy in I Sam. VIII', *VT* 24, 1974, 398–410.

— 'Deuteronomy and the Jerusalem Cult Tradition', *VT* 15, 1965, 300–12.

— Review of R. Rendtorff, *Das überlieferungsgeschichtliche Problem des Pentateuch*, *JSOT* 3, 1977, 46–56.

Coats, G. W., 'The Yahwist as Theologian? A Critical Reflection', *JSOT* 3, 1977, 28–32.

Cross, F. M., *Canaanite Myth and Hebrew Epic*, Harvard 1973.

Crüsemann, F., *Der Widerstand gegen das Königtum*, WMANT 49, 1978.

Culley, R. C., and Overholt, T. W. (eds), 'Anthropological Perspectives on Old Testament Prophecy', *Semeia* 21, 1981.

Debus, J., *Die Sünde Jeroboams*, FRLANT 93, 1967.

Dietrich, W., *Prophetie und Geschichte. Eine redaktionsgeschichtliche Untersuchung zum deuteronomistischen Geschichtswerk*, FRLANT 108, 1972.

— 'Josia und das Gesetzbuch (2 Reg. XXII)', *VT* 27, 1977, 13–35.

Driver, S. R., *Notes on the Hebrew Text and the Topography of the Books of Samuel*, Oxford 1913.

Eissfeldt, O., *Hexateuch Synopse*, Leipzig 1922.

— *Die Quellen des Richterbuches*, Leipzig 1925.

— *Die Komposition der Samuelisbücher*, Leipzig 1931.

— *The Old Testament: an Introduction*, Oxford 1965.

Emerton, J. A., 'Gideon and Jerubbaal', *JTS* 27, 1976, 289–312.

Engnell, I., *Critical Essays on the Old Testament*, London 1970.

Flanagan, J. W., 'Court History or Succession Document: a study of II Sam. 9–20 and I Kings 1–2', *JBL* 91, 1972, 172–81.

Fohrer, G., *Introduction to the Old Testament*, London 1970.

Freedman, D. N., 'Pentateuch', *IDB* 3, 711–27.

— 'Deuteronomic History', *IDBSuppl*, 226–28.

Friedman, R.E., *The Exile and Biblical Narrative: the formation of the deuteronomistic and priestly works*, Harvard Semitic Monographs 22, 1981.

de Geus, C. H. J., 'Richteren 1:1–2:5', *Vox Theologica* XXXVI, 1966, 32–54.

Gottwald, N., *The Tribes of Yahweh: a sociology of the Religion of liberated Israel 1250–1050 BCE*, London 1980.

Gray, J., *Joshua, Judges and Ruth*, New Century Bible, London 1967.

— *I & II Kings*,[2] Old Testament Library, London 1970.

Gressmann, H., *Die Anfänge Israels*. Die Schriften des Alten Testaments I, 2[2], 1922.

Gros Louis, K. R. R., 'The Book of Judges', *Literary Interpretations of Biblical Narratives*, ed., K. R. R. Gros Louis with J. S. Ackerman and T. S. Warshaw, Nashville 1974, 141–62.

Hayes, J., *Introduction to Old Testament Study*, Nashville 1979, and London 1982.

Hoffmann, H.-D., *Reform und Reformen: Untersuchungen zu einem Grundthema der deuteronomistischen Geschichtsschreibung*, ATANT 66, Zürich 1980.

Hollenstein, H., 'Literarkritische Erwägungen zum Bericht über die Reformmassnahmen Josias in 2 Kön.XXIII 4ff.', *VT* 27, 1977, 321–36.

Hölscher, G., 'Das Buch der Könige, seine Quellen und seine Redaktion', *Eucharisterion* I (Festschrift H. Gunkel), FRLANT 36, 1923, 158–213.

— *Die Anfänge der hebräischen Geschichtsschreibung*, 1942.

Hyatt, J. P., 'Were there an ancient historical credo in Israel and an independent Sinai tradition?', *Translating and Understanding the Old Testament*, ed., H. T. Frank and W. L. Reed, Nashville 1970, 152–70.

Bibliography

Jenni, E., 'Zwei Jahrzehnte Forschung an den Büchern Josua bis Könige', *ThR* NF 27, 1961, 1–32,97–146.

Jepsen, A., *Die Quellen des Königbuches*, Halle 1953.

Jones, G. H., ' "Holy War" or "Yahweh War" ', *VT* 25, 1975, 642–58.

Kittel, R., 'Die Pentateuchischen Urkunden in den Büchern Richter und Samuel', *Theologische Studien und Kritiken* 65, 1892, 44–71.

Kline, M. G., *The Treaty of the Great King. The Covenant Structure of Deuteronomy*, Grand Rapids 1963.

Kloppenborg, J. S., 'Joshua 22: the Priestly Editing of an Ancient Tradition', *Bib* 62, 1981, 347–71.

Kraus, H. J., *Geschichte der historisch-kritischen Erforschung des Alten Testaments*, Neukirchen 1956.

Kuenen, A., *Historisch-kritischen Onderzoek naar het antstaan en de Verzemeling van de Boeken des Ouden Verband*, 1861–65 (German translation: *Historisch-kritische Einleitung in die Bücher des Alten Testaments*, Leipzig 1887–1892.

Kutsch, E., *Verheissung und Gesetz*, BZAW 131, 1972.

Langlamet, F., 'Les récits de l'institution de la royauté (I Sam., VII–XII). De Wellhausen aux travaux récents', *RB* 77, 1970, 161–200.

Levenson, J. D., 'Who inserted the book of the Torah?', *HTR* 68, 1975, 203–33.

L'Hour, J., 'L'alliance de Sichem', *RB* 69, 1962, 5–36, 161–84, 350–68.

Lohfink, N., 'Darstellungskunst und Theologie in Dtn 1:6–3:29', *Bib* 41, 1960, 105–34.

—'Die deuteronomistischen Darstellung des Übergangs der Führung Israels von Moses auf Josue', *Scholastik* 37, 1962, 32–44.

—'Die Bundesurkunde des Königs Josias', *Bib* 44, 1963, 261–88, 461–98.

— *Das Hauptgebot. Eine Untersuchung literarischer Einleitungsfragen zu Dtn 5–11*, AnBib 20, Rome 1963.

— 'Die Wandlung des Bundesbegriffs im Buch Deuteronomium', *Gott in Welt* (Festgabe für Karl Rahner, hrsg von H. Vorgrimler) I, Freiburg 1964, 423–44.

— 'Zur Dekalogfassung von Dt 5', *BZ* 9, 1965, 17–32.

— *Höre Israel. Auslegung von Texten aus dem Buch Deuteronomium*, Dusseldorf 1965.

Lopez, F. Garcia, *Analyse litteraire de Deutéronome, V–XI*, Jerusalem 1978 (= *RB* 85, 1978, 5–49).

McCarter, P. K., *I Samuel*, AB 8, 1980.

McCarthy, D. J., 'I Samuel 7 and the Structure of the Deuteronomic History', *JBL* 84, 1965, 131–38.

— 'The Inauguration of Monarchy in Israel', *Interp* 27, 1973, 401–12.

— *Treaty and Covenant*[2], AnBib 21A, Rome 1978.

Macholz, G. C., *Untersuchungen zur Geschichte der Samuel-Überlieferungen*, Dissertation, Heidelberg, 1966.

Mayes, A. D. H., *Israel in the Period of the Judges*, SBT II/29, London 1974.

— 'The Period of the Judges and the Rise of the Monarchy', *Israelite and Judaean History*, ed., J. Hayes and J. M. Miller, London 1977, 285–331.

— 'The Rise of the Israelite Monarchy', *ZAW* 90, 1978, 1–19.

— *Deuteronomy*, New Century Bible, London 1979.

— 'Deuteronomy 5 and the Decalogue', *Proceedings of the Irish Biblical Association* 4, 1980, 68–83.

— 'Deuteronomy 4 and the Literary Criticism of Deuteronomy', *JBL* 100, 1981, 23–51.

— 'Deuteronomy: Law of Moses or Law of God?', *Proceedings of the Irish Biblical Association* 5, 1981, 36–54.

Mendelsohn, I., 'Samuel's Denunciation of Kingship in the Light of the Accadian Documents from Ugarit', *BASOR* 143, 1956, 17–22.

Merendino, R., *Das deuteronomische Gesetz*, BBB 31, 1969.

Mettinger, T. N. D., *King and Messiah*, Coniectanea Biblica; Old Testament Series 8, Lund 1976.

Miller, J. M., 'Saul's Rise to Power', *CBQ* 36, 1974, 157–74.

Miller, P. D., and Roberts, J. J. M., *The Hand of the Lord: a reassessment of the Ark Narrative of I Samuel*, Johns Hopkins University Press, 1977.

Minette de Tillesse, G., 'Sections "tu" et sections "vous" dans le Deutéronome', *VT* 12, 1962, 29–87.

Mittmann, S., *Deuteronomium 1.1–6.3 literarkritisch und traditionsgeschichtlich untersucht*, BZAW 139, 1975.

Mölle, H., *Der sogenannte Landtag zu Sichem*, Forschung zur Bibel 42, 1980.

Muilenburg, J., 'The Form and Structure of the Covenantal Formulations', *VT* 9, 1959, 347–65.

Nelson, R. D., *The Double Redaction of the Deuteronomistic History*, *JSOT* Supplement Series 18, Sheffield 1981.

Nicholson, E. W., *Deuteronomy and Tradition*, Oxford 1967.

— *Preaching to the Exiles*, Oxford 1970.

North, C. R., 'Pentateuchal Criticism', *The Old Testament and Modern Study*, ed., H. H. Rowley, Oxford 1951, 48–83.

Noth, M., *Das System der zwölf Stämme Israels*, BWANT IV/I, 1930.

— 'Studien zu den historisch-geographischen Dokumenten des Josuabuches', *ZDPV* 58, 1935, 183–255 (= *Aufsätze zur biblischen Landes- und Altertumskunde*, hrsg von H. W. Wolff, Neukirchen 1971, I, 229–80).

— *Überlieferungsgeschichtliche Studien*, Tübingen 1943, ²1957 (ET: *The Deuteronomistic History*, *JSOT* Supplement Series 15, Sheffield 1981.

— 'Das Amt des Richters Israels', Festschrift für A. Bertholet, Tübingen 1950, 404–17 (= *Gesammelte Studien II*, München 1969, 71–85).

— *Josua*, HAT 7, ²1953.

— *The History of Israel*², London 1960.

— 'The Background of Judges 17–18', *Israel's Prophetic Heritage*, ed., B. W. Anderson and W. Harrelson, London 1962, 68–85.

— *Numbers*, Old Testament Library, London 1968.

Otto, E., 'Stehen wir vor einem Umbruch in der Pentateuchkritik?', *Verkündigung und Forschung: Theologischer Jahresbericht* 22, 1977, 82–97.

Perlitt, L., *Bundestheologie im Alten Testament*, WMANT 36, 1969.

Polzin, R., *Moses and the Deuteronomist*, New York, 1980.

von Rad, G., *Old Testament Theology*, Edinburgh, I 1962; II 1965.

— 'The Form Critical Problem of the Hexateuch', *The Problem of the Hexateuch and Other Essays*, Edinburgh 1966, 1–78.

Bibliography

— 'There Remains still a Rest for the People of God', *The Problem of the Hexateuch and Other Essays*, 94–102.

Radjawane, A. N., 'Das deuteronomische Geschichtswerk', *ThR* NF 38, 1973, 177–216.

Rendtorff, R., 'Beobachtungen zur altisraelitischen Geschichtsschreibung anhand der Geschichte vom Aufstieg Davids', *Probleme biblischer Theologie* (G. von Rad zum 70. Geburtstag, hrsg von H. W. Wolff), München 1971, 428–39.

— 'The "Yahwist" as Theologian? The Dilemma of Pentateuchal Criticism', *JSOT* 3, 1977, 2–9.

— 'Pentateuchal Studies on the Move', *JSOT* 3, 1977, 43–5.

— *Das überlieferungsgeschichtliche Problem des Pentateuch*, BZAW 147, 1977.

Richter, W., *Die Bearbeitungen des 'Retterbuches' in der deuteronomischen Epoche*, BBB 21, 1964.

— 'Zu den "Richtern Israels" ', *ZAW* 77, 1965, 40–72.

— 'Die Überlieferungen um Jephtah, Ri 10,17–12,6', *Bib* 47, 1966, 485–556.

— *Traditionsgeschichtliche Untersuchungen zum Richterbuch*, BBB 18, ²1966.

Rose, M., *Die Ausschliesslichkeitsanspruch Jahwes*, BWANT 106, 1975.

— 'Bemerkungen zum historischen Fundament des Josia-Bildes in II Reg 22f.', *ZAW* 89, 1977, 50–63.

— *Deuteronomist und Jahwist*, ATANT 67, 1981.

Rösel, H. N., 'Die Überleitungen vom Josua im Richterbuch', *VT* 30, 1980, 342–50.

Rost, L., *Das kleine Credo und andere Studien zum Alten Testament*, Heidelberg, 1965.

Rowley, H. H., *From Joseph to Joshua*, London 1950.

Schlauri, I., 'Wolfgang Richters Beitrag zur Redaktionsgeschichte des Richterbuches', *Bib* 54, 1973, 367–403.

Schmid, H. H., *Der sogenannte Jahwist. Beobachtungen und Fragen zur Pentateuchforschung*, Zürich 1976.

— 'In search of new approaches in Pentateuchal research', *JSOT* 3, 1977, 33–42.

Schmidt, L., *Menschlicher Erfolg und Jahwes Initiative*, WMANT 38, 1970.

Schmidt, W. H., *Exodus*, BK II, 1974ff.

Schunck, K. D. 'Die Richter Israels und ihr Amt', SVT 15, 1966, 252–62.

Seitz, G., *Redaktionsgeschichtliche Studien zum Deuteronomium*, BWANT V/13, 1971.

van Seters, J., *Abraham in History and Tradition*, New Haven and London 1975.

— 'The Yahwist as Theologian? A Response', *JSOT* 3, 1977, 15–19.

Smend, R., 'Das Gesetz und die Völker. Ein Beitrag zur deuteronomistischen Redaktionsgeschichte', *Probleme biblischer Theologie* (G. von Rad zum 70. Geburtstag, hrsg von H. W. Wolff), München 1971, 494–509.

— *Die Entstehung des Alten Testaments*, Stuttgart 1978.

Soggin, J. A., *Joshua*, Old Testament Library, London 1972.

— 'Die Entstehungsort des deuteronomischen Geschichtswerkes', *ThLZ* 100, 1975, 3–8.

— *Introduction to the Old Testament*, London 1976.

— *Judges*, Old Testament Library, London 1981.

Stolz, F., *Jahwes und Israels Kriege. Kriegstheorien und Kriegserfahrungen im Glauben des alten Israel*, ATANT 60, 1972.

Sumner, W. A., 'Israel's Encounters with Edom, Moab, Ammon, Sihon and Og, according to the Deuteronomist', *VT* 18, 1968, 216–28.

Thiel, W., *Die soziale Entwicklung Israels in vorstaatlicher Zeit*, Neukirchen 1980.

Trompf, G. W., 'Notions of Historical Recurrence in classic Hebrew Historiography', *Studies in the Historical Books of the Old Testament*, SVT 30, 1979, 213–29.

de Vaux, R., *The Early History of Israel*, London 1976.

Veijola, T., *Die ewige Dynastie, David und die Entstehung seines Dynastie nach der deuteronomistischen Darstellung*, Helsinki 1975.

— *Das Königtum in der Beurteilung der deuteronomistischen Historiographie*, Helsinki 1977.

de Vries, S. J., 'The Hexateuchal Criticism of Abraham Kuenen', *JBL* 62, 1963, 31–57.

Wagner, N. E., 'A Response to Professor Rolf Rendtorff', *JSOT* 3, 1977, 20–27.

Weinfeld, M., 'The Period of the Conquest and of the Judges as seen by the earlier and later sources', *VT* 17, 1967, 93–113.

— *Deuteronomy and the Deuteronomic School*, Oxford 1972.

Weippert, H., 'Die "deuteronomistischen" Beurteilungen der Könige von Israel und Juda und das Problem der Redaktion der Königsbücher', *Bib* 53, 1972, 301–39.

Weippert, M.,' "Heiliger Krieg" in Israel und Assyria', *ZAW* 84, 1977, 460–93.

Weiser, A., *Introduction to the Old Testament*, London 1961.

— *Samuel. Seine geschichtliche Aufgabe und religiöse Bedeutung*, FRLANT 81, 1962.

Wellhausen, J., *Die Composition des Hexateuchs und der historischen Bücher des Alten Testaments*, ³1899.

— *Prolegomena to the History of Ancient Israel*, Meridian Books 1957.

de Wette, W. M. L., *Lehrbuch der historisch-kritischen Einleitung in die kanonischen und apokryphischen Bücher des Alten Testamentes* (1817), ⁶1845.

Wenham, G., 'The Deuteronomic Theology of the Book of Joshua', *JBL* 90, 1971, 140–48.

— Review of H. H. Schmid, *Der sogenannte Jahwist*, *JSOT* 3, 1977, 57–60.

Whybray, R. N., 'Response to Professor Rendtorff', *JSOT* 3, 1977, 11–14.

Wilson, R. R., *Prophecy and Society in Ancient Israel*, Philadelphia 1980.

Wright, G. E., 'Deuteronomy', IB 2, 311–537.

Würthwein, E., 'Die Josianische Reform und das Deuteronomium', *ZThK* 73, 1976, 395–423.

Zimmerli, W., *Grundriss der alttestamentliche Theologie*, Stuttgart 1972 (ET: *Old Testament Theology in Outline*, Edinburgh 1978).

Index of Names

Index of Subjects

Ark, ark narrative, 37f., 56, 79, 84f., 105, 160

Cities of refuge, 53f.
Conquest/settlement, 17f., 32, 42f., 45, 47, 48, 52, 54, 56, 77, 134f., 146, 157, 161
Covenant, 38f., 40, 41, 44, 50, 52, 56f., 59, 60, 69, 70, 74, 77f., 79, 92, 93, 105, 111, 125, 128, 133f., 159, 163, 168, 173
Covenant/treaty formulary, 25, 28, 34f., 37, 38f., 49, 153, 156, 158
Creed, 16f., 149

Decalogue, 31, 33, 34
Deuteronomic law, 22f., 24, 29f., 31f., 33, 34, 38, 40, 50, 54, 56, 108, 133f., 153, 155, 157
Deuteronomistic history: editions of, 3, 19, 110, 111, 112, 116, 118f., 131, 137, 141, 158, 170; history of study of, 1ff.; monarchy and, 85ff., 135f.; Pentateuch and, 14f., 15f., 16f., 37, 139ff., 144, 150, 175; prophecy and, 138f.; prophetic edition of, 87ff., 113ff., 135, 166, 167; Tetrateuch and, 9, 37, 141,

144f., 148f., 159, 160; theology of, 6f., 41ff., 50, 52, 138; unity of, 4ff.
Deuteronomistic school, social setting of, 137f.

Gibeonites, 42f., 44, 108f., 147, 157, 160

Hezekiah's reform, 122, 136
Holy war, 41ff., 62f., 157

Josiah's reform, 19, 53f., 108, 110f., 113, 123, 128ff., 131, 136, 155

Levites, 37f., 52, 54, 56f., 79, 156, 160

Pentateuch, 1, 2, 8, 14, 17f., 37, 86f., 139ff., 144
Priestly writing, 18, 37, 140, 141, 142, 143, 144, 145, 146, 152, 159
Rib, 70, 72, 78, 163

Sinai/Horeb covenant, 18, 32, 38, 133, 143, 159
Singular and plural forms of address, 29f., 32, 33f., 35

Index of Biblical References

Index of Biblical References

Joshua		21.45	48
	134, 159	22	160
8.31f.	51	22.1–34	41
9–10	145, 147	22.1–6	59, 160
9	44, 147	23	4, 45, 46, 48,
9.3	53		49, 50, 51, 56,
9.4	53		58, 60, 77f.,
10	53, 147		101, 157, 158,
10.1–5	160		161, 163
10.2	53	23.1f.	49
10.5	53	23.1	48, 49, 157
10.40–42	53	23.2	41, 46, 49
11.1–9	53	23.4	48
11.1	53	23.5	77
11.2	53	23.6f.	163
11.16–20	53, 160	23.6	41, 48
11.21–23	55	23.7	48, 76, 127
11.23	162	23.9	44, 48
12	4, 45	23.11–13	44, 111
12.1–6	55	23.12f.	48, 163
12.7–24	55	23.12	48, 60
13.21	44, 45, 58, 157	23.13	77
13–19	41, 49, 53f.,	23.14	44, 46, 48, 49
	158, 159	23.15–16	7, 44, 111
13	55, 158	23.16	41, 48, 76, 77,
13.1–7	47		127, 169
13.1–6	47, 48, 56, 58,	23.23	77
	77	24	12, 14, 157,
13.1	47, 49, 158		158, 159
13.7	47, 158	24.1–28	41, 46, 49, 50,
14	145		51f., 52, 56, 60,
14.6–15	55, 148, 154		134, 157, 158,
14.6–14	45		159, 161
14.10	6	24.1	49
14.15	162	24.2	169
15.21–62	53	24.10	169
17.14ff.	54, 160	24.16	169
18.21–28	53	24.20	169
19.2–7	53	24.23	169
19.41–46	53	24.26	51
20	53f., 55, 159	24.29–30(31)	160, 161
20.6	159	24.29–30	59, 78
21	53f., 55, 159	24.31	161
21.43–45	44, 47, 48, 55,	24.32–33	160
	58		
21.44	43, 48, 55, 77,	Judges	
	169	1.1–2.5	60, 61, 79, 135,

194

Index of Biblical References

7.3ff.	96		167
7.3–4	97, 98	9	152
7.3	97, 169	9.2	100
7.4	97, 169	9.15ff.	88
7.5–8.6	98	9.16	89
7.5	97	9.21	88
7.6	97, 98, 169	10	106
7.8	169	10.1	88
7.9	169	10.5–7	88
7.10–14	92, 93	10.8	86, 89
7.13	98, 169	10.17–27	85, 87, 88, 90,
7.15–8.3	98, 102, 105		92, 93, 96, 100
7.15	98	10.17–21	100
7.16	98	10.17ff.	9
7.17	98	10.18f.	100
8–12	9, 85f., 101,	10.18	92
	104, 166, 167,	10.19	91
	168	10.20f.	100
8	85, 86, 87, 90,	10.21–24	100
	92, 93, 96, 97,	10.21	100
	98, 106	10.22ff.	100
8.1–5	168	10.23	88, 100, 101,
8.1–3	94, 97, 98		167
8.3	94	10.24	88, 101, 167
8.4ff.	97	10.25ff.	100
8.5	97, 168	10.26f.	89, 168
8.6–22	168	10.27–11.15	87, 101
8.6–10	97, 98	10.27	90, 100, 168
8.6ff.	168	11	9, 85, 88, 89,
8.6	97, 168		101, 102, 105,
8.7	91, 94, 97, 100		167
8.8	169	11.1–11	167
8.9	168, 169	11.1ff.	168
8.11–22	98	11.7	88, 89
8.11–18	97	11.12–14	88, 89, 167
8.11–17	93, 94, 98, 99,	11.12	90
	102, 105, 168	11.15	88, 89, 167
8.11ff.	97	12	4, 9, 18, 82,
8.11	94, 97, 99		87, 92, 93, 96,
8.15	99		101, 105, 106,
8.16	99		116, 125, 131,
8.17	99		132, 136
8.20	90, 97	12.2–5	101
8.22	90, 97	12.2	101
9.1–10.16	9, 85, 86, 87,	12.3–5	94, 169
	88, 89, 99, 100,	12.3	90, 169
	101, 102, 105,	12.5	90, 101, 169

197

199

202

Web Site Analysis and Reporting

**Robin Nobles and
Kerri-Leigh Grady**

PRIMA TECH

A DIVISION OF PRIMA PUBLISHING

With sincere gratitude for everything he has done on our behalf, we dedicate this book to Richard Curtis...a true miracle worker.

 A Division of Prima Publishing

Prima Publishing and colophon are registered trademarks of Prima Communications, Inc. PRIMA TECH is a registered trademark of Prima Communications, Inc., Roseville, California 95661.

Microsoft, Windows, Internet Explorer, Notepad, VBScript, ActiveX, and FrontPage are trademarks or registered trademarks of Microsoft Corporation. Netscape is a registered trademark of Netscape Communications Corporation.

Important: Prima Publishing cannot provide software support. Please contact the appropriate software manufacturer's technical support line or Web site for assistance.

Prima Publishing and the author have attempted throughout this book to distinguish proprietary trademarks from descriptive terms by following the capitalization style used by the manufacturer.

Information contained in this book has been obtained by Prima Publishing from sources believed to be reliable. However, because of the possibility of human or mechanical error by our sources, Prima Publishing, or others, the Publisher does not guarantee the accuracy, adequacy, or completeness of any information and is not responsible for any errors or omissions or the results obtained from use of such information. Readers should be particularly aware of the fact that the Internet is an ever-changing entity. Some facts may have changed since this book went to press.

ISBN: 0-7615-2842-3

Library of Congress Catalog Card Number: 00-109083

Printed in the United States of America

01 02 03 04 05 HH 10 9 8 7 6 5 4 3 2 1

Publisher:
Stacy L. Hiquet

Associate Marketing Manager:
Heather Buzzingham

Managing Editor:
Sandy Doell

Acquisitions Editor:
Emi Smith

Developmental Editor:
Marla Reece-Hall

Project Editor:
Kelly Talbot

Technical Reviewer:
Dan Ransom

Copy Editor:
Fran Blauw

Interior Layout:
Scribe Tribe

Cover Design:
Prima Design Team

CD-ROM Producer:
Arlington Hartman

Indexer:
Tom Dinse

Proofreader:
Mitzi Foster